THE
QUOTABLE
WESLEY

DAVE ARMSTRONG, EDITOR

BEACON HILL PRESS
OF KANSAS CITY

Copyright 2014 by Dave Armstrong

ISBN 978-0-8341-3221-4

Printed in the
United States of America

Cover Design: Robbie Knight
Interior Design: Sharon Page

Note: To improve readability and consistency, quotations and excerpts from John Wesley's writings have been modestly adapted to contemporary style and punctuation standards.

Library of Congress Control Number: 2014930740

10 9 8 7 6 5 4 3 2 1

For all those Christians who have faithfully labored in the fruitful field of evangelization, sharing the gospel of Christ in the spirit and zeal of the one who exemplified that vision to an exceptional degree—John Wesley, with the power of God's grace and Holy Spirit.

And especially for my parents and four grandparents—Methodists all. I hope to have conveyed the best of that tradition in this volume.

And he said to them, "The harvest is plentiful, but the laborers are few; pray
therefore the Lord of the harvest to send out laborers into his harvest."
—Luke 10:2, RSV

I planted, Apol'los watered, but God gave the growth. So neither he who
plants nor he who waters is anything, but only God who gives the growth.
He who plants and he who waters are equal, and each shall receive his
wages according to his labor. For we are God's fellow workers;
you are God's field, God's building.
According to the grace of God given to me, like a skilled master builder
I laid a foundation, and another man is building upon it. Let each
man take care how he builds upon it. For no other foundation
can any one lay than that which is laid, which is Jesus Christ.
—1 Cor. 3:6-11, RSV

Contents

Biography*

John Wesley (1703-91), English divine, was born at Epworth Rectory on June 17, 1703. In June 1720 he went up to Christ Church, Oxford. On September 25, 1725, he was ordained deacon, and on March 17, 1726, he was elected fellow of Lincoln. He preached frequently in the churches near Oxford in the months succeeding his ordination.

In October 1726 he returned to Oxford, where he was appointed Greek lecturer and moderator of the classes. He gained considerable reputation in the disputation for his master's degree in February 1727. He was now free to follow his own course of studies and began to keep company almost solely with those who, like himself, were drawn to religion.

When he came into residence at Oxford in November 1729, he was recognized as the father of the Holy Club. The Holy Club was a society committed to devotional practices and ministry to the sick, imprisoned, and impoverished; its members sought to live lives of holiness. Because those in the Holy Club adhered to a methodical lifestyle, they were derisively called Methodists, a title that in due course became a badge of honor. The club met at first on Sunday evenings, and then every evening was passed in Wesley's room or that of some other member. They read the Greek New Testament and the classics, fasted on Wednesday and Friday, received the Lord's Supper every week, and brought all their life under review.

Looking back on these days in 1777, Wesley felt "the Methodists at Oxford were all one body, and, as it were, one soul—zealous for the religion of the Bible, of the primitive church, and, in consequence, of the Church of England, as they believed it to come nearer the scriptural and primitive plan than any other national church on earth" ("On Laying the Foundation of the New Chapel," sermon delivered April 21, 1777).

On Wednesday, May 24, 1738, he went to a society meeting in Aldersgate Street where Luther's "Preface to the Epistle of St. Paul to the Romans" was being read. "About a quarter before nine, while he was describing the change which God works in the heart through faith in Christ, I felt my heart strangely

---

*Abridged and adapted from *Encyclopaedia Britannica* (1911 ed.), s.v. "John Wesley," accessed January 27, 2014, http://encyclopedia.jrank.org/WAT_WIL/WESLEY_JOHN_1703_1791_.html.

warmed. I felt I did trust in Christ, Christ alone, for salvation; and an assurance was given me that he had taken away *my* sins, even *mine,* and saved *me* from the law of sin and death" (journal entry, May 24, 1738).

Wesley spent some time during the summer of 1738 in visiting the Moravian settlement at Herrnhut and returned to London on September 16, 1738, with his faith greatly strengthened. He preached in all the churches that were open to him, spoke in many religious societies, and visited Newgate and the Oxford prisons. On New Year's Day 1739, the Wesleys, George Whitefield, and other friends had a love feast (a meal of bread and water shared by Christians in a setting of fellowship, prayer, and worship) at Fetter Lane. In February, Whitefield went to Bristol, where his popularity was unbounded.

When the churches were closed against him, Whitefield spoke to the Kingswood coal miners in the open air and after six memorable weeks wrote Wesley and urged him to come and take up the work. Wesley was in his friend's congregation on April 1 but had commented earlier, "I could scarcely reconcile myself to this strange way of preaching in the fields . . . having been all my life (till very lately) so tenacious of every point relating to decency and order, that I should have thought the saving of souls almost a sin, if it had not been done in a church" (journal entry, March 29, 1739). Next day (April 2) Wesley followed Whitefield's example. His fears and prejudices melted away as he discerned that this was the very method needed for reaching the multitudes living in almost heathen darkness. He already had the means of shepherding those who were impressed by the preaching.

English Christianity seemed to have no power to uplift the people. Alcohol consumption was spreading like an epidemic. Freethinkers' clubs flourished. Some of the clergy in country parishes were devoted workers, but special zeal was resented or discouraged.

The doctrine of election had led to a separation between Whitefield and the Wesleys in 1741. Wesley believed that the grace of God could transform every life that received it. He preached the doctrine of conscious acceptance with God and daily growth in holiness. Victory over sin was the goal that he set before all his people. He made his appeal to the conscience in the clearest language, with the most cogent argument, and with all the weight of personal conviction. No preacher of the century had this mastery over his audience. His teaching may be described as evangelical Arminianism.

In August 1747, Wesley paid his first visit to Ireland, where he had such success that he gave more than six years of his life to the country and crossed the Irish Channel forty-two times. Wesley's first visit to Scotland was in 1751. He paid twenty-two visits, which stirred up all the Scottish churches.

As the work advanced, Wesley held a conference in 1744 at the Foundery (a building once used to cast guns that Wesley secured and transformed into a place of worship). Besides himself and his brother, four other clergymen were present and four "lay brethren." It was agreed that "lay assistants" were allowable, but only in cases of necessity. This necessity grew more urgent every year as Methodism extended. One of the preachers in each circuit was the "assistant," who had general oversight of the work; the others were "helpers." The conference became an annual gathering of Wesley's preachers (see Minutes of the Methodist Conference, June 25, 29, 1744).

In the early conversations doctrine took a prominent place, but as Methodism spread, the oversight of its growing organization occupied more time and attention. In February 1784, Wesley's deed of declaration gave the conference a legal constitution. He named one hundred preachers who after his death were to meet once a year, fill up vacancies in their number, appoint a president and secretary, station the preachers, admit proper persons into the ministry, and take general oversight of the societies. In October 1768, a Methodist chapel was opened in New York.

Wesley's account of his itinerancy is given in his famous *Journal*, of which the first part appeared about 1739. It is certainly Wesley's most picturesque biography and the most vivid account of the evangelical revival that we possess. The rapid development of his work made a tremendous strain on Wesley's powers. He generally traveled about five thousand miles a year and preached fifteen sermons a week. He had constant encounters with the mob, but his tact and courage never failed. His rule was always to look a mob in the face. Many delicious stories are told of his presence of mind and the skillful appeals that he made to the better feeling of the crowd.

Wesley's writings did much to open the eyes of candid men to his motives and his methods. Besides the incomparable *Journal*, his *Appeals to Men of Reason and Religion* also produced an extraordinary effect in allaying prejudice and winning respect. He constantly sought to educate his own people. No man in the eighteenth century did so much to create a taste for good reading and to supply it with books at the lowest prices.

As a social reformer Wesley was far in advance of his time. He provided work for the deserving poor and supplied them with clothes and food in seasons of special distress. The profits on his cheap books enabled him to give away as much as £1400 a year. He established a lending stock to help struggling businessmen and did much to relieve debtors who had been thrown into prison. He opened dispensaries in London and Bristol and was keenly interested in medicine.

Wesley's supreme gift was his genius for organization. Wesley's special power lay in his quickness to make use of circumstances and the suggestions made by those about him. The class meeting, the love feast, the watch night, the covenant service, leaders, stewards, lay preachers—all were the fruit of this readiness to benefit from suggestions made by men or events. Wesley skillfully wove these into his system and kept the whole machinery moving harmoniously. He inspired his preachers and his people with his own spirit and made everything subordinate to his overmastering purpose—the spread of scriptural holiness throughout the land.

During the last three years of his life John Wesley reaped the harvest he had sown. Honors were lavished on him. His people hailed every appearance among them with delight, and his visits to various parts of the country were public holidays. His interest in everything about him continued unabated. He had a wealth of happy stories that made him the most delightful of companions in the homes of his people.

He preached his last sermon in Mr. Belson's house at Leatherhead on Wednesday, February 23, 1791; wrote on the next day his last letter to Wilberforce, urging him to carry on his crusade against the slave trade; and died in his house at City Road on March 2, 1791, in his eighty-eighth year. He was buried on March 9 in the graveyard behind City Road chapel. His long life enabled him to perfect the organization of Methodism and to inspire his preachers and people with his own ideals. Moreover, he had conquered opposition by untiring patience and by close adherence to the principles he sought to teach.

Sources and Abbreviations

BIBLIOGRAPHY

B   Green, Richard, ed. *The Works of John and Charles Wesley: A Bibliography.* 2nd ed. London: Methodist Publishing House, 1906. http://books.google.com/books?id=uYguAAAAYAAJ &source=gbs_navlinks_s.

COLLECTIONS

Coll. A   Holden, Harrington William, ed. *John Wesley in Company with High Churchmen.* 5th ed. London: John Hodges, 1872. http://books.google.com/books?id=x3DuWp9qpAEC&source =gbs_navlinks_s.

Coll. B   Potts, James H., comp. *Living Thoughts of John Wesley.* New York: Eaton and Mains, 1891. http://books.google.com/books?id =qttzq3r679QC&dq=%22john+wesley%22&source=gbs _navlinks_s.

Coll. C   Welch, Herbert, comp. *Selections from the Writings of the Rev. John Wesley.* New York: The Methodist Book Concern, 1901. http:// books.google.com/books?id=e2RIAAAAYAAJ&dq =%22john+wesley%22&source=gbs_navlinks_s.

Coll. D   *Wesleyana: A Selection of the Most Important Passages in the Writings of the Late Rev. John Wesley, A.M.* 4th ed. London: Thomas Tegg, 1840. http://books.google.com/books?id=eCNMAAAAYAAJ &dq=%22john+wesley%22&source=gbs_navlinks_s.

MINUTES

Minutes   *Minutes of the Methodist Conferences, from the First, Held in London, by the Late John Wesley, A.M., in the Year 1744.* Vol. 1. London: John Mason, 1862. https://archive.org/details/minutesofmethod i00wesl.

WORKS BY JOHN WESLEY

Journal   Wesley, John. *The Journal of the Rev. John Wesley, A.M.* 4 vols. London and Toronto: J. M. Dent and Sons; New York: E. P. Dutton and Co., 1906.
- Vol. 1: http://archive.org/details/journalofrevjohnwesl
- Vol. 2: http://archive.org/details/journalofrevjohnwesl2
- Vol. 3: http://archive.org/details/journalofrevjohnwesl3
- Vol. 4: http://archive.org/details/journalofrevjohnwesl4

Letters	_____. *Letters of John Wesley*. Comp. George Eayrs. London: Hodder and Stoughton, 1915. http://books.google.com /books?id=zgYu6NpqWDEC&oe=UTF-8.
Letters (JT)	_____. *The Letters of the Rev. John Wesley, A.M.* 8 vols. Edited by John Telford. London: Epworth Press, 1931.
NT Notes	_____. *The New Testament, with Explanatory Notes*. 1754. Reprint, Halifax: William Nicholson and Sons, 1869. http: //archive.org/details/newtestamentwit00weslgoog.
Works, 12	_____. *The Works of the Rev. John Wesley*. Vol. 12, *The Appeals to Men of Reason and Religion, Answers to Mr. Church's Remarks, &c. &c.* London: Conference Office, 1812. http://books.google .com/books?id=35APAAAAIAAJ&oe=UTF-8.
Works, 13	_____. *The Works of the Rev. John Wesley*. Vol. 13, *Letters to Several Opponents, and Tracts on Various Subjects of Polemical Divinity*. London: Conference Office, 1812. http://books.google.com /books?id=bZEPAAAAIAAJ&oe=UTF-8.
Works, 15	_____. *The Works of the Rev. John Wesley*. Vol. 15, *Essays and Letters on Various Subjects*. London: Conference Office, 1812. http://books.google.com/books?id=CZEPAAAAIAAJ &oe=UTF-8.
Works, 16	_____. *The Works of the Rev. John Wesley*. Vol. 16, *Letters and Tracts on Various Subjects*. London: Conference Office, 1813. http://books.google.com/books?id=DZEPAAAAIAAJ &oe=UTF-8.
Works (B), 18	_____. *The Bicentennial Edition of the Works of John Wesley*. Vol. 18, *Journals and Diaries I (1735-38)*. Nashville: Abingdon Press, 1983–.
Works (S), 2	_____. *The Works of the Rev. John Wesley, A.M., in Seven Volumes*. Vol. 2 (sermons 59-140). 3rd American ed. New York: Carlton and Porter, 1856. http://books.google.com/books?id =uokYAAAAYAAJ&dq=sermons,+John+Wesley&source=gbs _navlinks_s.
Works (S), 5	_____. *The Works of the Rev. John Wesley, A.M., in Seven Volumes*. Vol. 5. 1st American ed. New York: J. Emory and B. Waugh, 1831. http://books.google.com/books?id=kHo9 AAAAYAAJ&source=gbs_navlinks_s.
Works (S), 7	_____. *The Works of the Rev. John Wesley, A.M., in Seven Volumes*. Vol. 7 (letters and tracts). 1st American ed. New York: B. Waugh and T. Mason, 1835. http://books.google.com /books?id=8rRaAAAAYAAJ&source=gbs_navlinks_s.
Works (T), 5	_____. *The Works of the Rev. John Wesley in Ten Volumes*. Vol. 5, *Forty-Two Sermons on Various Subjects* (sermons 1-42). 1st American ed. New York: J. and J. Harper, 1826. http://books.google .com/books?id=Pug7AAAAYAAJ&dq=sermons,+John+Wesley &source=gbs_navlinks_s.
Works (T), 6	_____. *The Works of the Rev. John Wesley in Ten Volumes*. Vol. 6, *Forty-Three Sermons on Various Subjects* (sermons 43-85). 1st American ed. New York: J. and J. Harper, 1826. http://books .google.com/books?id=0NFhAAAAIAAJ&source=gbs_nav links_s.

Sources

Works (T), 9   _____. *The Works of the Rev. John Wesley in Ten Volumes.* Vol. 9, *The Doctrine of Original Sin, and Tracts on Various Subjects of Polemical Divinity.* 1st American ed. New York: J. and J. Harper, 1827. http://books.google.com/books?id=T6M7AAAAYAAJ &source=gbs_navlinks_s.

Works (WL), 1   _____. *The Works of the Rev. John Wesley, A.M.: With the Last Corrections of the Author.* Vol. 1. 4th ed. London: John Mason, 1837. http://books.google.com/books?id=239PAAAAYAAJ &source=gbs_navlinks_s.

Works (WL), 7   _____. *The Works of the Rev. John Wesley, A.M.: With the Last Corrections of the Author.* Vol. 7. London: Wesleyan Conference Office, 1872. http://books.google.com/books?id =tI9KAAAAYAAJ&source=gbs_navlinks_s.

Works (WL), 10   _____. *The Works of the Rev. John Wesley, A.M.: With the Last Corrections of the Author.* Vol. 10. London: Wesleyan Conference Office, 1872. http://books.google.com/books?id=TZBKAA AAYAAJ&source=gbs_navlinks_s.

Works (WL), 11   _____. *The Works of the Rev. John Wesley, A.M.: With the Last Corrections of the Author.* Vol. 11. London: Wesleyan Conference Office, 1872. http://books.google.com/books?id=dJB KAAAAYAAJ&dq=The+Works+of+the+Rev.+John+Wesley %3B+Vol.+XI&source=gbs_navlinks_s.

Works (WL), 12   _____. *The Works of the Rev. John Wesley, A.M.: With the Last Corrections of the Author.* Vol. 12, *Letters to Various Persons.* 3rd ed. London: John Mason, 1830. http://books.google.com/books ?id=bKMOAAAAQAAJ&oe=UTF-8.

ABSOLUTION

We believe the absolution pronounced by the priest is only declarative and conditional. For judicially to pardon sin and absolve the sinner is a power God has reserved to himself. (*Popery Calmly Considered* [1779], in *Works*, 15:191)

One doctrine more of the Romish Church must not here be passed over—I mean that of *absolution* by a priest, as it has a clear, direct tendency to destroy both justice, mercy, and truth, yea, to drive all virtue out of the world. For if a man (and not always a very good man) has power to forgive sins—if he can at pleasure forgive any violation, either of truth or mercy or justice—what an irresistible temptation must this be to men of weak or corrupt minds! (197)

ALCOHOL

Distilled liquors have their use but are infinitely overbalanced by the abuse of them; therefore, were it in my power, I would banish them out of the world. (Letter to Thomas Taylor [December 11, 1787], in *Letters*, 217)

ANABAPTISTS

I desire that neither any preacher of ours nor any member of our Society would on any pretense go to an Anabaptist meeting. It is the way to destroy the Society. This we have experienced over and over. Let all that were of the [Anglican] Church keep to the Church. (Letter to Thomas Wride [June 23, 1771], in *Letters*, 186)

ANGELS

We honor the angels, as they are God's ministers; but we dare not worship or pray to them. It is what they themselves refuse and abhor. So when "St. John fell down at the feet of the angel to worship him, he said, See thou do it not. I am thy fellow-servant: worship God!" [see Rev. 19:10]. (*Popery Calmly Considered* [1779], in *Works*, 15:184)

Is it not their first care to minister to our souls? But we must not expect this will be done *with observation*—in such a manner as that we may clearly distinguish their working from the workings of our own minds. We have no more reason to look for this than for their appearing in a visible shape. Without this, they can, in a thousand ways, apply to our understanding. They may assist us in our search after truth, remove many doubts and difficulties, throw light on what was before dark and obscure, and confirm us in the truth that is after godliness. They may warn us of evil in disguise, and [they may] place what is good in a clear, strong light. They may gently move our will to embrace what is good and [to] fly from that which is evil. They may many times quicken our dull affections, increase our holy hope or filial fear, and assist us more ardently to love him, who has first loved us. . . .

May they not minister also to us, with respect to our bodies, in a thousand ways [that] we do not now understand? They may prevent our falling into many dangers, which we are not sensible of, and may deliver us out of many others, though we know not where our deliverance comes. How many times have we been strangely and unaccountably preserved, in sudden and dangerous falls! And it is well if we did not impute that preservation to chance or to our own wisdom or strength. Not so—it was God gave his angels charge over us, and in their hands they bore us up. . . .

And we may make one general observation: whatever assistance God gives to men by men, the same, and frequently in a higher degree, he gives to them by angels. Does he administer to us by men light when we are in darkness, joy when we are in heaviness, deliverance when we are in danger, ease and health when we are sick or in pain? It cannot be doubted but he frequently conveys the same blessings by the ministry of angels, not so sensibly, indeed, but full as effectually, though the messengers are not seen.

Does he frequently deliver us by means of men from the violence and subtlety of our enemies? Many times he works the same deliverance by those invisible agents. These shut the mouths of the human lions so that they have no power to hurt us. And frequently they join with our human friends (although neither they nor we are sensible of it), giving them wisdom, courage, or strength, without which all their labor for us would be unsuccessful. Thus do they secretly minister, in numberless instances, to the heirs of salvation, while we hear only but the voices of men and see none but men round about us. (Quoted in "Of Angels," chap. 18 in Coll. D, 343-44, 347)

ANGLICANISM

Had we been Dissenters of any kind, or even Low Church men (so called), it would have been a great stumbling block in the way of those who are zealous for the [Anglican] Church. And yet had we continued in the impetuosity of our High Church zeal, neither should we have been willing to converse with Dissenters, nor they to receive any good at our hands. (*A Farther Appeal to Men of Reason and Religion* [1745], pt. 3, in *Works*, 12:256)

But here another question occurs, "What is the Church of England?" It is not "all the people of England." Papists and Dissenters are no part thereof. It is not all the people of England except Papists and Dissenters. Then we should have a glorious church indeed! No; according to our twentieth article, a particular church is "a congregation of faithful people" (*caetus credentium*, the words in our Latin edition) "among whom the Word of God is preached, and the sacraments duly administered." Here is a true logical definition, containing both the essence and the properties of the church. What then, according to this definition, is the Church of England? Does it mean, "All the believers in England (except the Papists and Dissenters) who have the Word of God and the sacraments duly administered among them?" I fear this does not come up to your idea of "the Church of England." Well, what more do you include in that phrase? "Why, all the believers that adhere to the doctrine and discipline established by the Convocation under Queen Elizabeth." Nay, that discipline is well-nigh vanished away, and the doctrine both you and I adhere to. (Letter to Charles Wesley [August 19, 1785], in *Letters*, 91-92)

I do not advise our people to go to the Low Church. (Letter to Thomas Taylor [February 13, 1791], in *Letters*, 218)

ANGLICANISM: FAITHFULNESS TO

I exhorted our brethren to keep close to the [Anglican] Church and to all the ordinances of God; . . . A serious clergyman desired to know in what points we differed from the Church of England. I answered, "To the best of my knowledge, in none. The doctrines we preach are the doctrines of the Church of England; indeed, the fundamental doctrines of the Church, clearly laid down, both in her prayers, articles, and homilies." He asked, "In what points, then, do you differ from the other clergy of the Church of England?" I answered, "In none from that part of the clergy who adhere to the doctrines of the Church." (*Conditions of Justification* [1744], in Coll. B, 180)

I have now considered the most material objections I know which have been lately made against the great doctrines I teach. I have produced, so far as in me lay, the strength of those objections and then answered them, I hope, in the spirit of meekness. And now I trust it appears that these doctrines are no other than the doctrines of Jesus Christ; that they are all evidently contained in the Word of God, by which alone I desire to stand or fall; and that they are fundamentally the same with the doctrines of the Church of England, of which I do, and ever did, profess myself a member. (*Operations of the Holy Ghost* [1744], in Coll. B, 194)

We do not dispute concerning any of the externals or circumstantials of religion. There is no room, for we agree with you therein. We approve of, and adhere to, them all—all that we learned together when we were children, in our catechism and common-prayer book. We were born and bred up in your own church and desire to die therein. We always were, and are now, zealous for the [Anglican] Church, only not with a blind, angry zeal. We hold, and ever have done, the same opinions, which you and we received from our forefathers. (*A Farther Appeal to Men of Reason and Religion* [1745], pt. 3, in *Works*, 12:275)

In saying, "I teach the doctrines of the Church of England," I do, and always did, mean (without concerning myself whether others taught them or no, either this year or before the Reformation) I teach the doctrines which are comprised in those articles and homilies to which all the clergy of the Church of England solemnly profess to assent, and that in their plain, unforced, grammatical meaning. (Letter to John Smith [probably one of the archbishops of Canterbury, Thomas Herring or Thomas Secker] [December 30, 1745], in *Works* [WL], 12:64)

I cannot have a greater regard to any *human rules* than to follow them in all things, unless where I apprehend there is a *divine rule* to the contrary. I dare not *renounce communion* with the Church of England. As a *minister*, I teach her doctrines. I use her offices. I conform to her rubrics. I suffer reproach for my attachment to her. As a private *member* I hold her doctrines. I join in her offices, in prayer, in hearing, in communicating. I *expect* every reasonable man, touching these facts, to *believe his own eyes and ears*. But if these facts are so, how dare any man of common sense charge me with *renouncing* the Church of England? . . .

. . . Nay, nothing can prove I am no *member* of the Church, till I am either *excommunicated* or *renounce* her communion, and no longer join in her doctrine and in the breaking of bread and in prayer. Nor can anything prove I am no *minister* of the Church, till I either am *deposed* from my ministry or *voluntarily renounce* her, and wholly cease to teach her doctrines, use her offices, and obey her rubrics for conscience' sake. (*The Principles of a Methodist Farther Explained* [1746], in *Works*, 12:362-63)

They were all zealous members of the Church of England, not only tenacious of all her doctrines, so far as they knew them, but of all her discipline, to the minutest circumstance. . . .

At present those who remain with Mr. Wesley are mostly Church-of-England men. They love her articles, her homilies, her liturgy, [and] her discipline and unwillingly vary from it in any instance. (*A Short History of Methodism* [1764], in Coll. C, 200, 203)

I advise you to lose no opportunity of attending the service of the [Anglican] Church and receiving the Lord's Supper and of showing your regard for all her appointments. I advise steadily to adhere to her doctrine in every branch of it. (Letter to Mr. Knox [May 30, 1765], in *Works*, 16:98)

[My doctrine is] of the Bible, of the primitive church, and, in consequence, of the Church of England. (Quoted in "Steadfast unto the End," chap. 22 in Coll. A, 155)

If any of our lay preachers talk to her in public or private against the [Anglican] Church or the clergy or reading the church prayers or baptizing children, she require a promise from them to do it no more. [If] they will not promise it, then preach no more, and if they break their promise, let them be expelled [from] the society. (Letter "to an unnamed Inquirer" [March 4, 1784], in *Letters*, 232)

I am now, and have been from my youth, a member and minister of the Church of England, and I have no desire [or] design to separate from it, till my soul separates from my body. (Quoted in "Steadfast unto the End," chap. 22 in Coll. A, 156)

We are members of the Church of England, we are no particular sect or party, we are friends to all, we quarrel with none for their opinions or mode of worship, we love those of the Church wherein we were brought up. (Letter to Henry Brooke [June 14, 1786], *Letters* [JT], 7:333)

You cannot be too watchful against evil speaking or too zealous for the poor Church of England. . . . By all means go to church as often as you can and exhort all Methodists so to do. They that are enemies to the Church are enemies to *me*. I am a friend to it, and ever was. (Letter to William Percival [February 17, 1787], *Letters* [JT], 7:369-70)

I have uniformly gone on for fifty years never varying from the doctrine of the [Anglican] Church at all. (Quoted in "Steadfast unto the End," chap. 22 in Coll. A, 155)

Next after the primitive church, I esteemed our own, the Church of England, as the most scriptural national church in the world. I therefore not only assented to all the doctrines but observed all the rubric in the liturgy, and that with all possible exactness, even at the peril of my life. (*Farther Thoughts on Separation from the Church* [December 11, 1789], in Coll. C, 287)

ANGLICANISM: OPPOSITION TO SEPARATION AND A NEW DENOMINATION

And do they now forsake *that* assembling themselves together? You cannot, you dare not, say it. You know, they are more diligent therein than ever, it being one of the fixed rules of our societies, "that every member attend the ordinances of God," [that is], do *not divide from the [Anglican] Church*. And if any member of the Church does thus divide from or leave it, he hath no more place among us. (Quoted in "Institution and Design of Methodism," chap. 18 in Coll. A, 133)

How should an assistant (superintendent) be qualified for this charge? By loving the Church of England and resolving not to separate from it. Let this be well observed. I fear, when the Methodists leave the Church, God will leave them. [Oh,] use every means to prevent this. (1) Exhort all our people to keep close to the Church and sacrament. (2) Warn them all against niceness in hearing—a prevailing evil. (3) Warn them also against despising the prayers of the Church. (4) [Warn them] against calling our Society a church or the church. (5) [Warn them] against calling our preachers ministers; our houses, meeting houses—call them plain preaching houses. (Quoted in "Steadfast unto the End," chap. 22 in Coll. A, 158)

Such is our rule, that if any man separate from the [Anglican] Church, he is no longer a member of our Society. (Quoted in "Steadfast unto the End," chap. 22 in Coll. A, 156)

My brother and I closed the Conference by a solemn declaration of our purpose *never to separate* from the Church, and all our brethren cheerfully concurred therein. (Quoted in "Steadfast unto the End," chap. 22 in Coll. A, 159)

We look upon ourselves, not as the authors or ringleaders of a sect or party (it is the farthest thing from our thoughts), but as messengers of God to those who are Christians in name but heathens in heart and in life, to call them back to that from which they have fallen, to real, genuine Christianity. (*Reasons Against a Separation from the Church of England* [1758], quoted in Coll. C, 289n)

We, by such a separation should not only throw away the peculiar glorying [that] God hath given us . . . but should act in direct contradiction to that very end for which we believe God hath raised us up. The chief design of his providence in sending us out is undoubtedly to quicken our brethren—and the first message of all our preachers is to the lost sheep of the Church of England. (Quoted in "Institution and Design of Methodism," chap. 18 in Coll. A, 132)

The original Methodists were all of the Church of England; and the more awakened they were, the more zealously they adhered to it in every point, both of doctrine and discipline. Hence we insisted in the first rules of our Society, "They that leave the Church leave *us*." And this we did, not as a point of prudence, but a point of conscience. We believe it utterly unlawful to separate from the Church unless sinful terms of communion were imposed. (Letter to Mary Bishop [October 18, 1778], *Letters* [JT], 6:326)

I still think, when the Methodists leave the Church of England, God will leave them. Every year more and more of the clergy are convinced of the truth and grow well-affected toward us. It would be contrary to all common sense, as well as to good conscience, to make a separation now. (Letter to Samuel Bradburn [March 25, 1783], in *Letters*, 166)

But this does in nowise interfere with my remaining in the Church of England, from which I have no more desire to separate than I had fifty years ago. I still attend all the ordinances of the Church, at all opportunities, and I constantly and earnestly desire all that are connected with me to do so. When Mr. Smyth pressed us to "separate from the Church," he meant, "Go to Church no more." And this was what I meant seven-and-twenty years ago when I persuaded our brethren "not to separate from the Church." . . .

I openly declared in the evening that I had now no more thought of separating from the [Anglican] Church than I had forty years ago. (Quoted in "Steadfast unto the End," chap. 22 in Coll. A, 159)

I believe if we had *then* left the [Anglican] Church, we should not have done a tenth part of the good we have done; but I do not trouble myself on this head. I go calmly and quietly on my way, doing what I conceive to be the will of God. I do not, will not, concern myself with what will be when I am

A

dead. I take no thought about that. (Letter to Thomas Taylor [February 24, 1786], in *Letters*, 216)

Indeed I love the [Anglican] Church as sincerely as ever I did; and I tell our societies everywhere, "The Methodists will not leave the Church, at least while I live." (Letter to Charles Wesley [April 6, 1786], in *Works* [WL], 12:141)

We do not, will not, dare not separate from the [Anglican] Church till we see other reasons than we have seen yet. (Letter to Henry Brooke [June 14, 1786], *Letters* [JT], 7:333)

We *weighed* what was said about separating from the Church; but we all determined to continue therein, without one dissenting voice. (Quoted in "Steadfast unto the End," chap. 22 in Coll. A, 159)

It is easy to see that this would be a formal separation from the Church . . . and this I judge to be not only inexpedient but totally unlawful for me to do. (Quoted in "Steadfast unto the End," chap. 22 in Coll. A, 156-57)

A   All of these were, when they first set out, members of the established Church; . . . But they have been solicited again and again, from time to time, to separate from it and to form themselves into a distinct body, independent of all other religious societies. Thirty years ago, this was seriously considered among them at a general conference. All the arguments urged on one side and the other were considered at large; and it was determined, without one dissenting voice, that they "ought not to separate from the Church." ("Thoughts upon a Late Phenomenon" [July 13, 1788], in *Works* [S], 7:320)

In my youth I was not only a member of the Church of England but a bigot to it, believing none but the members of it to be in a state of salvation. I began to abate of this violence in 1729. But still I was as zealous as ever, observing every point of church discipline and teaching all my pupils so to do. When I was abroad, I observed every rule of the Church, even at the peril of my life. . . .

When the Rev. Mr. Edward Smyth came to live in Dublin, he earnestly advised me to leave the Church, meaning thereby (as all sensible men do) to renounce all connection with it, to attend the service of it no more, and to advise all our societies to take the same steps. I judged this to be a matter of great importance and would therefore do nothing hastily but referred it to the body of preachers, then met in conference. We had several meetings, in which he proposed all his reasons for it at large. They were severally considered and answered, and we all determined not to leave the Church.

. . . Some persons immediately began to cry out, "This is leaving the Church, which Mr. Wesley has continually declared he would never do." And I declare so still. . . .

. . . unless I see more reason for it than I ever saw yet, I will not leave the Church of England, as by law established, while the breath of God is in my nostrils. (Letter to the printer of the *Dublin Chronicle* [June 2, 1789], in *Works* [S], 7:322-24)

I never saw such a number of preachers before so unanimous in all points, particularly as to leaving the [Anglican] Church, which none of them had the least thought of. (Quoted in "Steadfast unto the End," chap. 22 in Coll. A, 159)

About a hundred preachers were present, and never was our Master more eminently present with us. The case of separation from the [Anglican] Church was largely considered, and we were all *unanimous* against it. (Quoted in "Steadfast unto the End," chap. 22 in Coll. A, 159)

I never had any design of separating from the [Anglican] Church; I have no such design now. I do not believe the Methodists in general design it, when I am no more seen. I do, and will do, all that is in my power to prevent such an event. Nevertheless, in spite of all I can do, many will separate from it, although I am apt to think not one-half, perhaps not a third of them. These will be so bold and injudicious as to form a separate party, which, consequently, will dwindle away into a dry, dull, separate party. In flat opposition to that, I declare, once more, that I live and die a member of the Church of England and that none who regard my judgment or advice will ever separate from it. (*Farther Thoughts on Separation from the Church* [December 11, 1789], in Coll. C, 290)

Ye were, fifty years ago, those of you that were then Methodist preachers, *extra*-ordinary messengers of God, not going in your own will, but *thrust* out, not to supersede, but "to provoke to jealousy" the ordinary messengers. In God's name, stop there. . . . Be Church-of-England-men still. Do not cast away the peculiar glory [that] God hath put upon you and *frustrate the design of providence—the very end for which God raised you up*. (Quoted in "Institution and Design of Methodism," chap. 18 in Coll. A, 132)

ANGLICANISM: PERSECUTION OF ANGLICAN METHODISTS

The truth is, you impute that hatred to us, which is in your own breasts. (I speak not this of all the clergy; God forbid! But let it fall on whom it concerns.) You, it is certain, have shown the utmost hatred to us, and in every possible way, unless you were actually to beat us (of which also we are not without precedent) or to shoot us through the head. And if you could prevail upon others to do this, I suppose you would think you did God service. I do not speak without ground. I have heard with my own ears such sermons (in Staffordshire particularly) that I should not have wondered if as soon as we came out of the church, the people had stoned me with stones. And it was a natural consequence of what that poor minister had lately heard at the bishop's visitation, as it was one great cause of the miserable riots and outrages [that] soon followed. . . .

"But what need is there (say even some of a milder spirit) of this preaching in fields and streets? Are there not churches enough to preach in?" No, my friend, there are not—not for *us* to preach in. You forget—we are not suffered to preach there, else we should prefer them to any places whatever. (*A Farther Appeal to Men of Reason and Religion* [1745], pt. 3, in *Works*, 12:258)

God begins a glorious work in our land. You set yourself against it with all your might—to prevent its beginning where it does not yet appear and to destroy it wherever it does. In part you prevail. You keep many from hearing the word that is able to save their souls. Others who had heard it, you induce to turn back from God and to list under the devil's banner again. Then you make the success of your own wickedness an excuse for not acknowledging the work of God! You urge "that not many sinners were reformed! And that some of those are now as bad as ever!"

Whose fault is this? Is it ours? Or your own? Why have not thousands more been reformed? Yea, for every one who is now turned to God, why are there not ten thousand? Because you and your associates labored so heartily in the cause of hell; because you and they spared no pains, either to prevent or to destroy the work of God! By using all the power and wisdom you had, you hindered thousands from hearing the gospel, which they might have found to be the power of God unto salvation. Their blood is upon your heads. By inventing or countenancing or [retelling] lies, some refined, some gross and palpable, you hindered others from profiting by what they did hear. You are answerable to God for these souls also. Many who began to taste the good word and run the way of God's commandments, you, by various methods, prevailed on to hear it no more. So they soon drew back to perdition. But know, that for every one of these also, God will require an account of you in the day of judgment. (*A Farther Appeal to Men of Reason and Religion* [1745], pt. 3, in *Works*, 12:268-69)

I learn from you that ignorance of another kind is a second reason why some of the clergy oppose us. They (like you) think us "enemies to the church." The natural consequence is that, in proportion to their zeal for the church, their zeal against us will be.

The zeal which many of them have for orthodoxy, or right opinions, is a third reason for opposing us. For they judge us heterodox in several points, maintainers of strange opinions. And the truth is, the old doctrines of the Reformation are now quite new in the world. Hence those who revive them cannot fail to be opposed by those of the clergy who know them not. (Letter to the Rev. Mr. Bailey [June 8, 1750], in *Works*, 13:164)

The Methodists will not separate from the [Anglican] Church, although continually reproached for doing it; although it would free them from abundance of inconveniences and make their path much smoother and easier; although many of their friends earnestly advise and their enemies provoke them to it, the clergy in particular, most of whom, far from thanking them for continuing in the Church, use all the means in their power, fair or unfair, to drive them out of it. ("Thoughts upon a Late Phenomenon" [July 13, 1788], in *Works* [S], 7:321)

The Methodists in general, my lord, are members of the Church of England. They hold all her doctrines, attend her service, and partake of her sacraments. They do not willingly do harm to anyone but do what good they can to all. To encourage each other herein, they frequently spend an hour together in prayer and mutual exhortation. Permit me then to ask, *Cui bono?* "For what reasonable end" would your lordship drive these people out of the Church? Are they not as quiet, as inoffensive, nay, as pious, as any of their neighbors, except perhaps here and there a harebrained man who knows not what he is about? Do you ask, "Who drives them out of the Church?" Your lordship does, and that in the most cruel manner, yea, and the most disingenuous manner. They desire a license to worship God after their own conscience. Your lordship refuses it and then punishes them for not having a license! So your lordship leaves them only this alternative, "Leave the Church or starve." And is it a Christian, yea, a Protestant bishop that so persecutes his own flock? I say *persecutes*, for it is persecution to all intents and purposes. You do not burn them indeed, but you starve them. And how small is the difference! (Letter to the bishop of [?] [June 26, 1790], in *Letters*, 133-34)

ANOINTING THE SICK WITH CONSECRATED OIL

As to the consecrated oil, you seem entirely to forget that it was neither St. Jerome nor St. Chrysostom but St. James who said, "Is any sick among you? Let him send for the elders of the church, and let them pray over him, anointing him with oil, in the name of the Lord. And the prayer of faith shall save the sick, and the Lord shall raise him up."

Anointing the sick with oil, you will not easily prove to be any corruption at all. (Quoted in "Of Anointing the Sick with Consecrated Oil," chap. 7 in Coll. A, 52)

ANTINOMIANISM (FALSITY OF)

"The first that I shall take notice of," says your lordship, "is the antinomian doctrine." . . . The second, "That Christ has done all, and left nothing for us to do, but to believe." . . . These belong not to me. I am unconcerned therein. I have earnestly opposed but did never teach or embrace them. (Letter to the bishop of London [June 11, 1747], in *Works*, 12:408)

Beware of antinomianism, "making void the law," or any part of it, "through faith." Enthusiasm naturally leads to this; indeed they can scarce be separated. This may steal upon you in a thousand forms, so that you cannot be too watchful against it. Take heed of everything, whether in principle or practice, which has any tendency thereto. Even that great truth that "Christ is the end of the law" may betray us into it, if we do not consider that he has adopted every point of the moral law and grafted it into the law of love. Beware of thinking, "Because I am filled with love, I need not have so much holiness. Because I pray always, therefore I need no set time for private prayer. Because I watch always, therefore I need no particular self-examination." Let us "magnify the law," the whole written word, "and make it honorable." Let this be our voice: "I prize thy commandments above gold or precious stones. [Oh,] what love have I unto thy law! All the day long is my study in it." (*A Plain Account of Christian Perfection* [1767; rev. 1777], in *Works* [WL], 11:430-31)

These were properly antinomians, absolute, avowed enemies to the law of God, which they never preached or professed to preach but termed all legalists who did. . . . They would "preach Christ," as they called it, but without one word either of holiness or good works. . . .

. . . they love the antinomians themselves, but it is with a love of compassion only, for they hate their doctrines with a perfect hatred; they abhor them as they do hell fire, being convinced nothing can so effectually destroy all faith, all holiness, and all good works. (*A Short History of Methodism* [1764], in Coll. C, 202-4)

The great hindrance to the inward work of God is antinomianism, wherever it breaks in. I am glad you are aware of it. Show your faith by your works. Fight the good fight of faith, and lay hold on eternal life. (Letter to Henry Eames [July 5, 1789], in *Works* [S], 7:99)

The imagination that faith *supersedes* holiness is the very marrow of antinomianism. ("On the Wedding Garment" [March 26, 1790], Sermon 124, in *Works* [S], 2:460)

APOCRYPHA (DEUTEROCANON)

Tobit and Judith, the book of Wisdom, Ecclesiasticus, Baruch, the two books of Maccabees, Esdras, and a new part of Esther and of Daniel: . . . We dare not receive them as part of the Holy Scriptures. For none of these books were received as such by the Jewish church, "to whom were committed the Oracles of God" [see Rom. 3:2]. Neither by the ancient Christian church, as appears from the sixtieth canon of the council of Laodicea, wherein is a catalog of the books of Scripture, without any mention of these. (*Popery Calmly Considered* [1779], in *Works*, 15:178. Note: the authenticity of canon 60 is widely questioned, due to inadequate manuscript evidence, and in fact, it *does* include Baruch and does *not* include Revelation.)

APOSTOLIC SUCCESSION

We believe it would not be right for us to administer either baptism or the Lord's Supper unless we had a commission so to do from those bishops whom we apprehend to be in a succession from the apostles. And yet we allow these bishops are the successors of those who were dependent on the bishop of Rome. But we would be glad to know on what reasons you believe this to be inconsistent with the Word of God. (Quoted in "Of Holy Orders," chap. 8 in Coll. A, 57)

Bishops are, and have been from the apostolic age, empowered to convey the requisite authority for the exercise of the priestly office. (Quoted in "Of Holy Orders," chap. 8 in Coll. A, 59)

ARMINIANISM

The errors charged upon these (usually termed Arminians) by their opponents are five: (1) that they deny *original sin*; (2) that they deny *justification by faith*; (3) that they deny *absolute predestination*; (4) that they deny the grace of God to be *irresistible*; and (5) that they affirm a believer may *fall from grace*.

With regard to the two first of these charges, they plead not guilty. They are entirely false. No man that ever lived, not John Calvin himself, ever asserted either original sin or justification by faith in more strong, more clear, and express terms than Arminius has done. These two points, therefore, are to be set out of the question—in these both parties agree. . . .

. . . The Calvinists hold, [firstly, that] God has absolutely decreed, from all eternity, to save such and such persons and no others and that Christ died for these, and none else. The Arminians hold [that] God has decreed from all eternity, touching all that have the written word. "He that believeth shall be saved; he that believeth not shall be condemned," and in order to this, "Christ died for all, all that were dead in trespasses and sins," that is, for every child of Adam, since *in Adam all died.*

The Calvinists hold, secondly, that the saving grace of God is absolutely *irresistible*—that no man is any more able to resist it than to resist the stroke of lightning. The Arminians hold that although there may be some moments wherein the grace of God acts irresistibly, yet in general any man may resist, and that to his eternal ruin, the grace whereby it was the will of God, he should have been eternally saved.

The Calvinists hold, thirdly, that a true believer in Christ cannot possibly fall from grace. The Arminians hold that a true believer may "make shipwreck of faith and a good conscience"—that he may fall, not only *foully* but *finally*, so as to perish forever. (*The Question, "What Is an Arminian?" Answered* [1770], in *Works* [T], 9:474-75)

ATONEMENT

But certainly the subject is of the last importance and deserves our most serious consideration. Indeed, nothing in the Christian system is of greater consequence than the doctrine of atonement. It is properly the distinguishing point between deism and Christianity. . . .

. . . the question is (the only question with me; I regard nothing else), What saith the Scripture? It says, "God was in Christ, reconciling the world unto himself"; that "he made him, who knew no sin, to be a sin offering for us." It says, "He was wounded for our transgressions and bruised for our iniquities." It says, "We have an Advocate with the Father, Jesus Christ the righteous; and he is the atonement for our sins." . . .

. . . undoubtedly, as long as the world stands, there will be a thousand objections to this scriptural doctrine. For still the preaching of Christ crucified will be foolishness to the wise men of the world. However, let us hold the precious truth fast in our hearts as well as in our understanding, and we shall find by happy experience that this is to us the wisdom of God and power of God. (Letter to Mary Bishop [February 7, 1778], *Letters* [JT], 6:297-99)

ATONEMENT: LIMITED (FALSITY OF)

If the Scripture nowhere speaks of a world of believers or elect, then we have no ground, reason, pretense, or excuse for saying Christ died only for a world of believers or elect. But the Scripture nowhere speaks of such a world. Therefore we have no ground or pretense for speaking thus.

. . . The Scripture saith, "Christ came to seek and to save that which was lost." But the elect, as elect, were not lost. Therefore Christ died not for the elect, as or because they were elect, for that had been to seek and save what was found and saved before. (*The Scripture Doctrine Concerning Predestination, Election, and Reprobation* [1741], in *Works* [T], 9:426)

I shall now briefly show the dreadful absurdities that follow from saying, *Christ died only for the elect.*

1. If Christ died not for all, then unbelief is no sin in them that perish; seeing there is not anything for those men to believe unto salvation, for whom Christ died not.

2. If Christ died not for all men, then it would be a sin in the greatest part of mankind to believe he died *for them*; seeing it would be to believe a lie.

3. If Christ died not for those that are damned, then they are not damned for unbelief. Otherwise, you say, that they are damned for not believing a lie.

4. If Christ died not for all, then those who obey Christ, by going and preaching the gospel to every creature, as glad tidings of grace and peace, of great joy *to all people*, do sin thereby, in that they *go to most people* with a lie in their mouth.

5. If Christ died not for all men, then God is not in earnest "in calling all men everywhere to repent"; for what good could repentance do those, for whom Christ died not?

6. If Christ died not for all, then why does he say, "He is not willing that any should perish"? Surely he is willing, yea resolved, that most men should perish; else he would have died for them also.

7. How shall "God judge the world by the man Christ Jesus," if Christ did not die for the world? Or how shall he judge them *according to the gospel*, when there was never any gospel or mercy for them? (*The Scripture Doctrine Concerning Predestination, Election, and Reprobation* [1741], in *Works* [T], 9:427-28)

XX. How will you reconcile reprobation with the following scriptures, which declare God's willingness that all should be saved?

[Matt. 22:9], "As many as ye shall find, bid (*invite*) to the marriage."

[Mark 16:15], "Go ye into all the world, and preach the gospel to every nation."

[Luke 19:41-42], "And when he came near, he beheld the city, and wept over it, saying, If (rather, *O that*) thou hadst known, at least in this thy day, the things which belong unto thy peace!"

[John 5:34], "These things I say, that ye may be saved," [namely,] those who persecuted him and sought to slay him [v. 16] and of whom he complains [v. 40], "Ye will not come unto me, that ye may have life."

[Acts 17:24, 26-27], "God that made the world and all things therein [. . .] giveth to all life, and breath, and all things, and hath made of one blood all nations of men for to dwell on all the face of the earth [. . .] That they should seek the Lord." Observe, this was God's end in creating all nations on all the earth.

[Rom. 5:18], "As by the offence of one judgment came upon all men to condemnation, so by the righteousness of one, the free gift came upon all men unto justification of life." [Rom. 10:12], "The same Lord over all is rich (in mercy) unto all that call upon him."

[1 Tim. 2:3-4], "This is good and acceptable in the sight of God our Saviour, who willeth all men to be saved." [1 Tim. 4:10], "Who is the Saviour of all men, especially of those that believe," [that is], intentionally of all and actually of believers. [James 1:5], "If any man lack wisdom, let him ask of God, who giveth to all men liberally, and upbraideth not." [2 Pet. 3:9], "The Lord is long-suffering toward us, not willing that any should perish, but that all should come to repentance." [1 John 4:14], "We have seen and do testify, that the Father sent the Son to be the Saviour of the world."

XXI. How will you reconcile reprobation with the following scriptures, which declare that Christ came to save all men, that he died for all, that he atoned for all, even for those that finally perish?

[Matt. 18:11], "The Son of man is come to save that which is lost," without any restriction. [John 1:29], "Behold the Lamb of God, which taketh away the sin of the world." [John 3:17], "God sent his Son into the world, that the world through him might be saved." [John 12:47], "I came not (now) to judge the world, but to save the world." [Rom. 14:15], "Destroy not him with thy meat, for whom Christ died." [1 Cor. 8:11], "Through thy knowledge shall thy weak brother perish, for whom Christ died."

[2 Cor. 5:14-15], "We thus judge, that if one died for all, then were all dead: and that he died for all, that those (or all) who live should live unto him which died for them." Here you see, not only that Christ died for all men, but likewise the end of his dying for them.

[1 Tim. 2:6], "Christ Jesus, who gave himself a ransom for all."

[Heb. 2:9], "We see Jesus made lower than the angels, that he might taste death for every man."

[2 Pet. 2:1], "There shall be false teachers among you, who shall privately bring in damnable heresies, even denying the Lord that bought them, and bring upon themselves swift destruction." You see, he bought, or redeemed, even those that perish, that bring upon themselves swift destruction.

[1 John 2:1-2], "If any man sin, we have an Advocate with the Father, Jesus Christ the righteous; and he is the propitiation for our sins" (who are elect, according to the knowledge of God) "and not for ours only, but also for the sins of the whole world."

You are sensible these are but a very small part of the scriptures which might be brought on each of these heads. But they are enough and they require no comment; taken in their plain, easy, obvious sense, they abundantly prove that there is not, cannot be any such thing as unconditional reprobation. (*Predestination Calmly Considered* [1752], in *Works* [T], 9:385-86)

To tear up the very roots of reprobation, and of all doctrines that have a necessary connection therewith, God declares in his word these three things, and that explicitly, in so many terms, (1) "Christ died for all" [2 Cor. 5:14], namely, all that *were dead* in sin, as the words immediately following fix the sense; here is the fact affirmed. (2) "He is the propitiation for the sins of the whole world" [1 John 2:2], even of all those for whom he died; here is the consequence of his dying for all. And, (3) "He died for all, that they should not live unto themselves, but unto him which died for them" [2 Cor. 5:15], that they might be saved from their sins; here is the design, the end of his dying for them. Now show me the scriptures wherein God declares in equally express terms, (1) "Christ did not die for all," but for some only. (2) "Christ is not the propitiation for the sins of the world"; and, (3) "He did not die for all, at least not with that intent, that they should live unto him who died for them." Show me, I say, the scriptures that affirm these three things in equally express terms. You know there are none. Nor is it possible to evade the force of those above recited . . .

. . . What an account does this doctrine give of the sincerity of God in a thousand declarations, such as these: "O that there were such a heart in them that they would fear me, and keep my commandments always, that it might be well with them, and with their children for ever!" [Deut. 5:29]. "My people would not hear my voice, and Israel would not obey me. So I gave them up unto their own hearts' lusts, and let them follow their own imaginations. O that my people would have hearkened unto me! For if Israel had walked in my ways, I should soon have put down their enemies, and turned my hand against their adversaries" [Ps. 81:11-14]. And all this time you suppose God had unchangeably ordained that there never should be *such a heart in them!* that it never should be possible for the people whom he thus *seemed* to lament over, to *hearken unto him*, or to *walk in his ways!* (*Predestination Calmly Considered* [1752], in *Works* [T], 9:393-94)

If anyone could show you, by plain Scripture and reason, a more excellent way than that you have received, you certainly would do well to receive it; and I trust I should do the same. But I think it will not be easy for anyone to show us either that Christ did not die for all or that he is not willing as well as able to cleanse from all sin, even in the present world. (Letter to Lady Maxwell [February 26, 1771], in *Letters*, 411)

But is it free *for all* as well as *in all*? The decree is past, and so it was before the foundation of the world. But what decree? Even this: "I will set before the sons of men, life and death, blessing and cursing. And the soul that chooseth life shall live, as the soul that chooseth death shall die." This decree, whereby "whom God did foreknow, he did predestinate," was indeed from everlasting: this, whereby all who suffer Christ to make them alive are "elect according to the foreknowledge of God," now standeth fast, even as the moon, and as the faithful witnesses in heaven; and when heaven and earth shall pass away, yet this shall not pass away, for it is as unchangeable and eternal as is the being of God that gave it. This decree yields the strongest encouragement to abound in all good works, and in all holiness; and it is a wellspring of joy, of happiness also, to our great and endless comfort. This is worthy of God: it is every way consistent with all the perfections of his nature. It gives us the noblest view both of his justice, mercy, and truth. To this agrees the whole scope of the Christian revelation, as well as all the parts thereof. To this Moses and all the Prophets bear witness, and our blessed Lord, and all his apostles. Thus Moses, in the name of his Lord, "I call heaven and earth to record against you this day, that I have set before you life and death, blessing and cursing; therefore choose life, that thou and thy seed may live." Thus Ezekiel (to cite one prophet for all), "The soul that sinneth, it shall die. The son shall not bear [eternally] the iniquity of the father. The righteousness of the righteous shall be upon him, and the wickedness of the wicked shall be upon him" [18:20]. Thus our blessed Lord: "If any man thirst, let him come unto me and drink" [John 7:37]. Thus his great Apostle St. Paul [Acts 17:30]: "God commandeth all men every where to repent"—"all men every where"; every man in every place, without any exception, either of place or person. Thus St. James: "If any of you lack wisdom, let him ask of God, who giveth to all men liberally, and upbraideth not, and it shall be given him" [James 1:5]. Thus St. Peter [2 Pet. 3:9]: "The Lord is not willing that any should perish, but that all should come to repentance." And thus St. John: "If any man sin, we have an Advocate with the Father; and he is the propitiation for our sins: and not for ours only, but for the sins of the whole world" [1 John 2:1-2].

O hear ye this, ye that forget God! Ye cannot charge your death upon him! "Have I any pleasure at all that the wicked should die? saith the Lord God" [Ezek. 18:23]. Repent, and turn from all your transgressions: so iniquity shall not be your ruin. Cast away from you all your transgressions whereby ye have transgressed—for why will ye die, O house of Israel? For I have no pleasure in the death of him that dieth, saith the Lord God. Wherefore turn yourselves, and live. "As I live, saith the Lord God, I have no pleasure in the death of the wicked. [. . .] Turn ye, turn ye, from your evil ways;

for why will ye die, O house of Israel?" [Ezek. 33:11]. (Quoted in "Of God," chap. 3 in Coll. D, 53-55)

But it is a poor case that you and I must be talking thus. Indeed, these things ought not so to be. It lay in your power to have prevented all, and yet to have borne testimony to what you call the truth. If you had disliked my sermon ["On Free Grace"], you might have printed another on the same text and have answered my proofs without mentioning my name. This had been fair and friendly. Whereas, to proceed as you have done is so far from friendship that it is not moral honesty. Moral honesty does not allow of a treacherous wound, or of the [revealing] of secrets. I will refer the point even to the judgment of Jews, Turk, infidel, or heretic.

Indeed among the latter (*i.e.*, heretics) you publicly place me; for you rank all the maintainers of *universal redemption* with Socinians themselves. Alas, my brother, do you not know even this—that the Socinians allow *no redemption* at all? that Socinus himself . . . says expressly Christ did not die *as a ransom* for any, but only as an *example* for all mankind? How easy were it for me to hit many other palpable blots in that which you call an answer to my sermon? And how above measure contemptible would you then appear to all impartial men either of sense or learning? But I spare you. Mine hand shall not be upon you. The Lord be judge between me and thee! (Letter to George Whitefield [April 27, 1741], in *Letters*, 106)

A

But for whose sins did Christ die? Did he die for *all* men, or but for *some*? . . .

First, the Prophet Isaiah saith thus, "Surely he hath borne our griefs, and carried our sorrows; yet did we esteem him stricken, smitten of God, and afflicted. But he was wounded for our transgressions, he was bruised for our iniquities: the chastisement of our peace was upon him; and with his stripes we are healed. All we like sheep have gone astray; we have turned every one to his own way; and the Lord hath laid on him the iniquity of us all" [Isa. 53:4-6]. Thus Isaiah shows plainly that the iniquities of all those who went astray were laid upon Christ. And to him the testimony of all the other prophets agrees: "To him gave all the prophets witness, that through his name whosoever believeth in him shall receive remission of sins" [Acts 10:43]. The same saith that great prophet, John the Baptist, who "came to bear witness of the light, that all men through it might believe" [John 1:7]. And again, "Behold," saith he, "the Lamb of God, that taketh away the sins of the world" [v. 29]. Thus have all the Prophets with one consent testified that God "laid upon Christ the iniquities of all that were gone astray," that he is "the Lamb of God, which taketh away the sins of the world," that "all men through him may believe," and that "through his name whosoever believeth in him, shall receive remission of sins."

Secondly, the angel of God testified the same thing, saying, "Fear not; for I bring you glad tidings of great joy, which shall be to all people," which were, that there was "born unto them a Saviour, even Christ the Lord" [Luke 2:10-11]. By this also it appears that Christ died for all men. For else it could not have been glad tidings of great joy, to all people; but rather sad tidings to all those for whom he died not.

Thirdly, we come now to the words of Christ himself, who knew his own business better than any man else; and therefore, if his testimony agree with these, we must needs be convinced that they are true. Now he speaks thus, "As Moses lifted up the serpent in the wilderness, even so must the Son of man be lifted up, that whosoever believeth in him should not perish, but have everlasting life. For God so loved the world, that he gave his only begotten Son, that whosoever believeth in him, should not perish, but have everlasting life. For God sent not his Son to condemn the world, but that the world through him might be saved" [John 3:14-17]. Thus we see the words of Christ agree with the words of the Prophets; therefore it must needs be owned that Christ died for all.

Fourthly, and now we will hear what the apostles say concerning this thing. "The love of Christ," saith the Apostle Paul, "constraineth us; because we thus judge, that if one died for all, then were all dead; and that he died for all, that they which live should not henceforth live unto themselves, but unto him that died for them, and rose again" [2 Cor. 5:14-15]. And to Timothy he saith, "There is one God, and one mediator between God and men, the man Christ Jesus, who gave himself a ransom for all, to be testified in due time" [1 Tim. 2:5-6]. Again, he saith to Titus, "The grace of God, which bringeth salvation to all men, hath appeared" [Titus 2:11]. And yet again to the Hebrews, "That he by the grace of God should taste death for every man" [Heb. 2:9]. And to this agreeth St. John, witnessing, "He is the propitiation for our sins, and not for ours only, but also for the sins of the whole world" [1 John 2:2]. And again, speaking of himself and the rest of the apostles, he saith, "We have seen and do testify that the Father sent the Son to be the Saviour of the world" [1 John 4:14]. Thus we have the testimony of all the Prophets, of the angel of God, of Christ himself, and of his holy apostles, all agreeing together in one to prove that Christ died for all mankind. (*The Scripture Doctrine Concerning Predestination, Election, and Reprobation* [1741], in *Works* [T], 9:424-26)

Thus having shown the grievous folly of those who say that *Christ died for none but the elect*, I shall now prove, by undeniable reasons, that *he died for all mankind.*

Reas. 1. Because all the Prophets, the angel of God, Christ himself, and his holy apostles, with one consent, affirm it.

Reas. 2. Because there is not one scripture, from the beginning of Genesis to the end of the Revelation, that denies it either negatively, by saying that *he did not die for all*, or affirmatively, by saying that *he died only for some*.

Reas. 3. Because he himself commanded that the gospel should be preached to *every creature*.

Reas. 4. *Because he calleth all men, everywhere to repent.*

Reas. 5. Because those who perish are damned for *not believing in the name of the only begotten Son of God*, therefore, he must have died for them. Else they would be damned *for not believing a lie*.

Reas. 6. Because they which are damned might have been saved. For thus saith the Word of God, "They received not the love of the truth, that they might be saved. Therefore God shall send them strong delusions, to believe a lie, that they all may be damned" [2 Thess. 2:10-12].

Reas. 7. Because some "deny the Lord that bought them, and bring upon themselves swift destruction." But they could not *deny the Lord that bought them*, if he had not bought them at all. (*The Scripture Doctrine Concerning Predestination, Election, and Reprobation* [1741], in *Works* [T], 9:427)

AUTHORITY: OBEDIENCE TO

Upon the whole we agree that Christ is the only *supreme Judge and Lawgiver* in the church; I may add, and in the world: for "there is no power," no secular power, but of God: of God who "was manifested in the flesh, who is over all, blessed for ever." But we do not at all agree in the inference which you would draw therefrom, namely, that there is no *subordinate judge* or *lawgiver* in the church. You may just as well infer that there is no subordinate judge or lawgiver in the *world*. Yea there is, both in the one and the other. And in obeying these *subordinate powers*, we do not, as you aver, renounce the *supreme*; no, but we obey them for *his* sake.

We believe it is not only innocent but our bounden duty so to do: in all things of an indifferent nature to "submit ourselves to every ordinance of man" and that for the Lord's sake, because we think he has not forbidden but expressly commanded it. Therefore "as a genuine fruit of our allegiance to Christ," we "submit" both "to the king and governors sent by him," so far as possibly we can without breaking some plain command of God. (*A Letter to the Rev. Mr. Toogood* [January 10, 1758], in *Works* [T], 9:153-54)

A

BAPTISM

It is the initiatory sacrament which enters as into covenant with God. It was instituted by Christ, who alone has power to institute a proper sacrament, a sign, seal, pledge, and means of grace, perpetually obligatory on all Christians. We know not, indeed, the exact time of its institution, but we know it was long before our Lord's ascension. And it was instituted in the room of circumcision. For, as that was a sign and seal of God's covenant, so is this. (*A Treatise on Baptism* [November 11, 1756], in Coll. B, 223)

BAPTISMAL REGENERATION

Be baptized and wash away thy sins: Baptism administered to real penitents is both a means and seal of pardon. Nor did God ordinarily in the primitive church bestow this on any, unless through this means. (Quoted in "Of Holy Baptism," chap. 3 in Coll. A, 9)

By baptism we, who were "by nature children of wrath," are made the children of God. And this regeneration, which our [Anglican] Church in so many places ascribes to baptism, is more than barely being admitted into the Church, though commonly connected therewith; being "grafted into the body of Christ's Church, we are made the children of God by adoption and grace." This is grounded on the plain words of our Lord, "Except a man be born again of water and of the Spirit, he cannot enter into the kingdom of God" [John 3:5]. By water then, as a means, the water of baptism, we are regenerated or born again; whence it is also called by the apostle "the washing of regeneration." Our Church, therefore, ascribes no greater virtue to baptism than Christ himself has done. Nor does she ascribe it to the outward washing, but to the inward grace, which, added thereto, makes it a sacrament. Herein a principle of grace is infused which will not be wholly taken away, unless we quench the Holy Spirit of God by long-continued wickedness. (*A Treatise on Baptism* [November 11, 1756], in Coll. B, 227)

By baptism we are admitted into the church, and consequently made members of Christ, its head. For "as many as are baptized into Christ," in his name, "have" thereby "put on Christ" [Gal. 3:27]—that is, are mystically united to Christ and made one with him. For "by one Spirit we are all baptized into one body" [1 Cor. 12:13], namely, the church, "the body of Christ." From which spiritual, vital union with him proceeds the influence of his grace on those that are baptized. . . .

By baptism we, who were "by nature children of wrath," are made the children of God. And this regeneration, which our [Anglican] Church in so many places ascribes to baptism, is more than barely being admitted into the Church, though commonly connected therewith; being "grafted into the body of Christ's Church, we are made the children of God by adoption and grace." . . . By water then, as a means—the water of baptism—we are regenerated, or born again: whence it is also called by the apostle "the washing of regeneration." Our Church, therefore, ascribes no greater virtue to baptism than Christ himself has done. Nor does she ascribe it to the outward washing, but to the inward grace, which added thereto makes it a sacrament. . . .

In consequence of our being made children of God, we are heirs of the kingdom of heaven. "If children" (as the apostle observes), "then heirs; heirs with God, and joint heirs with Christ." (*A Treatise on Baptism* [November 11, 1756], in Coll. B, 226-27)

The outward sign duly received is *always* accompanied with the inward grace. (Quoted in "Of Holy Baptism," chap. 3 in Coll. A, 7)

BAPTISM AND BEING "BORN AGAIN"

I baptized John Smith (late an Anabaptist) and four other adults at Islington. Of the adults I have known baptized lately, one only was at that time born again, in the full sense of the word; that is, found a thorough inward change by the love of God filling her heart. Most of them were only born again in a lower sense, [that is], received the remission of their sins. And some (as it has since too plainly appeared) neither in one sense nor the other. (*Journal,* January 25, 1739)

That these privileges—the being born again, born of God, born of the Spirit; the being a son or a child of God, or having the Spirit of adoption—are ordinarily annexed to baptism, we *know*. (Quoted in "Of Holy Baptism," chap. 3 in Coll. A, 9)

It is certain, our Church supposes that all who are baptized in their infancy are at the same time born again; and it is allowed, that the whole office for the baptism of infants proceeds upon this supposition. (Quoted in "Of Holy Baptism," chap. 3 in Coll. A, 8)

The expression, being born again, was not first used by our Lord in his conversation with Nicodemus. It was well known before that time and was in common use among the Jews when our Savior appeared among them. When an adult heathen was convinced that the Jewish religion was of God, and desired to join therein, it was the custom to baptize him first, before he was admitted to circumcision. And when he was baptized, he was said to be born again; by which they meant that he who was before a child of the devil was now adopted into the family of God and accounted one of his children. This expression, therefore, which Nicodemus, being "a teacher in Israel," ought to have understood well, our Lord uses in conversing with him, only in a stronger sense than he was accustomed to. And this might be the reason of his asking, "How can these things be?" They cannot be literally: a man cannot "enter a second time into his mother's womb, and be born"; but they may spiritually: a man may be born from above, born of God, born of the Spirit, in a manner which bears a very near analogy to the natural birth. (Quoted in "Of Regeneration," chap. 11 in Coll. D, 194-95)

The plain meaning of the expression, "except a man be born of water," is neither more nor less than this, "except he be baptized." And the plain reason why he ought to be thus *born of water* is because God hath appointed it. (Quoted in "Of Holy Baptism," chap. 3 in Coll. A, 8)

Of the new birth, you say, "The terms of being regenerated, of being born again, of being born of God, are often used to express the works of gospel righteousness." . . . I cannot allow this. I know not that they are ever used in Scripture to express any *outward work* at all. They always express an *inward work* of the Spirit, whereof baptism is the outward sign. . . . You proceed: "Our holy church doth teach us that by the laver of regeneration in baptism we are received into the number of the children of God—this is the first part of the new birth." . . .

. . . What is the *first part* of the new birth? *Baptism?* It is the *outward sign* of that inward and spiritual grace, but no *part* of it at all. It is impossible it should be. The outward sign is no more a part of the inward grace than the body is a part of the soul. Or do you mean that *regeneration* is a *part* of the new birth? Nay, this is the *whole* of it. Or is it the *laver of regeneration* which is the first *part* of it? That cannot be, for you suppose this to be the same with baptism. (A letter to the Rev. Mr. Potter [November 17, 1758], in *Works*, 13:75)

BAPTISM AND JUSTIFICATION

Infants indeed our [Anglican] Church supposes to be justified in baptism, although they cannot then either believe or repent. But she expressly requires both repentance and faith in those who come to be baptized when they are of riper years. (*A Farther Appeal to Men of Reason and Religion* [1745], pt. 1, in *Works*, 12:54)

Baptism administered to real penitents is both a means and seal of pardon. Nor did God ordinarily in the primitive church bestow this on any unless through this means. (Quoted in "Of Justification by Faith," chap. 11 in Coll. A, 78-79)

But "as by the offense of one, judgment came upon all men to condemnation, so by the righteousness of one, the free gift came upon all men, to justification of life." And the virtue of this free gift, the merits of Christ's life and death, are applied to us in baptism. "He gave himself for the Church, that he might sanctify and cleanse it with the washing of water by the word" [Eph. 5:25-26], namely, in baptism, the ordinary instrument of our justification. Agreeably to this, our [Anglican] Church prays in the baptismal office that the person to be baptized may be "washed and sanctified by the Holy Ghost and, being delivered from God's wrath, receive remission of sins and enjoy the everlasting benediction of his heavenly washing." (*A Treatise on Baptism* [November 11, 1756], in Coll. B, 226)

B

BAPTISM AND ORIGINAL SIN

What are the benefits we receive by baptism is the next point to be considered. . . . And the first of these is the washing away the guilt of original sin by the application of the merits of Christ's death. (*A Treatise on Baptism* [November 11, 1756], in Coll. B, 225)

It has been already proved that this original stain cleaves to every child of man; and that hereby they [infants] are children of wrath and liable to eternal damnation. It is true, the second Adam has found a remedy for the disease which came upon all by the offense of the first. But the benefit of this is to be received through the means which he hath appointed—through baptism in particular, which is the ordinary means he hath appointed for that purpose and to which God hath tied us, though he may not have tied himself. (*A Treatise on Baptism* [November 11, 1756], in Coll. B, 228)

BAPTISM AND SALVATION

You think the mode of baptism is necessary to salvation. I deny that even baptism is so. If it were, every Quaker must be damned, which I can in no wise believe. (Letter to Gilbert Boyce [May 22, 1750], *Letters* [JT], 3:36)

Our [Anglican] Church . . . declares in the rubric at the end of the office, "It is certain, by God's word, that children who are baptized, dying before they commit actual sin, are saved." And this is agreeable to the unanimous judgment of all the ancient fathers. . . . Baptism doth now save us, if we live answerable thereto; if we repent, believe, and obey the gospel, supposing this, as it admits us into the church here, so into glory hereafter. . . . In the ordinary way there is no other means of entering into the church or into heaven. (*A Treatise on Baptism* [November 11, 1756], in Coll. B, 226-28)

BAPTISM: INFANT

This, therefore, is our first ground. Infants need to be washed from original sin; therefore, they are proper subjects of baptism.

Secondly. If infants are capable of making a covenant, and were and still are under the evangelical covenant, then they have a right to baptism, which is the entering seal thereof. But infants are capable of making a covenant and were and still are under the evangelical covenant.

. . . But we have stronger proof than this, even God's own word: "Ye stand this day all of you before the Lord; your captains, with all the men of Israel; your little ones, your wives, and the stranger; that thou shouldest enter into covenant with the Lord thy God" [Deut. 29:10-12]. Now, God would never have made a covenant with little ones if they had not been capable of it. It is not said children only, but little children, the Hebrew word properly signifying infants.

. . . If it be objected, "There is no express mention in Scripture of any infants whom the apostles baptized," I would ask, Suppose no mention had been made in the Acts of those two women baptized by the apostles, yet might we not fairly conclude that when so many thousands, so many entire households, were baptized, women were not excluded, especially since it was the known custom of the Jews to baptize them? The same holds of children; nay, more strongly, on the account of circumcision. Three thousand were baptized by the apostles in one day, and five thousand in another. And can it be reasonably supposed that there were no children among such vast numbers? Again, the apostles baptized many families; nay, we hardly read of one master of a family who was converted and baptized, but his whole family (as was before the custom among the Jews) were baptized with him; thus the "jailer's household, he and all his; the household of Caius, of Stephanus, of Crispus." And can we suppose that in all these households, which, we read, were without exception baptized, there should not be so much as one child or infant? But to go one step farther: St. Peter says to the multitude, "Repent, and be baptized every one of you, for the remission of sins. For the promise is unto you, and to your children" [Acts 2:38-39]. Indeed, the answer is made directly to those who asked, "What shall we do?" But it reaches farther than to those who asked the question. And though children could not actually repent, yet they might be baptized. And that they are included appears, (1) Because the apostle addresses to "every one" of them, and in "every one" children must be contained. (2) They are expressly mentioned: "The promise is unto you, and to your children." (*A Treatise on Baptism* [November 11, 1756], in Coll. B, 229, 232)

BEATIFIC VISION

I doubt whether any embodied spirit can feel such entire self-abasement as is felt by those spirits that see the face of our Father which is in heaven. And undoubtedly, the nearer they approach the throne, the more abased they will be. (Letter to Miss Elizabeth Ritchie [October 6, 1778], *Works* [S], 7:180)

BISHOPS

We believe that the threefold order of ministers (which you seem to mean by papal hierarchy and prelacy) is authorized not only by its apostolic institution but also by the written Word. (Letter to Westley Hall, in *Journal*, December 30, 1745)

I know myself to be as real a Christian bishop as the Archbishop of Canterbury. (Letter to Barnabas Thomas [March 25, 1785], *Letters* [JT], 7:262)

I firmly believe I am a scriptural *episkopos* [bishop] as much as any man in England or Europe. (For the uninterrupted succession I know to be a fable, which no man ever did or can prove.) (Letter to Charles Wesley [August 19, 1785], in *Letters*, 91)

BISHOPS: LIBERAL OR NOMINAL

For these forty years I have been in doubt concerning the question: What obedience is due to "Heathenish priests and mitered infidels [unbelieving bishops]"?

I have from time to time proposed my doubts to the most pious and sensible clergymen I knew. But they gave me no satisfaction; rather they seemed to be puzzled as well as I. Some obedience I always paid to the bishops, in obedience to the laws of the land. But I cannot see that I am under any obligation to obey them farther than those laws require.

It is in obedience to those laws that I have never exercised in England the power which I believe God has given me. . . .

. . . I submit still (though sometimes with a doubting conscience) to mitered infidels. I do indeed vary from them in some points of doctrine and in some points of discipline—by preaching abroad, for instance, by praying extempore, and by forming societies; but not a hair's-breadth further than I believe to be meet, right, and my bounden duty. (Letter to Charles Wesley [August 19, 1785], in *Letters*, 91-92)

BISHOPS: OPPOSED IN METHODISM

How can you, how dare you, suffer yourself to be called bishop? I shudder; I start at the very thought! Men may call me a knave or a fool, a rascal, a scoundrel, and I am content; but they shall never, by my consent, call me *bishop!* For my sake, for God's sake, for Christ's sake, put a full end to this! Let the Presbyterians do what they please, but let the Methodists know their calling better. (Letter to the Rev. Francis Asbury [September 20, 1788], in Coll. C, 394)

BLESSINGS (PRIESTLY)

I then by imposition of hands, as *usual*, gave him a blessing. (Quoted in "Of Ritual," chap. 15 in Coll. A, 111)

BOWING (AT THE NAME OF JESUS)

May I . . . never mention Thy Venerable Name, unless on just, solemn, and devout occasions, nor even then without *acts of adoration.* (Quoted in "Of Ritual," chap. 15 in Coll. A, 110)

BUFFOONERY AND FOOLS

I immediately saw there was no encountering a buffoon, by serious reason and argument. This would naturally have furnished both him and his admirers with fresh matter of ridicule. On the other hand, if I should let myself down to a level with him, by a less serious manner of writing than I was accustomed to, I was afraid of debasing the dignity of the subject. Nay, and I knew not but I might catch something of his spirit. I remembered the advice, "Answer not a fool according to his folly, lest thou also be like unto him" [Prov. 26:4]. And yet I saw there must be an exception in some cases, as the words immediately following show: "Answer a fool according to his folly, lest he be wise in his own conceit" [v. 5]. I conceive, as if he had said, Yet it is needful in some cases, to "answer a fool according to his folly," otherwise he will be "wiser in his own conceit, than seven men that can render a reason." I therefore constrained myself to approach as near as I dared, to his own manner of writing. And I trust the occasion will plead my excuse with your lordship, and all reasonable men. (*A Second Letter to the Author of* The Enthusiasm of Methodists and Papists Compared [November 27, 1750], in *Works,* 13:21)

CALLING (WESLEY'S)

I have both an ordinary call and an extraordinary. My ordinary call is my ordination by the bishop, "Take thou authority to preach the Word of God." My extraordinary call is witnessed by the works God doeth by my ministry: which prove that he is with me of a truth in this exercise of my office.

Perhaps this might be better expressed in another way: God bears witness in an extraordinary manner, that my thus exercising my ordinary call is well pleasing in his sight. (Letter to Charles Wesley [June 23, 1739], in *Letters*, 71)

CALVIN, JOHN

That Michael Servetus was "one of the wildest antitrinitarians that ever appeared" is by no means clear. I doubt of it, on the authority of Calvin himself, who certainly was not prejudiced in his favor. For if Calvin does not misquote his words, he was no antitrinitarian at all. Calvin himself gives a quotation from one of his letters, in which he expressly declares, "I do believe the Father is God, the Son is God, and the Holy Ghost is God. But I dare not use the word *Trinity* or *Person*." I dare, and I think them very good words. But I should think it very hard to be burnt alive for not using them: especially with a slow fire, made of moist, green wood!

I believe Calvin was a great instrument of God and that he was a wise and pious man. But I cannot but advise those who love his memory to let Servetus alone. (*Some Remarks on a Defense of the Preface to the Edinburgh Edition of* Aspasio Vindicated [May 1766], in *Works*, 13:117)

CALVINISM: CRITICISMS OF

Q. 23. Wherein may we come to the very edge of Calvinism?

A. (1) In ascribing all good to the free grace of God. (2) In denying all natural free-will, and all power antecedent to grace. And, (3) In excluding all merit from man; even for what he has or does by the grace of God. (*Minutes of Some Late Conversations* [August 2, 1745], in *Works* [S], 5:201)

I did attack predestination eight and twenty years ago. And I do not believe now, any predestination which implies irrespective reprobation. But I do not believe it is *necessarily subversive* of all religion. I think hot disputes are much more so. Therefore I never willingly dispute with anyone about it. And I advise all my friends, not in Scotland only but all over England and Ireland, to avoid all contention on the head, and let every man remain in his own opinion. Can any man of candor blame me for this? Is there anything *unfair* or *disingenuous* in it? (Letter to Rev. Mr. Plendeleith [May 23, 1768], in *Works*, 16:78)

Both my brother and I still indulged the fond hope of living in peace with our *warm Calvinist* brethren, but we now give it up. Our eyes are open; we see what we have to expect. We look for neither mercy nor justice at their hands; if we find any, it will be clear gains. (*Some Remarks on Mr. Hill's Review of All the Doctrines Taught by Mr. John Wesley* [September 9, 1772], in *Works* [T], 9:501)

Has *the truth* . . . a natural tendency to *spoil the temper*? To inspire pride, haughtiness, superciliousness? To make a man wiser *in his own eyes than seven men that can render a reason*? Does it naturally turn a man into a cynic, a bear, a Toplady? Does it at once set him free from all the restraints of good nature, decency, and good manners? Cannot a man hold *distinguishing grace*, as it is called, but he must distinguish himself for passion, sourness, bitterness? Must a man as soon as he looks upon himself to be an absolute favorite of heaven, look upon all that oppose him as *Diabolonians*, as predestinated dogs of hell? Truly, the melancholy instance now before us would almost induce us to think so. For who was of a more amiable temper than Mr. Hill, a few years ago? When I first conversed with him in London, I thought I had seldom seen a man of fortune who appeared to be of a more humble, modest, gentle, friendly disposition. And yet this same Mr. H. when he has once been grounded in the *knowledge of the* truth, is of a temper as totally different from this, as light is from darkness! He is now haughty, supercilious, disdaining his opponents, as unworthy to be set with the dogs of his flock! He is violent, impetuous, bitter of spirit! In a word, the author of *the Review*!

[Oh,] Sir, what a commendation is this of your doctrine? Look at Mr. H. the *Arminian!* The loving, amiable, generous, friendly man. Look at Mr. H. the *Calvinist!* Is it the same person? This spiteful, morose, touchy man? Alas, what has *the knowledge of the truth* done? What a deplorable change has it made? Sir, I love you still; though I cannot esteem you as I did once. Let me entreat you, if not for the honor of God, yet for the honor of your cause, avoid for the time to come, all anger, all spite, all sourness and bitterness, all contemptuous usage of your opponents, not inferior to you, unless in fortune. (*Some Remarks on Mr. Hill's Review of All the Doctrines Taught by Mr. John Wesley* [September 9, 1772], in *Works* [T], 9:506-7)

For who will dare to affirm that none of these are truly religious men? Not only many of them in the last century were burning and shining lights, but many of them are now real Christians, loving God and all mankind. And yet what are all the absurd opinions of all the Romanists in the world, compared to that one, that the God of Love, the wise, just, merciful Father of the spirits of all flesh, has, from all eternity, fixed an absolute, unchangeable, irresistible decree, that part of mankind shall be saved, do what they will, and the rest damned, do what they can! ("On the Trinity" [May 8, 1775], Sermon 59, in *Works* [T], 6:208)

Q. 26. Calvinism has been the greatest hindrance of the work of God. What makes men swallow it so greedily?

A. Because it is so pleasing to flesh and blood; the doctrine of final perseverance in particular.

Q. 27. What can be done to stop its progress?

A. (1) Let all our preachers carefully read our tracts and Mr. Fletcher's and Sellon's.

(2) Let them preach universal redemption frequently and explicitly, but in love and gentleness, taking care never to return railing for railing. Let the Calvinists have all this on their side. (*An Answer to Mr. Rowland Hill's Tract, Entitled, "Imposture Detected"* [June 28, 1777], in *Works* [WL], 10:449)

Calvinism is not the gospel; nay, it is farther from it than most of the sermons I hear at church. These are very frequently unevangelical, but they are not anti-evangelical. They are (to say no more) equally wrong, and they are far more dangerously wrong. Few of the Methodists are now in danger from imbibing error from the [Anglican] Church ministers, but they are in great danger of imbibing the grand error—Calvinism—from the Dissenting ministers. (Letter to Mary Bishop [October 18, 1778], in *Letters* [JT], 6:326)

Of Calvinism, mysticism, and antinomianism, have a care, for they are the bane of true religion; and one or the other of them has been the grand hindrance of the work of God, wherever it has broken out. (Letter to William Black [February 26, 1783], in *Letters*, 260)

There is no part of Calvinism or antinomianism which is not fully answered in some part of our writings; particularly in the *Preservative against Unsettled Notions in Religion* [1758]. (Letter to William Black [May 11, 1784], in *Letters*, 261)

CATHOLICISM (ROMAN); CATHOLICS

I can in no degree justify these things. And yet neither can I look upon them in the same light that you do, as "some of the very worst things which are objected to the Church of Rome." They are exceedingly great mistakes: yet in as great mistakes have holy men both lived and died: Thomas à Kempis, for instance, and Francis [de] Sales. And yet I doubt not, they are now in Abraham's bosom. (*Answer to the Rev. Mr. Church's "Remarks on the Rev. Mr. Wesley's Last Journal"* [February 2, 1745], in *Works*, 12:286)

I must here take notice of . . . your instances of popish enthusiasm. . . . "That not a word fell from St. Katharine of Sienna that was not religious and holy." . . . I would to God the comparison between the Methodists and Papists would hold in this respect! Yea, that you, and all the clergy in England, were guilty of such enthusiasm. (*A Letter to the Author of* The Enthusiasm of Methodists and Papists Compared [1750], in *Works*, 13:4)

It is true that for thirty years last past I have "gradually put on a more catholic spirit," finding more and more tenderness for those who differed from me either in opinions or modes of worship. But it is not true that I "reject any design of converting others from any communion." I have, by the blessing of God, converted several from popery, who are now alive and ready to testify it. (*A Second Letter to the Author of* The Enthusiasm of Methodists and Papists Compared [November 27, 1750], in *Works*, 13:62)

There are excellent things in most of the mystic writers. As almost all of them lived in the Romish Church, they were lights whom the gracious providence of God raised up to shine in a dark place. But they did not give a clear, a steady, or a uniform light. (Letter to Miss Bishop [September 19, 1773], in *Works* [S], 7:165)

The Church of Rome is no more the *church in general* than the Church of England is. It is only one particular branch of the catholic, or universal, church of Christ, which is the whole body of believers in Christ scattered over the whole earth. We therefore see no reason to refer any matter in dispute to the Church of Rome more than any other church, especially as we know neither the bishop nor the Church of Rome to be any more infallible than ourselves. (*Popery Calmly Considered* [1779], in *Works*, 15:179-80)

That many members of that church have been holy men, and that many are so now, I firmly believe. . . . by the tender mercies of God, many members of the Church of Rome have been and are now holy men, notwithstanding their principles; yet I fear many of their principles have a natural tendency to undermine holiness; greatly to hinder, if not utterly to destroy, the essential branches of it, to destroy the love of God and the love of our neighbor, with all justice and mercy and truth. (*Popery Calmly Considered* [1779], in *Works*, 15:193-94)

On the other hand, how many writers of the Romish Church (as Francis [de] Sales and Juan de Castaniza, in particular) have written strongly and scripturally on sanctification, who, nevertheless, were entirely unacquainted with the nature of justification! insomuch that the whole body of their Divines at the Council of Trent, in their *Catechismus ad Parochos* (Catechism which every parish priest is to teach his people) totally confound sanctification and justification together. But it has pleased God to give the Methodists a full and clear knowledge of each, and the wide difference between them. ("On God's Vineyard" [October 17, 1787], Sermon 107, in *Works* [WL], 7:204)

I have often been pained for you, fearing you did not set out the right way. I do not mean with regard to this or that set of opinions, Protestant or Romish. All these I trample under foot. But with regard to those weightier matters, wherein if they go wrong, either Protestants or Papists will perish everlastingly. I feared you were not *born again*; and "except a man be born again," if we may credit the Son of God, "he cannot see the kingdom of heaven"; except he experience that inward change of the earthly, sensual mind, for the mind which was in Christ Jesus. You might have thoroughly understood the scriptural doctrine of the new birth, yea, and experienced it long before now, had you used the many opportunities of improvement which God put into your hand, while you believed both your father and me to be teachers sent from God. But, alas! what are you now? Whether of this church or that, I care not; you may be saved in either or damned in either; but I fear you are not born again and except ye be born again you cannot see the kingdom of God. You believe the Church of Rome is right. What then? If you are not born of God, *you* are of *no Church*. Whether Bellarmine or Luther be right, you are certainly wrong if you are not *born of the Spirit*, if you are not renewed in the spirit of your mind in the likeness of him that created you.

I doubt you were never convinced of the necessity of this great change. And there is now greater danger than ever that you never will be, that you will be diverted from the thought of it by a train of new notions, new practices, new modes of worship—all which put together (not to consider whether they are unscriptural, superstitious, and idolatrous, or no), all I say put together do not amount to one grain of true, vital, spiritual religion.

. . . My dear Sammy, your first point is to repent and believe the gospel. Know yourself a poor, guilty, helpless sinner! Then know Jesus Christ and him crucified! Let the Spirit of God bear witness with your spirit that you are a child of God, and let the love of God be shed abroad in your heart by the Holy Ghost, which is given unto you; and then, if you have no better work, I will talk with you of transubstantiation or purgatory. (Letter to Samuel Wesley Jr. [August 19, 1784], in *Letters*, 443-44)

The faith of the Roman Catholics in general seems to be above that of the ancient Jews. If most of these are volunteers in faith, believing more than God has revealed, it cannot be denied that they believe all which God has revealed as necessary to salvation. In this we rejoice on their behalf; we are glad that none of those new articles which they added at the Council of Trent to "the faith once delivered to the saints," does so materially contradict any of the ancient articles as to render them of no effect. ("On Faith" [April 9, 1788], Sermon 106, in Coll. D, 178-79)

CELIBACY AND SINGLENESS

To this happy few I say, . . . Know the advantages you enjoy, many of which are pointed out by the apostle himself. You may be without carefulness. You are under no necessity of "caring for the things of the world." You have only to "care for the things of the Lord, how you may please the Lord." One care alone lies upon you, how you "may be holy both in body and spirit."

You may "attend upon the Lord without distraction" . . .

You enjoy a blessed liberty from the "trouble in the flesh," which must more or less attend a married state, from a thousand nameless domestic trials which are found, sooner or later, in every family. You are exempt from numberless occasions of sorrow and anxiety, with which heads of families are entangled; especially those who have sickly or weak or unhappy or disobedient children. . . .

You may give all your worldly substance to God; nothing need hinder. You have no increasing family; you have no wife or children to provide for, which might occasion a thousand doubts (without any extraordinary measure of divine light) whether you had done either too much or too little for them. (*Thoughts on a Single Life* [1743], in *Works* [WL], 11:458-59)

Blessed are they who have made themselves eunuchs for the kingdom of heaven's sake; who abstain from things lawful in themselves, in order to be more devoted to God. Let these never forget those remarkable words: "Peter said, Lo we have left all and followed thee." And Jesus answered and said, "Verily I say unto you," a preface denoting the certainty and importance of what is spoken, "There is no man that hath left" (either by giving them up, or by not accepting them) "house, or brethren, or sisters, or father, or mother, or wife, or children, or lands, for my sake and the gospel's, but he shall receive an hundredfold—now, in this time; and, in the world to come, eternal life."

When the apostles said, "If the case be so, it is good not to marry, he said unto them, All men cannot receive this saying . . . He that is able to receive it, *let* him receive it." To this happy few I say, Know the advantages you enjoy, many of which are pointed out by the apostle himself: You may be *without carefulness*. You are under no necessity of *caring for the things of the world*. You have only to *care for the things of the Lord, how you may please the Lord*. One care alone lies upon you, how you *may be holy both in body and spirit*.

And let it be a matter of daily thanksgiving to God that he has made you a partaker of these benefits. Indeed the more full and explicit you are herein, the more sensible you will be of the cause you have to be thankful; the more lively conviction you will have of the greatness of the blessing. (Quoted in "Of the Celibate State," chap. 9 in Coll. A, 64-65)

My scraps of time this week I employed in setting down my present *Thoughts upon a single life*, which indeed are just the same as they have been these thirty years. And the same they must be, unless I give up my Bible. (Quoted in "Of the Celibate State," chap. 9 in Coll. A, 68)

CHEERFULNESS (AND CHRISTIANITY)

You seem to apprehend that I believe religion to be inconsistent with cheerfulness and with a sociable, friendly temper. So far from it that I am convinced as true religion or holiness cannot be without cheerfulness, so steady cheerfulness, on the other hand, cannot be without holiness or true religion. And I am equally convinced, that religion has nothing sour, austere, unsociable, unfriendly in it; but, on the contrary, implies the most winning sweetness, the most amiable softness and gentleness. Are you for having as much cheerfulness as you can? So am I. (Letter to Mrs. Chapman [March 39, 1737], in Coll. C, 315)

By the grace of God I never fret; I repine at nothing, I am discontented with nothing. And to hear persons at my ear fretting and murmuring at everything is like tearing the flesh off my bones. I see God sitting upon his throne and ruling all things well. Although therefore I can bear this also, to hear his government of the world continually found fault with (for in blaming the things which he alone can alter, we in effect blame him), yet it is such a burden to me as I cannot bear without pain; and I bless God when it is removed. (Letter to Ebenezer Blackwell [August 31, 1755], in *Letters*, 329)

CHILD KILLING

They were as a nation . . . *"Void of natural affection,"* even to their own bowels. Witness the universal custom, which obtained for several ages in Rome and all its dependencies (as it had done before through all the cities of Greece), when in their highest repute for wisdom and virtue, of *exposing* their own newborn children, more or fewer of them, as every man pleased, when he had as many as he thought good to keep, throwing them out to perish by cold and hunger, unless some more merciful wild beast shortened their pain and provided them a sepulchre. Nor do I remember a single Greek or Roman, of all those that occasionally mention it, ever complaining of this diabolical custom or fixing the least touch of blame upon it. Even the tender mother in Terence, who had some compassion for her helpless infant, does not dare to acknowledge it to her husband, without that remarkable preface, *Ut misere superstitiosae sumus omnes*, as we women are all miserably superstitious.

I would desire those gentlemen who are so very severe upon the Israelites for killing the children of the Canaanites at their entrance into the land of Canaan, to spend a few thoughts on this. Not to insist, that the Creator is the absolute Lord and Proprietor of the lives of all his creatures: that as such he may at any time, without the least injustice, take away the life which he has given; that he may do this in whatsoever manner and by whatever instruments he pleases and consequently may inflict death on any creature by whom he pleases without any blame either to him or them; not to insist, I say, on this or many other things which might be offered, let us at present fix on this single consideration. The Israelites destroyed the children for some weeks or months, the Greeks and Romans for above a thousand years. The one put them out of their pain at once, doubtless by the shortest and easiest way. The others were not so compassionate as to cut their throats, but left them to pine away by a lingering death. Above all, the Hebrews destroyed only the children of their enemies; the Romans destroyed their own. (*The Doctrine of Original Sin: According to Scripture, Reason, and Experience* [1757], in *Works* [T], 9:175-76)

CHRISTIAN

A Christian! Are you so? Do you understand the word? Do you know what a Christian is? If you are a Christian, you have the mind that was in Christ and you so walk as he also walked. You are holy as he is holy both in heart and in all manner of conversation. Have you then the mind that was in Christ? And do you walk as Christ walked? Are you inwardly and outwardly holy? I fear, not even outwardly. No; you live in known sin. Alas! How then are you a Christian? What a railer, a Christian! A common swearer, a Christian! A sabbath breaker, a Christian! A drunkard or whoremonger, a Christian! Thou art a heathen barefaced; the wrath of God is on thy head and the curse of God upon thy back. Thy damnation slumbereth not. By reason of such Christians it is that the holy name of Christ is blasphemed. (*A Farther Appeal to Men of Reason and Religion* [1745], pt. 1, in *Works*, 12:134)

None can deny that the people of England, in general, are *called* Christians. They are *called* so, a few only excepted, by others as well as by themselves. But I presume no man will say that the *name* makes the *thing*, that men *are* Christians barely because they are *called* so. It must be . . . allowed that the people of England, generally speaking, have been *christened* or baptized. But neither can we infer these were once *baptized*; therefore they *are* Christians now. It is . . . allowed that many of those who were once *baptized* and are *called Christians* to this day *hear* the word of God, attend *public prayers*, and partake of the *Lord's Supper*. But neither does this prove that they *are* Christians. For notwithstanding this, some of them live in open sin: and others (though not conscious to themselves of *hypocrisy*, yet) are utter strangers to the *religion of the heart*: are full of pride, vanity, covetousness, ambition; of hatred, anger, malice, or envy; and consequently are no more *scriptural* Christians than the open drunkard or common swearer. (*The Principles of a Methodist Farther Explained* [1746], in *Works*, 12:389-93)

Those who are holy or righteous in the judgment of God himself; those who are endued with the faith that purifies the heart, that produces a good conscience; those who are grafted into the good Olive tree, the spiritual, invisible church; those who are branches of the true Vine, of whom Christ says, "I am the Vine, ye are the branches"; those who so effectually know Christ, as by that knowledge to have escaped the pollutions of the world; those who see the light of the glory of God in the face of Jesus Christ and who have been made partakers of the Holy Ghost, of the witness and fruits of the Spirit; those who live by faith in the Son of God; those who are sanctified by the blood of the covenant. (*Serious Thoughts upon the Perseverance of the Saints* [1751], in *Works* [T], 9:439)

Who then is a Christian, according to the light which God hath vouchsafed to this people? He that, being "justified by faith, hath peace with God through our Lord Jesus Christ"; and, at the same time, is "born again," "born from above," "born of the Spirit"; inwardly changed from the image of the devil, to that "image of God wherein he was created"; he that finds the love of God shed abroad in his heart by the Holy Ghost which is given unto him; and whom this love sweetly constrains to love his neighbor, every man, as himself; he that has learned of his Lord to be meek and lowly in heart and in every state to be content; he in whom is that whole mind, all those tempers which were also in Christ Jesus; he that abstains from all appearance of evil in his actions and that offends not with his tongue; he that walks in all the commandments of God and in all his ordinances blameless; he that in all his intercourse with men does to others as he would they should do to him; and in his whole life and conversation, whether he eats or drinks or whatsoever he doeth, doeth all to the glory of God. ("On God's Vineyard" [October 17, 1787], Sermon 107, in *Works* [WL], 7:205-6)

I care not a rush for your being called a Papist or Protestant. But I am grieved at your being a heathen. Certain it is that the general religion both of Protestants and Catholics is no better than refined heathenism. (Letter to Samuel Wesley Jr. [April 29, 1790], *Letters* [JT], 8:218)

CHRISTIANITY AND SECULAR KNOWLEDGE

Some of those [lay Methodist preachers] who now preach are unlearned. They neither understand the ancient languages nor any of the branches of philosophy. And yet this objection might have been spared by many of those who have frequently made it, because they are unlearned too (though accounted otherwise). They have not themselves the very thing they require in others.

Men in general are under a great mistake with regard to what is called "the Learned World." They do not know, they cannot easily imagine, how little learning there is among them. I do not speak of abstruse learning but of what all Divines, at least of any note, are supposed to have, [namely], the knowledge of the tongues, at least Latin, Greek, Hebrew, and of the common arts and sciences.

How few men of learning, so called, understand Hebrew! Even so far as to read a plain chapter in Genesis! Nay, how few understand Greek! Make an easy experiment. Desire that grave man who is urging this objection only to tell you the English of the first paragraph that occurs in one of Plato's Dialogues! I am afraid we may go farther still. How few understand Latin! Give one of them an Epistle of Tully and see how readily he will explain it without his dictionary. If he can hobble through that, 'tis odds but a georgic [poem] in Virgil or a satire of Persius sets him fast.

And with regard to the arts and sciences: how few understand so much as the general principles of logic? Can one in ten of the clergy (O grief of heart!) or of the masters of arts in either university, when an argument is brought, tell you even the mood and figure wherein it is proposed? Or complete an enthymeme? Perhaps, you do not so much as understand the term: supply the premise which is wanting, in order to make it a full categorical syllogism. Can one in ten of them demonstrate a problem or theorem in Euclid's Elements? Or define the common terms used in metaphysics? Or intelligibly explain the first principles of it? Why then will they pretend to that learning which they are conscious to themselves they have not? Nay, and censure others who have it not and do not pretend to it? Where are sincerity and candor fled?

It will easily be observed that I do not depreciate learning of any kind. The knowledge of the languages is a valuable talent; so is the knowledge of the arts and sciences. Both the one and the other may be employed to the glory of God and the good of men. But yet I ask, Where hath God declared in his word that he cannot or will not make use of men that have it not? Has Moses or any of the Prophets affirmed this? Or our Lord? Or any of his apostles? You are sensible all these are against you. You know the apostles themselves, all except St. Paul, were . . . common, unphilosophical, unlettered men. (*A Farther Appeal to Men of Reason and Religion* [1745], pt. 3, in *Works*, 12:246-48)

CHURCH, THE

I do not think either the Church of England or the People called Methodist or any other particular Society under heaven to be the true church of Christ. For that church is but one and contains all the true believers on earth. But I conceive every society of true believers to be a branch of the one true Church of Christ. (Letter to Gilbert Boyce [May 22, 1750], *Letters* [JT], 3:35)

Not to admit into the society called *The Church of England*, or not to administer the Lord's Supper to them, is not the same thing with "excluding men from the church of Christ," unless this society be *the whole church* of Christ, which neither you nor I will affirm. This society therefore may scruple to receive those as members who do not observe her rules in things indifferent, without pretending "to set aside or alter the terms which Christ has fixed" for admission into the Christian church. (*A Letter to the Rev. Mr. Toogood* [January 10, 1758], in *Works* [T], 9:153)

Sometimes the word *church* is taken in Scripture in a still more extensive meaning, as including all the Christian congregations that are upon the face of the earth. And in this sense we understand it in our liturgy, when we say, "Let us pray for the whole state of Christ's church militant here on earth." In this sense it is unquestionably taken by St. Paul, in his exhortation to the elders of Ephesus [Acts 20:28], "Take heed to the church of God, which he has purchased with his own blood." The church here undoubtedly means the catholic or universal church, that is, all the Christians under heaven. ("Of the Church" [September 28, 1785], Sermon 74, in *Works* [T], 6:374-75)

CLOTHING

The sin of "superfluous apparel" lies chiefly in the *superfluous expense*. To make it therefore a point of conscience, to differ from others as to the *shape* or *color* of your apparel, is mere superstition: let the difference lie in the *price*, that you may have the more wherewith to clothe them that have none. (*A Letter to a Person Lately Joined to the People Called Quakers* [February 2, 1748], in *Works* [T], 9:117)

COMMUNION, HOLY: DAILY RECEPTION

A second reason why every Christian should do this, as often as he can, is because the benefits of doing it are so great to all that do it in obedience to him, [namely], the forgiveness of our past sins, the present strengthening and refreshing of our souls. (Quoted in "Of Christian Duties," chap. 15 in Coll. D, 275-76)

C

In the ancient church everyone who was baptized communicated daily. . . . Let everyone therefore who has either any desire to please God, or any love for his own soul, obey God and consult the good of his own soul by communicating every time he can, like the first Christians, with whom the Christian sacrifice was a constant part of the service of the Lord's Day. And for several centuries they received it almost every day. Four times a week always and every Saint's day beside. Accordingly, those that joined in the prayers of the faithful never failed to partake of the blessed sacrament.

. . . Are we not to obey every command of God as often as we can? Are not all the promises of God made to those, and those only, who *give all diligence*; that is, to those who do all they can to obey his commandments? Our power is the one rule of our duty. Whatever we can do, that we ought. With respect either to this or any other command, he that, when he may obey it if he will, does not, will have no place in the kingdom of heaven.

[Another] objection, which some have made against constant Communion is that "the [Anglican] Church enjoins it only three times a year." The words of the Church are, "Note that every parishioner shall communicate, at the least, three times in the year." To this I answer, first, What if the Church had not enjoined it at all, is it not enough that God enjoins it? We obey the Church only for God's sake. And shall we not obey God himself? . . . But, secondly, we cannot conclude from these words that the Church excuses him who receives only thrice a year. The plain sense of them is that he who does not receive thrice at least shall be cast out of the Church.

. . . Reverence for the sacrament may be of two sorts: either such as is owing purely to the newness of the thing—such as men naturally have for anything they are not used to—or such as is owing to our faith or to the love and fear of God. Now, the former of these is not properly a religious reverence, but purely natural. And this sort of reverence for the Lord's Supper, the constantly receiving of it must lessen. But it will not lessen the true reverence, but rather confirm and increase it.

I ask then, Why do you not accept of his mercy as often as ever you can? God now offers you his blessing; why do you refuse it? You have now an opportunity of receiving his mercy; why do you not receive it? You are weak; why do you not seize upon every opportunity of increasing your strength? In a word, considering this as a command of God, he that does not communicate—not once a month but as often as he can—has no piety; considering it as a mercy, he that does not communicate as often as he can has no wisdom. (Quoted in "Of the Holy Communion," chap. 5 in Coll. A, 25-26)

How often did the first Christians receive the Lord's Supper? Every day; it was their "Daily Bread." How often did they join in public prayers? Twice a day, as many of them as could. How did they search the Scriptures? They heard or read them every day and meditated therein day and night. How long is every Christian to use these means of grace? To his life's end. (Quoted in "Of the Order of Public Services and of Church Arrangements," chap. 14 in Coll. A, 92)

It was the judgment of many of the ancient fathers that we are here ["Give us this day our daily bread"] to understand the sacramental bread also, daily received in the beginning by the whole church of Christ and highly esteemed (till the love of many waxed cold) as the grand channel whereby the grace of the Spirit was conveyed to the souls of all the children of God. (Quoted in "Of the Holy Communion," chap. 5 in Coll. A, 22)

We had the Lord's Supper daily, a little emblem of the primitive church. (Quoted in "Of the Holy Communion," chap. 5 in Coll. A, 24)

COMMUNION, HOLY: MEANS OF GRACE

The grace of God given herein confirms to us the pardon of our sins and enables us to leave them. As our bodies are strengthened by bread and wine, so are our souls by these tokens of the body and the blood of Christ. This is the food of our souls; this gives strength to perform our duty and leads us on to perfection. If, therefore, we have any regard for the plain command of Christ, if we desire the pardon of our sins, if we wish for strength to believe, to love and obey God, then we should neglect no opportunity of receiving the Lord's Supper; then we must never turn our backs on the feast which our Lord has prepared for us. We must neglect no occasion, which the good providence of God affords us for this purpose. (Quoted in "Of Christian Duties," chap. 15 in Coll. D, 276)

What is to be inferred from this undeniable matter of fact, one that had not faith received it in the Lord's Supper? Why, (1) that there are means of grace, [that is], outward ordinances whereby the inward grace of God is ordinarily conveyed to man, whereby the faith that brings salvation is conveyed to them who before had it not; (2) that one of these means is the Lord's Supper; and (3) that he who has not this faith ought to wait for it, in the use both of this and of the other means which God hath ordained. (*Journal,* November 7, 1739)

All who desire an increase of the grace of God are to wait for it in partaking of the Lord's Supper. . . .
   And that this is also an ordinary, stated mean of receiving the grace of God is evident from those words of the apostle, . . . "The cup of blessing which we bless, is it not the communion [or *communication*] of the blood of Christ? The bread which we break, is it not the communion of the body of Christ?" [1 Cor. 10:16]. Is not the eating of that bread and the drinking of that cup the outward, visible mean whereby God conveys into our souls all that spiritual grace, that righteousness and peace and joy in the Holy Ghost which were purchased by the body of Christ once broken and the blood of Christ once shed for us? Let all, therefore, who truly desire the grace of God eat of that bread and drink of that cup. ("The Means of Grace" [November 15, 1739], Sermon 16, in *Works* [T], 5:157)

But in latter times many have affirmed that the Lord's Supper is not a converting but a confirming ordinance.
   And among us it has been diligently taught that none but those who are converted, who have received the Holy Ghost, who are believers in the full sense ought to communicate.
   But experience shows the gross falsehood of that assertion, that the Lord's Supper is not a converting ordinance. Ye are the witnesses. For many now present know, the very beginning of your conversion to God (perhaps, in some, the first deep conviction) was wrought at the Lord's Supper. Now one single instance of this kind overthrows the whole assertion.
   The falsehood of the other assertion appears both from Scripture precept and example. Our Lord commanded those very men who were then unconverted, who had not yet received the Holy Ghost, who (in the full sense of the word) were not believers, to "do this in remembrance of him." Here

the precept is clear. And to these he delivered the elements with his own hands. Here is example, equally indisputable. (*Journal,* April 27, 1740)

I showed at large: (1) That the Lord's Supper was ordained by God to be a means of conveying to men, either preventing or justifying or sanctifying grace, according to their several necessities. (2) That the persons for whom it was ordained are, all those who know and feel that they want the grace of God, either to restrain them from sin or to show their sins forgiven or to renew their souls in the image of God. (3) That inasmuch as we come to his table, not to give him anything, but to receive whatsoever he sees best for us, there is no previous preparation indispensably necessary; but a desire to receive whatsoever he pleases to give. (*Journal,* April 28, 1740)

COMMUNION, HOLY: PREPARATION AND FITNESS FOR RECEPTION

Only *let a man* first *examine himself,* whether he understand the nature and design of this holy institution and whether he really desire to be himself made conformable to the death of Christ: *and so,* nothing doubting, "let him eat of that bread, and drink of that cup" [1 Cor. 11:28]. ("The Means of Grace" [November 15, 1739], Sermon 16, in *Works* [T], 5:157)

No fitness is required at the time of communicating, but a sense of our state, of our utter sinfulness and helplessness; everyone who knows he is fit for hell, being just fit to come to Christ, in this as well as all other ways of his appointment. (*Journal,* April 28, 1740)

So many as intend to be partakers of the Holy Communion shall signify their names to the curate at least some time the day before:
And if any of these be an open and notorious evil liver—the curate shall advertise him, that in any wise he presume not to come to the Lord's Table until he hath openly declared himself to have truly repented. (Quoted in "Of Obedience to Church Authority," chap. 17 in Coll. A, 121-22)

[Everyone should partake] with due preparation—that is, with solemn prayer, with careful examination, with deep repentance suited thereto, with earnest and deliberate self-devotion. (Quoted in "Of the Holy Communion," chap. 5 in Coll. A, 21)

Who dares repel any one of the great men in his parish from the Lord's Table? Even though he be a drunkard or a common swearer? Yea, though he openly deny the Lord that bought him? (*A Farther Appeal to Men of Reason and Religion* [1745], pt. 2, in *Works,* 12:194)

The persons for whom it was ordained are all those who know and feel that they *want* the *grace* of God either to *restrain* them from sin or to *show their sins forgiven* or to *renew their souls* in the image of God. (Quoted in "Of the Holy Communion," chap. 5 in Coll. A, 21)

COMMUNION, HOLY: REAL PRESENCE

Do you in communicating *discern* the Lord's body? (Quoted in "Of the Holy Communion," chap. 5 in Coll. A, 13)

"A Methodist, says Mr. Wesley, went to receive the sacrament—when God was pleased to let him see a crucified Savior." Very well, and what is this brought to prove? Why, (1) that I am an enthusiast; (2) that I "encourage the notion of the real, corporeal presence in the sacrifice of the mass." How so? (*A Letter to the Author of* The Enthusiasm of Methodists and Papists Compared [1750], in *Works*, 13:10)

COMMUNION, HOLY: TRANSUBSTANTIATION (FALSITY OF)

No such change of the bread into the body of Christ can be inferred from his words, "This is my body." For it is not said, "This is *changed* into my body," but, "This *is* my body," which, if it were to be taken literally, would rather prove the substance of the bread to be his body. But that they are not to be taken literally is manifest from the words of St. Paul, who calls it bread not only before but likewise after the consecration [1 Cor. 10:17; 11:26-28]. Here we see that what was called his body was bread at the same time. And accordingly these elements are called by the Fathers, "the images, the symbols, the figure of Christ's body and blood."

Scripture and antiquity, then, are flatly against transubstantiation. And so are our very senses. Now, our Lord himself appealed to the senses of his disciples: "Handle me and see; for a spirit hath not flesh and bones, as ye see me have" [Luke 24:39]. Take away the testimony of our senses, and there is no discerning a body from a spirit. But if we believe transubstantiation, we take away the testimony of all our senses.

And we give up our reason too, for if every particle of the host is as much the whole body of Christ as the whole host is before it is divided, then a whole may be divided, not into parts, but into wholes. For divide and sub-divide it over and over, and it is whole still! It is whole before the division, whole in the division, whole after the division! Such nonsense, absurdity, and self-contradiction all over is the doctrine of transubstantiation! (*Popery Calmly Considered* [1779], in *Works*, 15:189-90)

COMMUNION, HOLY: WEEKLY RECEPTION

The judgment of our own [Anglican] Church is quite in favor of *constant* Communion. She takes all possible care that the sacrament be duly administered, wherever the Common Prayer is read, every Sunday and Holyday in the year. (Quoted in "Of the Holy Communion," chap. 5 in Coll. A, 22)

It would be worthwhile to talk at large with that young man who neglects the Lord's Supper. But if he obstinately persists in that neglect, you can't give him any more tickets for our society. (Letter to David Gordon [February 29, 1788], in *Letters,* 230)

CONCUPISCENCE

Then desire having conceived by our own will joining therewith, *bringeth forth actual sin*—It doth not follow that the *desire* itself is not sin. He that begets a man is himself a man. *And sin being perfected* (grown up to maturity, which it quickly does), *bringeth forth death*—Sin is born big with death. (*NT Notes,* 574, comment on James 1:14)

CONFESSION

How dare any man deny this [confession to one another] to be (as to the substance of it) *a means of grace, ordained by God?* Unless he will affirm with Luther in the fury of his solifidianism, that St. James's Epistle is "an epistle of straw"? (Quoted in "Of Confession," chap. 6 in Coll. A, 38n)

Do not they yet know that the only popish confession is the confession made by a single person to a priest? and this itself is in no wise condemned by our [Anglican] Church; nay, she recommends it in some cases. (*A Plain Account of the People Called Methodists* [1748], in Coll. C, 186)

Although it is often of use to confess our sins to a spiritual guide, yet [for Catholics] to make confessing to a priest necessary to forgiveness and salvation is "teaching for doctrines the commandments of men." And to make it necessary in all cases is to lay a dangerous snare both for the confessor and the confessed. (*Popery Calmly Considered* [1779], in *Works,* 15:191)

CONFIRMATION (RITE)

And when they believed, they were to be baptized with the baptism of Christ; the next thing was to lay hands upon them, that they might receive the Holy Ghost; after which they were more fully instructed. (Quoted in "Of Confirmation," in chap. 1 of Coll. A, 11)

But it must be allowed Christ did not institute confirmation; therefore, it is no sacrament at all. (*Popery Calmly Considered* [1779], in *Works,* 15:189)

CONVERSION

Do you know what *conversion* is? (A term indeed which I very rarely use, because it rarely occurs in the New Testament.) . . . A man is usually converted long before he is a perfect man. It is probable, most of those Ephesians to whom St. Paul directed his Epistle were converted. Yet they were not "come (few, if any) to a perfect man, to the measure of the stature of the fulness of Christ." (*A Letter to the Author of* The Enthusiasm of Methodists and Papists Compared [1750], in *Works,* 13:9)

"Your followers, however, do pretend to the grace of a miraculous conversion." Is there any conversion that is not *miraculous*? Is conversion a natural or *supernatural* work: I suppose all who allow there is any such thing believe it to be supernatural. And what is the difference between a *supernatural* and a *miraculous* work, I am yet to learn. (A letter to the Rev. Mr. Potter [November 17, 1758], in *Works,* 13:77-78)

C

DEMONIACS

At St. Thomas's was a young woman, raving mad, screaming and tormenting herself continually. I had a strong desire to speak to her. The moment I began she was still. The tears ran down her cheeks all the time I was telling her, "Jesus of Nazareth is able and willing to deliver you." (*Journal,* December 5, 1738)

I could not but be under some concern, with regard to one or two persons who were tormented in an unaccountable manner and seemed to be indeed lunatic as well as sore-vexed. Soon after I was sent for to one of these, who was so strangely torn of the devil, that I almost wondered her relations did not say, Much religion *hath made thee mad.* We prayed God to *bruise Satan* under her feet. Immediately *we had the petition we asked of him.* She cried out vehemently, "He is gone, he is gone," and was filled with the spirit of *love, and of a sound mind.* I have seen her many times since strong in the Lord. When I asked abruptly, "What do you desire now?" She answered, "Heaven." I asked, "What is in your heart?" She replied, "God." (*A Farther Appeal to Men of Reason and Religion* [1745], pt. 1, in *Works,* 12:66-67)

The account of people falling down in fits you cite as a fifth instance of my enthusiasm: it being "plain," you say, that I "look upon both the disorders and the removals of them to be supernatural" . . . I answered, "It is not quite plain. I look upon some of these cases as wholly natural, on the rest as mixed; both the disorders and the removals being partly natural and partly not" . . . You reply, "It would have been kind to have let us know your rule by which you distinguish these." I will. I distinguish them by the circumstances that precede, accompany, and follow. "However, some of these you here allow to be in part supernatural. Miracles therefore are not wholly ceased." Can you prove they are? By Scripture or reason? You then refer to two or three cases related in the third Journal [Wesley's journal entries for April 26–May 1, 1739]. . . . I believe there was a *supernatural* power on the minds of the persons there mentioned, which occasioned their bodies to be so affected by the *natural* laws of the vital union. This point, therefore, you have to prove, or here is no enthusiasm; that there was no *supernatural* power in the case.

. . . For more than three hundred years after Christ, you know demoniacs were common in the church; and I suppose that you are not unapprised that, during this period (if not much longer), they were continually relieved by the prayers of the faithful. Nor can I doubt but demoniacs will remain so long as Satan is the *god of this world*. I doubt not but there are such at this day. And I believe John Haydon was one. But of whatever sort his disorder was, that it was removed by prayer is undeniable. Now, Sir, you have only two points to prove, and then your argument will be conclusive: (1) That to think or say, "There are *demoniacs* now, and they are now relieved by prayer," is enthusiasm; (2) that to say, "*Demoniacs* were or are relieved on prayer made by Cyprian, or their parish minister," is to parallel the actions of Cyprian or that minister "with the highest miracles of Christ and his disciples." (*The Principles of a Methodist Farther Explained* [1746], in *Works*, 12:374-75)

It is well that Satan is constrained to show himself so plainly in the case of those poor demoniacs. Thereby he weakens his own kingdom and excites us to assault him more zealously. In the beginning of the work in England and Ireland we had many cases of the kind. But he now chooses to assault us by subtlety more than by strength. (Letter to William Black [March 19, 1788], in *Letters*, 276)

DIALOGUE AND ARGUMENT

I am grieved at your extreme warmth; you are in a thorough ill-humor from the very beginning of your book to the end. This cannot hurt me, but it may yourself. And it does not at all help your cause. If you denounce against me all the curses from Genesis to the Revelation, they will not amount to one argument. I am willing (so far as I know myself) to be reproved either by you or any other. But whatever you do, let it be done in love, in patience, in meekness of wisdom. (*A Farther Appeal to Men of Reason and Religion* [1745], pt. 1, in *Works*, 12:81)

(1) My first desire (and prayer to God) is that I may live peaceably with all men. My next, that if I must dispute at all, it may be with a man of understanding. Thus far therefore, I rejoice on the present occasion. I rejoice also in that I have confidence of your sincerity, of your real desire, to promote the glory of God, by peace and goodwill among men. I am likewise thankful to God for your calm manner of writing (a few paragraphs excepted), and yet more for this, that *such* an opponent should by writing in *such* a manner give me an opportunity of explaining myself on those very heads whereon I wanted an occasion so to do.

(2) I do not want indeed (though perhaps you think I do) to widen the breach between us or to represent the difference of the doctrines we severally teach as greater than it really is. So far from it that I earnestly wish there were none at all; or if there must be some, that it may be as small as possible, being fully persuaded that could we once agree in doctrines, other differences would soon fall to the ground. (*Answer to the Rev. Mr. Church's "Remarks on the Rev. Mr. John Wesley's Last Journal"* [February 2, 1745], in *Works*, 12:281-82)

Are you persuaded you see more clearly than me? It is not unlikely that you may. Then treat me as you would desire to be treated yourself upon a change of circumstances. Point me out a better way than I have yet known. Show me it is so by plain proof of Scripture. And if I linger in the path I have been accustomed to tread and am therefore unwilling to leave it, labor with me a little; take me by the hand and lead me as I am able to bear. But be not displeased if I entreat you not to beat me down in order to quicken my pace—I can go but feebly and slowly at best—then I should not be able to go at all. May I not request of you, farther, not to give me hard names in order to bring me into the right way. Suppose I were ever so much in the wrong, . . . it would make me run so much the farther from you and so get more and more out of the way. (Preface to a publication of Wesley's sermons [1747], in Coll. C, 15-16)

I am sensible, in speaking on so tender a point as this must needs be, to those who believe the Christian system, there is danger of a warmth which does no honor to our cause, nor is it at all countenanced by the revelation which we defend. I desire neither to show, nor to feel this, but to "speak the truth in love" (the only warmth which the gospel allows) and to write with calmness, though not with indifference. There is likewise a danger of despising our opponents and of speaking with an air of contempt or disdain. I would gladly keep clear of this also, well knowing that a diffidence of ourselves is far from implying a diffidence of our cause; I distrust myself, not my argument. (Preface [November 30, 1756], *The Doctrine of Original Sin: According to Scripture, Reason, and Experience* [1757], in *Works* [T], 9:167-68)

For several years I was moderator in the disputations which were held six times a week at Lincoln College in Oxford. I could not avoid acquiring hereby some degree of *expertness* in arguing and especially in discerning and pointing out well-covered and plausible fallacies. I have since found abundant reason to praise God for giving me this *honest art.* By this, when men have hedged me in by what they called *demonstrations*, I have been many times able to dash them in pieces; in spite of all its covers to touch the very point where the fallacy lay, and it flew open in a moment. This is the *art* which I have used with Bishop Warburton. . . . When Dr. E. twisted truth and falsehood together in many of his propositions, it was by this *art* I untwisted the one from the other and showed just how far each was true. At doing this, I bless God, I am *expert,* as those will find who attack me without rhyme or reason. But *shifting, subtlety,* and *disguise* I despise and abhor, fully as much as Dr. E. (*Some Remarks on a Defense of the Preface to the Edinburgh Edition of* Aspasio Vindicated [May 1766], in *Works,* 13:120)

I was told yesterday that you are sick of the conversation even of them who profess religion, that you find it quite unprofitable—if not hurtful—to converse with them three or four hours together and are sometimes almost determined to shut yourself up as the less evil of the two.

I do not wonder at it at all, especially considering with whom you have chiefly conversed for some time past, namely, the hearers of Mr. _____ and Mr. _____. The conversing with them I have rarely found to be profitable to my soul. Rather, it has damped my desires and has cooled my resolutions, and I have commonly left them with a dry, dissipated spirit.

And how can you expect it to be otherwise? For do we not naturally catch their spirit with whom we converse? And what spirit can we expect them to be of, considering the preaching they sit under?

. . . One had need to be an angel, not a man, to converse three or four hours at once to any good purpose. In the latter part of such a conversation, we shall be in great danger of losing all the profit we had gained before. (Letter to the Rev. John Fletcher [March 20, 1768], in *Works* [WL], 12:146-47)

ECUMENISM; RELIGIOUS TOLERANCE

Will you aver in cool blood, that everyone who dies a Quaker, a Baptist, an Independent, or a Presbyterian is as infallibly damned as if he died in the act of murder or adultery? Surely you start at the thought! It makes even nature recoil. How then can you reconcile it to the love that hopeth all things? (*A Farther Appeal to Men of Reason and Religion* [1745], pt. 3, in *Works*, 12:266)

You have heard ten thousand stories of us who are commonly called Protestants, of which, if you believe only one in a thousand, you must think very hardly of us. But this is quite contrary to our Lord's rule, "Judge not, that ye be not judged," and has many ill consequences; particularly this, it inclines us to think as hardly of you. Hence we are on both sides less willing to help one another and more ready to hurt each other. Hence brotherly love is utterly destroyed; and each side looking on the other as monsters gives way to anger, hatred, malice, to every unkind affection, which have frequently broken out in such inhuman barbarities as are scarce named among the heathens.

Now, can nothing be done, even allowing us on both sides to retain our own opinions, for the softening our hearts toward each other, the giving a check to this flood of unkindness, and restoring at least some small degree of love among our neighbors and countrymen? Do not you wish for this? Are you not fully convinced that malice, hatred, revenge, bitterness—whether in us or in you, in our hearts or yours—are an abomination to the Lord? Be our opinions right or be they wrong, these tempers are undeniably wrong. They are the broad road that leads to destruction, to the nethermost hell.

I do not suppose all the bitterness is on your side. I know there is too much on our side also; so much that I fear many Protestants (so called) will be angry at me too for writing to you in this manner and will say, "It is showing you too much favor; you deserve no such treatment at our hands."

But I think you do. I think you deserve the tenderest regard I can show, were it only because the same God hath raised you and me from the dust of the earth and has made us both capable of loving and enjoying him to eternity; were it only because the Son of God has bought you and me with his own blood. How much more, if you are a person fearing God (as without question many of you are) and studying to have a conscience void of offense toward God and toward man?

I shall therefore endeavor, as mildly and inoffensively as I can, to remove in some measure the ground of your unkindness by plainly declaring what our belief and what our practice is, that you may see we are not altogether such monsters as perhaps you imagined us to be. (*A Letter to a Roman Catholic* [July 18, 1749], in Coll. C, 303-4)

Are we not thus far agreed? Let us thank God for this and receive it as a fresh token of his love. But if God still loveth us, we ought also to love one another. We ought, without this endless jangling about opinions, to provoke one another to love and to good works. Let the points wherein we differ stand aside; here are enough wherein we agree, enough to be the ground of every Christian temper and of every Christian action.

[Oh,] brethren, let us not still fall out by the way! I hope to see you in heaven. And if I practice the religion above described, you dare not say I shall go to hell. You cannot think so. None can persuade you to it. Your own conscience tells you the contrary. Then if we cannot as yet think alike in all things, at least we may love alike. Herein we cannot possibly do amiss. For one point none can doubt a moment, "God is love; and he that dwelleth in love, dwelleth in God, and God in him."

In the name, then, and in the strength of God, let us resolve, first, not to hurt one another, to do nothing unkind or unfriendly to each other, nothing which we would not have done to ourselves. Rather let us endeavor after every instance of a kind, friendly, and Christian behavior toward each other.

Let us resolve, secondly, God being our helper, to speak nothing harsh or unkind to each other. The sure way to avoid this is to say all the good we can both of and to one another—in all our conversation, either with or concerning each other, to use only the language of love; to speak with all softness and tenderness; with the most endearing expression—which is consistent with truth and sincerity.

Let us, thirdly, resolve to harbor no unkind thought, no unfriendly temper, toward each other. Let us lay the axe to the root of the tree: let us examine all that rises in our heart and suffer no disposition there which is contrary to tender affection. Then shall we easily refrain from unkind actions and words, when the very root of bitterness is cut up.

Let us, fourthly, endeavor to help each other on in whatever we are agreed leads to the kingdom. So far as we can, let us always rejoice to strengthen each other's hands in God. Above all, let us each take heed to himself (since each must give an account of himself to God) that he fall not short of the religion of love; that he be not condemned in that he himself approveth. [Oh,] let you and I (whatever others do) press on to the prize of our high calling! that, being justified by faith, we may have peace with God through our Lord Jesus Christ; that we may rejoice in God through Jesus Christ, by whom we have received the atonement; that the love of God may be shed abroad in our hearts by the Holy Ghost which is given unto us. Let us count all things but loss for the excellency of the knowledge of Jesus Christ our Lord, being ready for him to suffer the loss of all things and counting them but dung that we may win Christ.

I am your affectionate servant, for Christ's sake. (*A Letter to a Roman Catholic* [July 18, 1749], in Coll. C, 309-11)

I dare not, therefore, presume to impose my mode of worship on any other. I believe it is truly primitive and apostolic, but my belief is no rule for another. I ask not, therefore, of him with whom I would unite in love, "Are you of my church, of my congregation? Do you receive the same form of church government and allow the same church officers with me? Do you join in the same form of prayer wherein I worship God?" I inquire not, "Do you receive the supper of the Lord in the same posture and manner that I do?" Nor whether, in the administration of baptism, you agree with me in admitting sureties for the baptized? In the manner of administering it? Or the age of those to whom it should be administered? Nay, I ask not of you (as clear as I am in my own mind), whether you allow baptism and the Lord's Supper at all. Let all these things stand by; we will talk of them, if need be, at a more convenient season. My only question at present is this, "Is thine heart right, as my heart is with thy heart?"

. . . We must both act as each is fully persuaded in his own mind. Hold you fast that which you believe is most acceptable to God, and I will do the same.
. . . I believe infants ought to be baptized and that this may be done either by

dipping or sprinkling. If you are otherwise persuaded, be so still, and follow your own persuasion. It appears to me that forms of prayer are of excellent use, particularly in the great congregation. If you judge extemporary prayer to be of more use, act suitable to your own judgment. My sentiment is that I ought not to forbid water wherein persons may be baptized and that I ought to eat bread and drink wine as a memorial of my dying Master; however, if you are not convinced of this act according to the light you have, I have no desire to dispute with you one moment upon any of the preceding heads. Let all these smaller points stand aside. Let them never come into sight "If thine heart is as my heart," if thou lovest God and all mankind, I ask no more; "give me thine hand." ("Catholic Spirit" [1750], Sermon 41, in *Works* [T], 5:414, 416)

A catholic spirit is not indifference to all congregations. This is another sort of latitudinarianism no less absurd and unscriptural than the former.

. . . But while he is steadily fixed in his religious principles, in what he believes to be the truth as it is in Jesus; while he firmly adheres to that worship of God which he judges to be most acceptable in his sight; and while he is united by the tenderest and closest ties to one particular congregation, his heart is enlarged toward all mankind, those he knows and those he does not; he embraces with strong and cordial affection neighbors and strangers, friends and enemies. This is catholic or universal love. And he that has this is of a catholic spirit. For love alone gives the title to this character: catholic love is a catholic spirit. ("Catholic Spirit" [1750], Sermon 41, in *Works* [T], 5:418-19)

As far as is possible, let us join in destroying the works of the devil and in setting up the kingdom of God upon earth, in promoting righteousness, peace, and joy in the Holy Ghost.

Of whatever opinion or denomination we are, we must serve either God or the devil. If we serve God, our agreement is far greater than our difference. Therefore, as far as may be, setting aside the difference, let us unite in destroying the works of the devil, in bringing all we can from the power of darkness into the kingdom of God's dear Son. And let us assist each other to value more and more the glorious grace whereby we stand, and daily to grow in that grace and in the knowledge of our Lord Jesus Christ. (*Predestination Calmly Considered* [1752], in *Works* [T], 9:420)

Whenever I meet with any whom I have reason to believe "children of God," I do not ask of him with whom I would unite in love (never at the entrance upon our conversation, seldom till we are a little acquainted), "Do you agree with my opinions and mode of worship? Particularly with regard to church government, baptism, and the Lord's Supper." I "let all these stand by" till we begin to know and have confirmed our love to each other. Then may come "a more convenient season" for entering into controversy. My only question *at present* is, "Is thy heart right?"

. . . Could any man answer those questions, "Dost thou believe in the Lord Jesus Christ, God over all, blessed forever" (which indeed no Arian or Semi-Arian, and much less, Socinian, can do)? "Is God the center of thy soul? The sum of all thy desires? Art thou more afraid of displeasing God than either of death or hell?" . . . (which no wicked man can possibly do; none who is not a real child of God). If, I say, a man could answer these in the affirmative, I would then gladly give "him my hand." (Letter to the Rev. Mr. Clarke [July 3, 1756], in *Works*, 16:26-27)

I have labored after union with all whom I believe to be united with Christ. I have sought it again and again; but in vain. They were resolved to stand aloof. And when one and another sincere minister of Christ has been inclined to come nearer to me, others have diligently kept them off, as though thereby they did God service.

. . . I impose my notions upon none. I will be bold to say, there is no man living farther from it. I make no opinion the term of union with any man: I think and let think. What I want is holiness of heart and life. They who have this are my brother, sister, and mother.

. . . I am not satisfied with, "Be very civil to the Methodists but have nothing to do with them." No. I desire to have a league offensive and defensive with every soldier of Christ. We have not only one faith, one hope, one Lord but are directly engaged in one warfare. We are carrying the war into the devil's own quarters, who therefore summons all his hosts to war. Come then, ye that love him, to the help of the Lord, to the help of the Lord against the mighty! (Letter to the Rev. Mr. Venn [June 22, 1765], in *Works*, 16:59-60, 62)

How can any man know what Arminius held who has never read one page of his writings? Let no man bawl against Arminians till he knows what the term means, and then he will know that Arminians and Calvinists are just upon a level. And Arminians have as much right to be angry at Calvinists as Calvinists have to be angry at Arminians. John Calvin was a pious, learned, sensible man; and so was James Harmens [Jacob Arminius]. Many Calvinists are pious, learned, sensible men, and so are many Arminians. Only the former hold absolute predestination; the latter, conditional.

One word more: Is it not the duty of every Arminian preacher, first, never in public or in private to use the word *Calvinist* as a term of reproach; seeing it is neither better nor worse than *calling names*?—a practice no more consistent with good sense or good manners than it is with Christianity. Secondly, to do all that in him lies to prevent his hearers from doing it, by showing them the sin and folly of it? And is it not equally the duty of every Calvinist preacher, first, never in public or in private, in preaching or in conversation, to use the word *Arminian* as a term of reproach? Secondly, to do all that in him lies to prevent his hearers from doing it, by showing them the sin and folly thereof, and that the more earnestly and diligently if they have been accustomed so to do? perhaps encouraged therein by his own example? (*The Question, "What Is an Arminian?" Answered* [1770], in *Works* [T], 9:475)

EDUCATION: METHODIST

1. Our design is, with God's assistance, to train up children in every branch of useful learning.

2. We teach none but boarders. These are taken in, being between the years of six and twelve, in order to be taught reading, writing, arithmetic, English, French, Latin, Greek, Hebrew, history, geography, chronology, rhetoric, logic, ethics, geometry, algebra, physics, music.

3. The school contains eight classes.

In the first class the children read "Instructions for Children" and "Lessons for Children" and begin learning to write.

In the second class they read "The Manners of the Ancient Christians," go on in writing, learn the "Short English Grammar," the "Short Latin Grammar," read *"Praelectiones Pueriles,"* translate them into English and the "Instructions for Children" into Latin, part of which they transcribe and repeat.

In the third class they read Dr. Cave's "Primitive Christianity," go on in writing, perfect themselves in the English and Latin Grammar, read *"Corderii Colloquia Selecta"* and *"Historiae Selectae,"* translate *"Historiae Selectae"* into English and "Lessons for Children" into Latin, part of which they transcribe and repeat.

In the fourth class they read "The Pilgrim's Progress," perfect themselves in writing, learn Dilworth's Arithmetic, read Castellio's Kempis and Cornelius Nepos, translate Castellio into English and "Manners of the Ancient Christians" into Latin, transcribe and repeat select portions of "Moral and Sacred Poems."

In the fifth class they read "The Life of Mr. Haliburton"; perfect themselves in arithmetic; read Select Dialogues of Erasmus, Phaedrus, and Sallust; translate Erasmus into English and "Primitive Christianity" into Latin; transcribe and repeat select portions of "Moral and Sacred Poems."

In the sixth class they read "The Life of Mr. De Renty" and Kennet's "Roman Antiquities"; they learn Randal's Geography; read Caesar, select parts of Terence and Valleius Paterculus; translate Erasmus into English and "The Life of Mr. Haliburton" into Latin; transcribe and repeat select portions of "Sacred Hymns and Poems."

In the seventh class they read Mr. Law's "Christian Perfection" and Archbishop Potter's "Greek Antiquities," they learn *"Bengelii Introductio ad Chronologiam"* with Marshall's "Chronological Tables," read Tully's Offices and Virgil's Aeneid, translate Bengelius into English and Mr. Law into Latin; learn (those who have a turn for it) to make verses, and the "Short Greek Grammar," read the Epistles of St. John, transcribe and repeat select portions of Milton.

In the eighth class they read Mr. Law's "Serious Call" and Lewis's "Hebrew Antiquities"; they learn to make themes and to declaim; learn Vossius's Rhetoric; read Tully's Tusculan Questions and *"Selecta ex Ovirlio, Virgilio, Horatio, Juvenale, Persia, Martiale"*; perfect themselves in the Greek Grammar; read the Gospels and six books of Homer's Iliad; translate Tully into English and Mr. Law into Latin; learn the "Short Hebrew Grammar" and read Genesis; transcribe and repeat *"Selecta ex Virgilio, Horatio, Juvenale."* . . .

The following method may be observed by those who design to go through a course of academic learning:

First Year. Read Lowth's English Grammar; Latin, Greek, Hebrew, French grammars; Cornelius Nepos; Sallust; Caesar; Tully's Offices; Terence; Phaedrus; Aeneid; Dilworth; Randal; Bengel; Vossius; Aldrich and Wallis's Logic; Langbaine's Ethics; Hutchinson on the Passions; Spanheim's "Introduction to Ecclesiastical History"; Puffendorf's "Introduction to the History of Europe"; "Moral and Sacred Poems"; Hebrew Pentateuch, with the Notes; Greek Testament—Matthew to the Acts, with the Notes; Xenophon's Cyrus; Homer's Iliad; Bishop Pearson on the Creed; ten volumes of the "Christian Library"; *Telemaque.*

Second Year. Look over the grammars; read Velleius Paterculus; Tusculan Questions; *Excerpta*; *"Vidae Opera"*; *"Lusus Westmonasterienses"*; Chronological Tables; Euclid's Elements; Wells's Tracts; Newton's *"Principia"*; Mosheim's "Introduction to Church History"; Usher's "Annals"; Burnet's "History of the Reformation"; Spenser's "Fairy Queen"; Historical Books of the Hebrew Bible; Greek Testament, *ad finem*; . . . Homer's Odyssey; twelve volumes of the "Christian Library"; Ramsay's Cyrus; Racine.

Third Year. Look over the grammars; Livy; Suetonius; Tully *"De Finibus"*; *"Musae Anglicanae"*; Dr. Burton's *"Poemata"*; Lord Forbes's Tracts; Abridgment of Hutchinson's Works; "Survey of the Wisdom of God in the Creation"; Rollin's "Ancient History"; Hume's "History of England"; Neal's "History of the Puritans"; Milton's Poetical Works; Hebrew Bible—Job to the Canticles; Greek Testament; Plato's Dialogues; Greek Epigrams; twelve volumes of the "Christian Library"; Pascal; Corneille.

Fourth Year. Look over the grammars; Tacitus; *"Grotii Historia Belgica"*; Tully *"De Naturâ Deorum"*; *"Praedium Rusticum"*; *"Carmina Quadragesimalia"*;

"Philosophical Transactions Abridged"; Watts's Astronomy, [etc.]; "*Compendium Metaphysicae*"; Watts's Ontology; Locke's Essay; Malebranche; Clarendon's History; Neal's "History of New-England"; Antonio Solis's "History of Mexico"; Shakespeare; rest of the Hebrew Bible; Greek Testament; Epictetus; Marcus Antoninus; *Poetae Minores*; end of the "Christian Library"; "*La Fausseté de les Vertues Humaines*"; *Quesnell sur les Evangiles*.

Whoever carefully goes through this course will be a better scholar than nine in ten of the graduates at Oxford or Cambridge. (*A Short Account of the School in Kingswood, Near Bristol* [1768], in *Works* [S], 7:332-33, 335-36)

EDUCATION: SECULARIZATION OF

Every part of the nation abounds with masters of this kind; men who are either uninstructed in the very principles of Christianity or quite indifferent as to the practice of it . . .

. . . But it is not only with regard to instruction in religion, that most of our great schools are defective. They are defective likewise . . . with regard to learning, and that in several respects. In some, the children are taught little or no arithmetic; in others, little care is taken even of their writing. In many, they learn scarce the elements of geography and as little of chronology. . . .

. . . The masters not only take no care to train up their scholars in true religion, but they themselves teach them what is utterly destructive of all religion whatever: they put authors into their hands that—with all the beauty of language, all the sweetness of expression—instill into their tender minds both obscenity and profaneness: Virgil's *Alexis*, the lewd epigrams of Martial, and the shameless satires of Juvenal (even the sixth), so earnestly recommending sodomy as well as adultery! (*A Plain Account of Kingswood School* [1781], in *Works* [S], 7:337-38)

ELECTION: CONDITIONAL

The scripture saith, "God hath chosen us in Christ before the foundation of the world, that we should be holy and without blame before him in love" [Eph. 1:4]. And St. Peter calls the saints, "Elect according to the foreknowledge of God the Father, through sanctification of the Spirit unto obedience" [1 Pet. 1:2]. And St. Paul saith unto them, "God hath from the beginning chosen you to salvation through sanctification of the Spirit and belief of the truth: whereunto he hath called you by our gospel, to the obtaining of the glory of our Lord Jesus Christ" [2 Thess. 2:13-14].

From all these places of Scripture it is plain that God hath chosen some to life and glory, before or from the foundation of the world. (Quoted in "Of God," chap. 3 in Coll. D, 64)

As Christ was called "The Lamb slain from the foundation of the world" and yet not slain till several thousands of years after, so also men are called "Elect from the foundation of the world" and yet are not elected perhaps till several thousands of years after, till the day of their conversion to God. (*The Scripture Doctrine Concerning Predestination, Election, and Reprobation* [1741], in *Works* [T], 9:421)

But here some may object, that I hold our faith and obedience to be the cause of God's electing us to glory.

I answer, I do hold that faith in Christ producing obedience to him is *a cause without which* God electeth none to glory, for we never read of God's electing to glory any who lived and died a disobedient unbeliever. But I do not hold that it is *the cause for which* he elects any . . .

I do not hold God chose any man to life and salvation for any good which he had done or for any which was in him before he put it there. (*The Scripture Doctrine Concerning Predestination, Election, and Reprobation* [1741], in *Works* [T], 9:422-23)

I believe *election* means . . . a divine appointment of some men to eternal happiness. But I believe this election to be conditional, as well as the reprobation opposite thereto. I believe the eternal decree concerning both is expressed in these words: "He that believeth shall be saved: he that believeth not shall be damned." And this decree without doubt God will not change, and man cannot resist. According to this, all true *believers* are in Scripture termed *elect*, as all who continue *in unbelief* are so long properly *reprobates*, that is, *unapproved* of God and *without discernment* touching the things of the Spirit. (*Predestination Calmly Considered* [1752], in *Works* [T], 9:381-82)

ELECTION: UNCONDITIONAL (FALSITY OF)

Now, then, without any extenuation on the one hand or exaggeration on the other, let us look upon this doctrine, call it what you please, naked and in its native color. Before the foundations of the world were laid, God, of his own mere will and pleasure, fixed a decree concerning all the children of men who should be born unto the end of the world. This decree was unchangeable with regard to God and irresistible with regard to man. And herein it was ordained that one part of mankind should be saved from sin and hell and all the rest left to perish for ever and ever, without help, without hope. That none of these should have that grace which alone could prevent their dwelling with everlasting burnings God decreed for this cause alone, "because it was his good pleasure!" and for this end, "to show forth his glorious power, and his sovereignty over all the earth."

. . . Now can you, upon reflection, believe this? Perhaps you will say, "I do not think about it." That will never do. You not only think about it (though it

E

may be confusedly) but speak about it too, whenever you speak of unconditional election. (*Predestination Calmly Considered* [1752], in *Works* [T], 9:381)

Unconditional election I cannot believe, not only because I cannot find it in Scripture, but also (to waive all other considerations) because it necessarily implies unconditional reprobation. Find out any election which does not imply reprobation, and I will gladly agree to it. But reprobation I can never agree to while I believe the Scripture to be of God, as being utterly irreconcilable to the whole scope of the Old and New Testaments. (*Predestination Calmly Considered* [1752], in *Works* [T], 9:382)

Do you think it will cut the knot to say, "Why, if God might justly have passed by all men (speak out, 'if God might *justly* have *reprobated* all men,' for it comes to the same point), then he may justly pass by some. But God might *justly* have passed by all men." Are you sure he might? Where is it written? I cannot find it in the Word of God. Therefore I reject it as a bold, precarious assertion utterly unsupported by Holy Scripture.

If you say, "But you know in your own conscience, God might justly have passed by *you*," I deny it. That God might *justly,* for my unfaithfulness to his grace, *have given me up* long ago, I grant; but this concession supposes me to have had that grace which you say a reprobate never had.

But besides, in making this supposition of what God might have justly done, you suppose his justice might have been separate from his other attributes, from his mercy in particular. But this never was nor ever will be, nor indeed is it possible it should. All his attributes are inseparably joined; they cannot be divided, no, not for a moment. Therefore this whole argument stands not only on an unscriptural but on an absurd, impossible supposition. (*Predestination Calmly Considered* [1752], in *Works* [T], 9:387)

"ENTHUSIASM" (OPPOSITION TO)

Every proposition which I have anywhere advanced concerning those *operations* of the Holy Ghost which, I believe, are *common* to all Christians in all ages, is here clearly maintained by our own [Anglican] Church.

Under a full sense of this I could not well understand for many years how it was that on the mentioning any of these great truths, even among men of education, the cry immediately arose, "An enthusiast! An enthusiast!" But I now plainly perceive this is only an old fallacy in a new shape. To object *enthusiasm* to any person or doctrine is but a decent method of begging the question. It generally spares the objector the trouble of reasoning and is a shorter and easier way of carrying his cause.

For instance, I assert that "till a man 'receives the Holy Ghost' he is without God in the world; that he cannot know the things of God unless God reveal them unto him by the Spirit; no, nor have even one holy or heavenly temper without the inspiration of the Holy One." Now, should one who is conscious to himself that he has experienced none of these things attempt to confute these propositions, either from Scripture or antiquity, it might prove a difficult task. What, then, shall he do? Why, cry out, "Enthusiasm! Enthusiasm!" and the work is done.

But what does he mean by *enthusiasm*? Perhaps nothing at all; few have any distinct idea of its meaning. Perhaps "something very bad" or "something I never experienced and do not understand." Shall I tell you then what that "terrible something" is? I believe thinking men mean by *enthusiasm* a sort of religious madness, a *false imagination* of being inspired by God; and by *an enthusiast*, one that *fancies* himself under the influence of the Holy Ghost when, in fact, he is not.

Let him prove me guilty of this who can. I will tell you once more the whole of my belief on these heads; and if any man will show me (by arguments, not hard names) what is wrong, I will thank God and him. (*Operations of the Holy Ghost* [1744], in Coll. B, 192-93)

How greatly then was I surprised some months ago when I was shown a kind of circular letter which one of those whom the Holy Ghost hath made overseers of his church, I was informed, had sent to all the clergy of his diocese! Part of it ran (nearly, if not exactly) thus: "There is great indiscretion in preaching up a sort of religion, as the true and only Christianity, which in their own account of it consists in an enthusiastic ardor, to be understood or attained by very few and not to be practiced without breaking in upon the common duties of life." . . . what manner of words are these? Supposing candor and love out of the question, are they words of truth? I dare stake my life upon it—there is not one true clause in all this paragraph. (*A Farther Appeal to Men of Reason and Religion* [1745], pt. 1, in *Works,* 12:60-61)

Are you not convinced, Sir, that you have laid to my charge things which I know not? I do not gravely tell you, as much an enthusiast as you over and over affirm me to be, "That I sensibly feel, in your sense, the motions of the Holy Spirit." Much less do I "make this, any more than convulsions, agonies, howlings, roarings, and violent contortions of the body," either "certain signs of men's being in a state of salvation" or "necessary in order thereunto." You might with equal justice and truth inform the world, and the Worshipful the Magistrates of Newcastle, that I make seeing the wind or feeling the light necessary to salvation. Neither do I "confound the extraordinary with the ordinary operations of the Spirit." And as to your last inquiry, "What is the best proof of our being led by the Spirit?" I have no exception to that just and scriptural answer which you yourself have given, "A thorough change and renovation of mind and heart, and the leading a new and holy life." (*A Farther Appeal to Men of Reason and Religion* [1745], pt. 1, in *Works*, 12:83-84)

Every proposition which I have anywhere advanced concerning those operations of the Holy Ghost which I believe are common to all Christians in all ages is here clearly maintained by our own [Anglican] Church. Under a full sense of this, I could not well understand for many years how it was that on the mentioning of any of these great truths, even among men of education, the cry immediately arose, "an Enthusiast! an Enthusiast!" but I now plainly perceive this is only an old fallacy in a new shape. To object enthusiasm to any person or doctrine is but a decent method of begging the question. It generally spares the objector the trouble of reasoning and is a shorter and easier way of carrying his cause. For instance, I assert that "till a man *receives the Holy Ghost* he is without God in the world, that he cannot know the things of God unless God reveal them unto him by his Spirit; no, nor have even one holy or heavenly temper without the inspiration of the Holy One." Now should one who is conscious to himself, that he has experienced none of these things, attempt to confute these propositions either from Scripture or antiquity, it might prove a difficult task. What then shall he do? Why, cry out, "Enthusiasm! Enthusiasm!" and the work is done. But what does he mean by enthusiasm? Perhaps nothing at all; few have any distinct idea of its meaning. Perhaps "something very bad" or "something I never experienced and do not understand." Shall I tell you then what that "terrible something" is? I believe thinking men mean by enthusiasm a sort of religious madness, a false imagination of being inspired by God; and by an enthusiast, one that fancies himself under the influence of the Holy Ghost when, in fact, he is not. Let him prove me guilty of this who can. . . . if any man will show me (by arguments, not hard names) what is wrong, I will thank God and him. (*A Farther Appeal to Men of Reason and Religion* [1745], pt. 1, in *Works*, 12:114-15)

Fanaticism, if it mean anything at all, means the same with *enthusiasm* or religious madness . . . It is a convenient word to be thrown out upon anything we do not like, because scarce one reader in a thousand has any idea of what it means. (*A Farther Appeal to Men of Reason and Religion* [1745], pt. 3, in *Works*, 12:242)

You have drawn, Sir, (in the main) a true picture of an *enthusiast.* But it is no more like me, than I am like a centaur. Yet you say, "they are these very things which have been charged upon you and which you could never yet disprove"; I will try for once and to that end will go over these articles one by one.

. . . "Instead of making the word of God the rule of his actions, he follows only his secret impulse." In the whole compass of language there is not a proposition which less belongs to me than this. I have declared again and again that I make the Word of God the rule of all my actions and that I no more follow any "secret impulse" instead thereof than I follow Mahomet or Confucius. . . .

"Instead of judging of his spiritual estate by the improvement of his heart, he rests only on ecstasies." Neither is this my case. I rest not on them at all. Nor did I ever experience any. I do judge of my spiritual estate by the improvement of my heart and the tenor of my life conjointly. . . . "He is very difficult to be convinced by reason and argument, as he acts upon a supposed principle superior to it—the direction of God's Spirit." I am very difficult to be convinced by dry blows or hard names (both of which I have not wanted) but not by reason and argument. At least that difficulty cannot spring from the cause you mention. For I claim no other direction of God's Spirit than is common to all believers. "Whoever opposes him is charged with rejecting the Spirit." What! whoever opposes *me*, John Wesley? Do I charge every such person with rejecting the Spirit? No more than I charge him with robbing on the highway. I cite you yourself, to confute your own words. For do I charge *you* with rejecting the Spirit? "His own dreams must be regarded as oracles?" Whose? I desire neither my dreams nor my waking thoughts may be regarded at all unless just so far as they agree with the oracles of God. (*Answer to the Rev. Mr. Church's "Remarks on the Rev. Mr. Wesley's Last Journal"* [February 2, 1745], in *Works*, 12:318-19)

Every enthusiast, then, is properly a madman. Yet his is not an ordinary but a religious madness. By religious I do not mean that it is any part of religion; quite the reverse. Religion is the spirit of a sound mind and consequently stands in direct opposition to madness of every kind. But I mean it has religion for its object; it is conversant about religion. And so the enthusiast is generally talking of religion, of God, or of the things of God but talking in such a manner that every reasonable Christian may discern the disorder of his mind. Enthusiasm, in general, may then be described in some such manner as this: a religious madness arising from some falsely imagined influence or inspiration of God, at least from imputing something to God which ought not to be imputed to him or expecting something from God which ought not to be expected from him. ("The Nature of Enthusiasm" [1750], Sermon 39, in *Works* [T], 5:392)

That there are enthusiasts among the Methodists I doubt not and among every other people under heaven, but that they are "made such either by our doctrine or discipline" still remains to be proved. If they are such in spite

of our doctrine and discipline, their madness will not be laid to our charge.
(Second letter to the Rev. Mr. Clarke [September 10, 1756], in *Works* [S], 7:285)

A sixth charge [against the Methodists] is: "They treat Christianity as a wild, enthusiastic scheme, which will bear no examination." . . . Where or when? In what sermon? In what tract, practical or polemical? I wholly deny the charge. . . .

Nearly allied to this is the threadbare charge of enthusiasm, with which you frequently and largely compliment us. But as this also is asserted only, and not proved, it falls to the ground of itself. Meantime, your asserting it is a plain proof that you know nothing of the men you talk of. Because you know them not, you so boldly say, "One advantage we have over them, and that is reason." Nay, that is the very question. I appeal to all mankind, whether you have it or no. However, you are sure we have it not and are never likely to have. For "reason," you say, "cannot do much with an enthusiast, whose first principle is to have nothing to do with reason but resolve all his religious opinions and notions into immediate inspiration." Then, by your own account, I am no enthusiast; for I resolve none of my notions into immediate inspiration. I have something to do with reason, perhaps as much as many of those who make no account of my labors. And I am ready to give up every opinion which I cannot by calm, clear reason defend. Whenever, therefore, you will try what you can do by argument, which you have not done yet, I wait your leisure, and will follow you step by step, which way soever you lead. (Letter to the Rev. Mr. Downes [November 17, 1759], in Coll. C, 245)

Beware of that daughter of pride, enthusiasm! [Oh,] keep at the utmost distance from it! Give no place to a heated imagination. Do not hastily ascribe things to God. Do not easily suppose dreams, voices, impressions, visions, or revelations to be from God. They may be from him. They may be from nature. They may be from the devil. Therefore, "believe not every spirit, but try the spirits whether they be of God." Try all things by the written word, and let all bow down before it. You are in danger of enthusiasm every hour if you depart ever so little from Scripture, yea, or from the plain, literal meaning of any text taken in connection with the context. And so you are, if you despise or lightly esteem reason, knowledge, or human learning—every one of which is an excellent gift of God and may serve the noblest purposes. . . .

One general inlet to enthusiasm is expecting the end without the means; the expecting knowledge, for instance, without searching the Scriptures and consulting the children of God; the expecting spiritual strength without constant prayer and steady watchfulness; the expecting any blessing without hearing the Word of God at every opportunity.

Some have been ignorant of this device of Satan. They have left off searching the Scriptures. They said, "God writes all the Scriptures on my heart. Therefore, I have no need to read it." Others thought they had not so much need of hearing and so grew slack in attending the morning preaching. [Oh,] take warning, you who are concerned herein! You have listened to the voice of a stranger. Fly back to Christ, and keep in the good old way which was "once delivered to the saints"—the way that even a heathen bore testimony of, "That the Christians rose early every day to sing hymns to Christ as God." . . .

I say yet again, beware of enthusiasm. Such is the imagining you have the gift of prophesying or of discerning of spirits which I do not believe one of you has; no, nor ever had yet. Beware of judging people to be either right or wrong by your own feelings. This is no scriptural way of judging. [Oh,] keep close to "the law and to the testimony"! (*A Plain Account of Christian Perfection* [1767; rev. 1777], in *Works* [WL], 11:429-30)

I am afraid you are in danger of enthusiasm. We know there are divine dreams and impressions. But how easily may you be deceived herein! How easily where something is from God may we mix something which is from nature! especially if we have a lively imagination and are not aware of any danger. (Letter to Mrs. R____ [June 28, 1766], in Coll. B, 528)

There is a danger of every believer's mistaking the voice of the enemy, or of their own imagination, for the voice of God. And you can distinguish one from the other not by any written rule but only by the unction of the Holy One. This only teaches Christian prudence, consistent with simplicity and godly sincerity. (Letter to a young disciple [May 2, 1771], in *Works* [S], 7:89)

There is a threefold leading of the Spirit. Some he leads by giving them, on every occasion, apposite texts of Scripture; some by suggesting reasons for every step they take—the way by which he chiefly leads me; and some by impressions; but he judges the last to be the least desirable way, as it is often impossible to distinguish dark impressions from divine or even diabolical. (Letter to the Rev. Freeborn Garrettson [July 15, 1789], in *Letters*, 284)

EUCHARISTIC ADORATION (WRONGNESS OF)

But the greatest abuse of all in the Lord's Supper is the *worshipping the consecrated bread.* And this the Church of Rome not only practices but positively enjoins. . . .

The Romanists themselves grant that if Christ is not corporally present in the Lord's Supper, this is idolatry. And that he is not corporally present anywhere but in heaven, we learn from Acts [1:11; 3:21]. (*Popery Calmly Considered* [1779], in *Works*, 15:190-91)

EUCHARISTIC SACRIFICE

Do you neglect no opportunity of attending and partaking of the Christian sacrifice? (Quoted in "Of the Order of Public Services and of Church Arrangements," chap. 14 in Coll. A, 93)

We believe there is and always was in every Christian church (whether dependent on the bishop of Rome or not) an outward priesthood ordained by Jesus Christ and an outward sacrifice offered therein by men authorized to act as ambassadors of Christ and stewards of the mysteries of God. (Quoted in "Of Holy Orders," chap. 8 in Coll. A, 54)

EVANGELISM AND PREACHING, LAY

Was Mr. Calvin ordained? Was he either priest or deacon? And were not most of those whom it pleased God to employ in promoting the Reformation abroad laymen also? Could that great work have been promoted at all in many places if laymen had not preached? (*A Farther Appeal to Men of Reason and Religion* [1745], pt. 3, in *Works*, 12:250)

Suppose, I say, this minister . . . for some years, . . . saves no soul at all, saves no sinners from their sins; but after he has preached all this time to five or six hundred persons cannot show that he has converted one from the error of his ways; many of his parishioners dying as they lived and the rest remaining just as they were before he came.

. . . Will you condemn a man who, having compassion on dying souls and some knowledge of the gospel of Christ, without any temporal reward, saves them from their sins whom the minister *could* not save?

. . . Will you condemn such a preacher because he has not learning or has not had a university education?

. . . I think he is a true, evangelical minister, . . . to save souls from death, to reclaim sinners from their sins and that every Christian, if he is able to do it, has authority to save a dying soul. (*A Letter to a Clergyman* [May 4, 1748], in Coll. C, 251-52)

It is not clear to us that Presbyters, so circumstanced as we are, may *appoint* or *ordain* others; but it is, that we may *direct*, as well as *suffer* them to do what we conceive they are *moved to by the Holy Ghost*. It is true that in *ordinary* cases both an *inward* and an *outward* call are requisite. But we apprehend there is something far from *ordinary* in the present case. And upon the calmest view of things, we think they who are only called of God and not of man have *more* right to preach than they who are only called of man and not of God. Now that many of the clergy, though called of man, are not called of God to preach his gospel is undeniable: (1) Because they themselves utterly disclaim, nay, and ridicule the inward call. (2) Because they do not know what the gospel is; of consequence they *do not* and *cannot* preach it.

. . . Soul-damning clergymen lay me under more difficulties than soul-saving laymen! (Letter to Mr. T. Adams [October 31, 1755], in *Works,* 16:41-42)

Do you not observe that all the lay preachers who are connected with me are maintainers of general redemption? And it is undeniable that they are instrumental of saving souls. God is with them and he works by them and he has done so for near these thirty years; therefore, the opposing them is neither better nor worse than fighting against God. (Letter to the Rev. John Fletcher [March 20, 1768], in Coll. B, 530)

I think the strength of the cause rests there, on your having an extraordinary call. So I am persuaded has every one of our lay preachers; otherwise, I could not countenance his preaching at all. It is plain to me that the whole work of God called Methodism is an extraordinary dispensation of his providence. Therefore, I do not wonder if several things occur therein which do not fall under ordinary rules of discipline. St. Paul's ordinary rule was, "I permit not a woman to speak in the congregation." Yet, in extraordinary cases, he made a few exceptions—at Corinth in particular. (Letter to Mrs. Mary Fletcher [June 13, 1771], in *Letters,* 360)

Give me one hundred preachers who fear nothing but sin and desire nothing but God, and I care not a straw whether they be clergymen or laymen, such alone will shake the gates of hell and set up the kingdom of heaven upon earth. (Letter to Alexander Mather [August 6, 1777], *Letters* [JT], 6:272)

But we have reason to believe there were, in every age, two sorts of prophets. The extraordinary, such as Nathan, Isaiah, Jeremiah, and many others on whom the Holy Ghost came in an extraordinary manner. Such was Amos in particular, who saith of himself [7:14-15], "I was no prophet, neither a prophet's son. But I was a herdman, and the Lord said unto me, Go, prophesy unto my people Israel." The ordinary were those who were educated in "the schools of the prophets," one of which was at Ramah, over which Samuel presided [1 Sam. 19:18]. These were trained up to instruct the people and were the ordinary preachers in their synagogues. In the New Testament they are usually termed scribes, . . . "expounders of the law." But few if any of them were priests. These were all along a different order.

. . . Many learned men have shown at large that our Lord himself and all his apostles built the Christian church as nearly as possible on the plan of the Jewish. So the great High Priest of our profession sent apostles and evangelists to proclaim glad tidings to all the world and then pastors, preachers, and teachers to build up in the faith the congregations that should be founded. But I do not find that ever the office of an evangelist was the same with that of a pastor, frequently called a bishop. He presided over the flock and administered the sacraments; the former assisted him and preached the word either in one or more congregations. I cannot prove from any part of the New Testament or from any author of the three first centuries that the office of an evangelist gave any man a right to act as a pastor or bishop. I believe these offices were considered as quite distinct from each other till the time of Constantine. ("The Ministerial Office" [May 4, 1789], Sermon 115, in *Works* [S], 2:540-41)

EXAMINATION OF CONSCIENCE; SELF-EXAMINATION

It is good to renew ourselves, from time to time, by closely examining the state of our souls, as if we had never done it before. For nothing tends more to the full assurance of faith than to keep ourselves by this means in humility and the exercise of all good works.

. . . They ought continually to regard each other in God, and closely to examine themselves, whether all their thoughts are pure and all their words directed with Christian discretion. Other affairs are only the things of men, but these are peculiarly the things of God. (*A Plain Account of Christian Perfection* [1767; rev. 1777], in *Works* [WL], 11:439)

Be serious and frequent in the examination of your heart and life. There are some duties like those parts of the body, the want of which may be supplied by other parts; but the want of these nothing can supply. Every evening review your carriage through the day: what you have done or thought that was unbecoming your character; whether your heart has been instant upon religion and indifferent to the world. Have a special care of two portions of time, namely, morning and evening: the morning to forethink what you have to do and the evening to examine whether you have done what you ought. (Quoted in "Of Christian Duties," chap. 15 in Coll. D, 278)

EXPERIENCE: RELIGIOUS

"We are assured that the doing what God commands is the sure way of knowing that we have received his Spirit." We have doubtless received it, if we love God (as he commands) with all our heart, mind, soul, and strength, "And not by any sensible impulses or feelings whatsoever." "Any sensible impulses whatsoever?" Do you then exclude *all sensible impulses?* Do you reject *inward feelings* [as a whole]? Then you reject both the *love* of God and of our neighbor. For if these cannot be *inwardly felt*, nothing can. You reject all *joy* in the Holy Ghost. For if we cannot be sensible of this, it is no joy at all. You reject the peace of God which if it be not felt in the inmost soul, is a dream, a notion, an empty name. You therefore reject the whole *inward kingdom* of God, that is, in effect, the whole gospel of Jesus Christ.

You have, therefore, yourself abundantly shown (what I do not *insinuate* but proclaim on the housetop) that I am charged with *enthusiasm*, for *asserting the power* (as well as the form) *of godliness.* (*Answer to the Rev. Mr. Church's "Remarks on the Rev. Mr. Wesley's Last Journal"* [February 2, 1745], in *Works*, 12:320)

What reasonable assurance can you have of things whereof you have not personal experience? . . .

. . . And those who were blind but now see, those who were sick many years but now are healed, those who were miserable but now are happy will afford you also a very strong evidence of the truth of Christianity—as strong as can be in the nature of things, till you experience it in your own soul; and this, though it be allowed they are but plain men and, in general, of weak understanding; nay, though some of them should be mistaken in other points and hold opinions which cannot be *defended.* (*A Plain Account of Genuine Christianity* [1749], in Coll. C, 327)

Do I here "advance impressions, impulses, feelings, [etc.], into certain rules of conduct"? Or anywhere else? You may just as well say I advance them into certain proofs of transubstantiation. Neither in writing nor in private conversation have I ever "taught any of my followers to depend upon them as sure guides or infallible proofs" of anything.

Nay, you yourself own, I have taught quite the reverse: and that at my very first setting out. Then, as well as ever since, I have told the societies, "They were not to judge by their own inward feelings. I warned them, all these were in themselves of a doubtful, disputable nature. They might be from God or they might not and were therefore to be tried by a further rule, to be brought to the only certain test, the Law and the Testimony." . . .

This is what I have taught from first to last. (*A Second Letter to the Author of* The Enthusiasm of Methodists and Papists Compared [November 27, 1750], in *Works*, 13:37-38)

In the afternoon God was eminently present with us, though rather to comfort than convince. But I observed a remarkable difference, since I was here [Everton] before, as to the manner of the work. None now were in trances, none cried out, none fell down or were convulsed; only some trembled exceedingly, a low murmur was heard, and many were refreshed with the multitude of peace.

The danger was to regard extraordinary circumstances too much—such as outcries, convulsions, visions, trances—as if these were essential to the inward work, so that it could not go on without them. Perhaps the danger is to regard them too little, to condemn them altogether, to imagine they had nothing of God in them and were a hindrance to his work. Whereas the truth is (1) God suddenly and strongly convinced many that they were lost sinners; the natural consequence whereof were sudden outcries and strong bodily convulsions; (2) to strengthen and encourage them that believed and to make his work more apparent, he favored several of them with divine dreams, others with trances and visions; (3) in some of these instances, after a time, nature mixed with grace; (4) Satan likewise mimicked this work of God in order to discredit the whole work; and yet it is not wise to give up this part any more than to give up the whole. At first it was, doubtless, wholly from God. It is partly so at this day; and he will enable us to discern how far, in every case, the work is pure and where it mixes or degenerates. (*Journal*, November 25, 1759)

And with respect to *inward feelings*, whoever denies them in the sense wherein alone I defend them must deny all the life and power of religion and leave nothing but a dead, empty form. For take away the love of God and our neighbor, the peace of God and joy in the Holy Ghost, or (which comes to the same) deny that they are felt, and what remains but a poor, lifeless shadow? (Letter to the Rev. Dr. Rutherforth [March 28, 1768], in *Works*, 13:139)

EXTREME UNCTION (FALSITY OF)

When the apostles were sent forth "they anointed with oil many that were sick, and healed them" [Mark 6:13], using this as a sign of the miraculous cures to be wrought. And St. James accordingly directs: "Is any sick among you? let him call for the elders of the church; let them pray over him, anointing him with oil in the name of the Lord: and the prayer of faith shall save the sick" [5:14-15]. But what has this to do with the extreme unction of the Church of Rome? In the first church this anointing was a mere rite; in the Church of Rome it is made a sacrament! It was used in the first church for the body; it is used in the Church of Rome for the soul. It was used then for the recovery of the sick; now, for those only that are thought past recovery. It is easy, therefore, to see that the Romish extreme unction has no foundation in Scripture. (*Popery Calmly Considered* [1779], in *Works*, 15:192)

FAITH

Christian faith is then not only an assent to the whole gospel of Christ but also a full reliance on the blood of Christ; a trust in the merits of his life, death, and resurrection; a recumbency upon him as our atonement and our life, *as given for us* and *living in us*. It is a sure confidence which a man hath in God, that through the merits of Christ *his* sins are forgiven and *he* reconciled to the favor of God. ("Salvation by Faith" [June 18, 1738], sermon, in Coll. C, 20)

Now, faith (supposing the Scripture to be of God) is . . . "the demonstrative evidence of things unseen," the supernatural evidence of things invisible, not perceivable by eyes of flesh or by any of our natural senses or faculties. Faith is that divine evidence whereby the spiritual man discerneth God and the things of God. It is with regard to the spiritual world, what sense is with regard to the natural. It is the spiritual sensation of every soul that is born of God. (*An Earnest Appeal to Men of Reason and Religion* [1743], in Coll. C, 210)

Faith, in general, is a divine, supernatural . . . (evidence, or conviction) of things not seen, nor discoverable by our bodily senses, as being either past, future, or spiritual. Justifying faith implies . . . a sure trust and confidence that Christ died for my sins, that he loved me and gave himself for me. And the moment a penitent sinner believes this, God pardons and absolves him. (*Conditions of Justification* [1744], in Coll. B, 179)

The term *faith* I likewise use in the scriptural sense, meaning thereby "the evidence of things not seen." And that it is scriptural appears to me a sufficient defense of any way of speaking whatever. For however the propriety of those expressions may vary which occur in the writings of men, I cannot but think those which are found in the Book of God will be equally proper in all ages. . . .

. . . I believe, (1) that a rational assent to the truth of the Bible is one ingredient of Christian faith; (2) that Christian faith is a moral virtue in that sense wherein hope and charity are; (3) that men ought to yield the utmost attention and industry for the attainment of it; and yet, (4) that this, as every Christian grace is properly supernatural, is an immediate gift of God which he commonly gives in the use of such means as he hath ordained.

I believe it is generally given in an instant, but not arbitrarily, in your sense of the word; not without any regard to the fitness (I should say, the previous qualifications) of the recipient.

. . . Christian, saving faith, is a divine conviction of invisible things, a supernatural conviction of the things of God with a filial confidence in his love. Now, a man may have a full assent to the truth of the Bible (probably attained by the slow steps you mention), yea, an assent which has some influence on his practice, and yet not have one grain of this faith. (Letter to John Smith [probably one of the archbishops of Canterbury, Thomas Herring or Thomas Secker] [September 28, 1745], in *Works* [WL], 12:58-59, 61)

The faith by which the promise is attained is represented by Christianity as a power wrought by the Almighty in an immortal spirit inhabiting a house of clay, to see through that veil into the world of spirits, into things invisible and eternal; a power to discern those things which with eyes of flesh and blood no man hath seen or can see, either by reason of their nature, which (though they surround us on every side) is not perceivable by these gross senses; or by reason of their distance, as being yet afar off in the bosom of eternity.

This is Christian faith in the general notion of it. In its more particular notion, it is a divine evidence or conviction wrought in the heart that God is reconciled to me through his Son; inseparably joined with a confidence in him, as a gracious reconciled Father, as for all things, so especially for all those good things which are invisible and eternal.

To believe (in the Christian sense) is, then, to walk in the light of eternity and to have a clear sight of and confidence in the Most High, reconciled to me through the Son of his love.

. . . It gives a more extensive knowledge of things invisible, showing what eye had not seen, nor ear heard, neither could it before enter into our heart to conceive. And all these it shows in the clearest light, with the fullest certainty and evidence. (*A Plain Account of Genuine Christianity* [1749], in Coll. C, 320-23)

FAITH ALONE (FALSITY OF)

I observed every day more and more . . . the advantage Satan has gained over us . . . almost all these had left off the means of grace, saying, "They must now cease from their own works; they must now trust in Christ alone; they were poor sinners and had nothing to do but to lie at his feet." (Quoted in "Of Justification by Faith," chap. 11 in Coll. A, 75)

In flat opposition [to "faith alone"] . . . I began . . . to expound the Epistle of St. James, the great antidote against this poison. (Quoted in "Of Justification by Faith," chap. 11 in Coll. A, 75-76)

Beware of solifidianism; crying nothing but, "Believe, believe!" and condemning those as ignorant or legal who speak in a more scriptural way. At certain seasons, indeed, it may be right to treat of nothing but repentance or merely of faith or altogether of holiness, but, in general, our call is to declare the whole counsel of God and to prophesy according to the analogy of faith. The written word treats of the whole and every particular branch of righteousness, descending to its minutest branches; as to be sober, courteous, diligent, patient, to honor all men. So, likewise, the Holy Spirit works the same in our hearts, not merely creating desires after holiness in general, but strongly inclining us to every particular grace, leading us to every individual part of "whatsoever is lovely." And this with the greatest propriety, for as "by works faith is made perfect," so the completing or destroying the work of faith and enjoying the favor or suffering the displeasure of God greatly depends on every single act of obedience or disobedience. (*A Plain Account of Christian Perfection* [1767; rev. 1777], in *Works* [WL], 11:431-32)

Here is the masterpiece of Satan; farther than this he cannot go. Men are holy without a grain of holiness in them! Holy in Christ, however unholy in themselves; they are in Christ without one jot of the mind that was in Christ. In Christ, though their nature is whole in them. They are "complete in him," though they are in themselves as proud, as vain, as covetous, as passionate as ever; it is enough. They may be unrighteous still, seeing Christ has "fulfilled all righteousness." (*A Blow at the Root* [1762], in *Works* [T], 9:455)

FAITH AND JUSTIFICATION

Faith, therefore, is the "necessary" condition of justification; yea, and the "only necessary" condition thereof. . . . the very moment God giveth faith (for "it is the gift of God") to the "ungodly" that "worketh not," that "faith is counted to him for righteousness." He hath no righteousness at all, antecedent to this, not so much as negative righteousness or innocence. But "faith is imputed to him for righteousness," the very moment that he believeth. Not that God . . . thinketh him to be what he is not. But as "he made Christ to be a sin-offering for us," that is, treated him as a sinner, punishing him for our sins; so he counteth us righteous, from the time we believe in him; that is, he doth not punish us for our sins; yea, treats us as though we are guiltless and righteous.

. . . For he that cometh unto God by this faith must fix his eye singly on his own wickedness, on his guilt and helplessness, without having the least regard to any supposed good in himself, to any virtue or righteousness whatsoever. He must come as a "mere sinner," inwardly and outwardly, self-destroyed and self-condemned, bringing nothing to God but ungodliness only, pleading nothing of his own but sin and misery. Thus it is, and thus alone, when his "mouth is stopped," and he stands utterly "guilty before" God, that he can "look unto Jesus" as the whole and sole "Propitiation for his sins." Thus only can he be "found in him" and receive the "righteousness which is of God by faith." ("Justification by Faith" [1746], Sermon 5, in *Works* [T], 5:53-54)

F FAITH AND REASON

There are many, it is confessed (particularly those who are styled mystic divines), that utterly decry the use of reason, thus understood, in religion; nay, that condemn all reasoning concerning the things of God as utterly destructive of true religion.

But we can in no wise agree with this. We find no authority for it in holy writ. So far from it, that we find there both our Lord and his apostles continually reasoning with their opposers. . . . And the strongest reasoner whom we have ever observed (excepting only Jesus of Nazareth) was that Paul of Tarsus . . .

We therefore not only allow but earnestly exhort all who seek after true religion to use all the reason which God hath given them in searching out the things of God. (*An Earnest Appeal to Men of Reason and Religion* [1743], in Coll. C, 221)

Christianity, considered as an inward principle, . . . is holiness and happiness, the image of God impressed on a created spirit; a fountain of peace and love springing up into everlasting life.

. . . And this I conceive to be the strongest evidence of the truth of Christianity. I do not undervalue traditional evidence. Let it have its place and its due honor. It is highly serviceable in its kind and in its degree. And yet I cannot set it on a level with this. . . .

Traditional evidence is of an extremely complicated nature, necessarily including so many and so various considerations that only men of a strong and clear understanding can be sensible of its full force. On the contrary, how plain and simple is this; and how level to the lowest capacity! Is not this the sum: *One thing I know; I was blind, but now I see*? An argument so plain that a peasant, a woman, a child, may feel all its force.

The traditional evidence of Christianity stands, as it were, a great way off; and therefore, although it speaks loud and clear, yet makes a less lively impression. It gives us an account of what was transacted long ago, in far distant times as well as places. Whereas the inward evidence is intimately present to all persons at all times and in all places. It is nigh thee, in thy mouth and in thy heart, if thou believest in the Lord Jesus Christ. "This," then, "is the record," this is the evidence, emphatically so called, "that God hath given unto us eternal life; and this life is in his Son." . . .

I have sometimes been almost inclined to believe that the wisdom of God has, in most later ages, permitted the external evidence of Christianity to be more or less clogged and encumbered for this very end, that men (of reflection especially) might not altogether rest there but be constrained to look into themselves also and attend to the light shining in their hearts.

Nay, it seems (if it may be allowed for us to pry so far into the reasons of the divine dispensations) that, particularly in this age, God suffers all kinds of objections to be raised against the traditional evidence of Christianity, that men of understanding, though unwilling to give it up, yet, at the same time they defend this evidence, may not rest the whole strength of their cause thereon but seek a deeper and firmer support for it. (*A Plain Account of Genuine Christianity* [1749], in Coll. C, 323-25)

"Child," said my father to me, when I was young, "you think to carry everything by dint of argument. But you will find, by and by, how very little is ever done in the world by clear reason." Very little indeed! It is true of almost all men, except so far as we are taught of God. . . .

Passion and prejudice govern the world, only under the name of reason. It is our part, by religion and reason joined, to counteract them all we can. (Letter to Joseph Benson [1770], in Coll. B, 533)

It is doubtless the will of the Lord we should be guided by our reason, so far as it can go. But in many cases it gives us very little light, and in others none at all. In all cases it cannot guide us right but in subordination to the unction of the Holy One. So that in all our ways we are to acknowledge him, and he will direct our paths.

I do not remember to have heard or read anything like my own experience. Almost ever since I can remember I have been led in a peculiar way.

I go on in an even line, being very little raised at one time or depressed at another. Count Zinzendorf observes there are three different ways wherein it pleases God to lead his people. Some are guided almost in every instance by apposite texts of Scripture. Others see a clear and plain reason for everything they are to do. And yet others are led not so much by Scripture or reason as by particular impressions. I am very rarely led by impressions but generally by reason and by Scripture. I see abundantly more than I feel. I want to feel more love and zeal for God. (Letter to Miss Elizabeth Ritchie [February 24, 1786], in Coll. B, 554-55)

I wish to be, in every point, great and small, a scriptural, rational Christian. (Letter to the Rev. Freeborn Garrettson [January 24, 1789], in Coll. B, 560)

FAITH AND SALVATION

I am now to consider what has been lately objected with regard to the nature of saving faith.

The author [of the pamphlet *The Notions of the Methodists Disproved*] "cannot understand how those texts of St. John are at all to the purpose." [1 John 3:1], "Behold what manner of love the Father hath bestowed upon us, that we should be called the sons of God." [1 John 4:19], "We love him, because he first loved us." I answer, (1) These texts were not produced in the Appeal by way of proof but of illustration only. But, (2) I apprehend they may be produced as a proof both that Christian faith implies a confidence in the love of God and that such a confidence has a direct tendency to salvation, to holiness both of heart and life. (*A Farther Appeal to Men of Reason and Religion* [1745], pt. 1, in *Works*, 12:75)

FAITH AND WORKS

Our gospel, as it knows no other foundation of good works than faith or of faith than Christ, so it clearly informs us, we are not his disciples while we either deny him to be the Author or his Spirit to be the Inspirer and Perfecter both of our faith and works. ("The Circumcision of the Heart" [January 1, 1733], Sermon 17, in *Works* [T], 5:169)

The first usual objection to this is that to preach salvation or justification by faith only is to preach against holiness and good works. To which a short answer might be given: It would be so if we spake, as some do, of a faith which was separate from these, but we speak of a faith which is not so but necessarily productive of all good works and all holiness. ("Salvation by Faith" [June 18, 1738], sermon, in Coll. C, 23)

I considered the . . . assertion, that there is but one commandment in the New Testament, [namely], "To believe," that no other duty lies upon us, and that a believer is not obliged to do anything as commanded.

How gross, palpable a contradiction is this to the whole tenor of the New Testament, every part of which is full of commandments, from St. Matthew to the Revelation! But it is enough to observe, (1) That this bold affirmation is shamelessly contrary to our Lord's own words: "Whosoever shall break one of the least of these commandments shall be called the least in the kingdom of heaven," for nothing can be more evident than that he here speaks of more than one of several commandments, which every soul, believer or not, is obliged to keep as commanded. (2) That this whole scheme is overturned from top to bottom by that other sentence of our Lord, "When ye have done all that is commanded you, say, We have done no more than it was our duty to do." (3) That, although to do what God commands is a believer's privilege, that does not affect the question. He does it nevertheless as his bounden duty and as a command of God. (4) That this is the surest evidence of his believing, according to our Lord's own words: "If ye love me (which cannot be unless ye believe), keep my commandments." (5) That to desire to do what God commands, but not as a command, is to affect not freedom, but independency—such independency as St. Paul had not; for, though "the Son had made him free," yet was he not without law to God, but "under the law to Christ," such as the holy angels have not, for they "fulfill his commandments" and hearken to the voice of his words; yea, such as Christ himself had not, for "as the Father had given him commandment, so he spake." (*Journal,* April 23, 1740)

I read over Martin Luther's Comment on the Epistle to the Galatians. I was utterly ashamed. How have I esteemed this book. . . . how blasphemously does he speak of good works and of the law of God! . . . Here (I apprehend) is the real spring of the grand error of the Moravians. They follow Luther, for better for worse. (Quoted in "Of Justification by Faith," chap. 11 in Coll. A, 76)

In strictness therefore, neither our faith nor our works justify us, [that is], deserve the remission of our sins. But God himself justifies us of his own mercy through the merits of his Son only. (Quoted in "Of Justification by Faith," chap. 11 in Coll. A, 75)

St. Paul requires nothing on the part of man but only a true and living faith. Yet this faith does not shut out repentance, hope, and love, which are joined with faith in every man that is justified. But it shuts them out from the office of justifying. So that although they are all present together in him that is justified, yet they justify not all together.

. . . Neither does faith shut out good works necessarily to be done afterward. But we may not do them to this intent—to be justified by doing them. Our justification comes freely of the mere mercy of God . . .

But it should also be observed what that faith is whereby we are justified. Now that faith which brings forth not good works is not a living faith but a dead and devilish one. (*The Principles of a Methodist* [1743], in Coll. B, 41-42)

Q. 11. Are works necessary to the continuance of faith?

A. Without doubt, for a man may forfeit the free gift of God either by sins of omission or commission. . . .

Q. 13. How is faith "made perfect by works"?

A. The more we exert our faith, the more it is increased. "To him that hath shall be given." (*Minutes of Some Late Conversations* [June 25, 1744], in *Works* [S], 5:195)

You add, "It is plain then that good works are always, in St. Paul's judgment, joined with faith." (So undoubtedly they are, that is, as an effect is always joined with its cause.) (*A Farther Appeal to Men of Reason and Religion* [1745], pt. 1, in *Works*, 12:74)

Faith may be . . . the sole condition of justification, and yet not only repentance be our duty *before*, but all obedience *after* we believe. (*Answer to the Rev. Mr. Church's "Remarks on the Rev. Mr. Wesley's Last Journal"* [February 2, 1745], in *Works*, 12:298)

Q. 25. Does faith supersede (set aside the necessity of) holiness or good works?

A. In nowise. So far from it, that it implies both, as a cause does its effects. (*Minutes of Some Late Conversations* [August 2, 1745], in *Works* [S], 5:201)

Q. Is not the whole dispute of salvation by faith or by works a mere strife of words?

A. In asserting salvation by faith we mean this: (1) That pardon (salvation begun) is received by faith producing works. (2) That holiness (salvation continued) is faith working by love. (3) That heaven (salvation finished) is the reward of this faith. (*Minutes of Some Late Conversations* [May 13, 1746], in *Works* [S], 5:205)

Q. 24. But do you consider that we are under the covenant of grace and that the covenant of works is now abolished?

A. All mankind were under the covenant of grace from the very hour that the original promise was made. If by the covenant of works you mean that of unsinning obedience made with Adam before the fall, no man but Adam was ever under that covenant, for it was abolished before Cain was born. Yet it is not so abolished but that it will stand, in a measure, even to the end of the world, that is, if we "do this," we shall live; if not, we shall die eternally; if we do well, we shall live with God in glory; if evil, we shall die the second death. For every man shall be judged in that day and rewarded "according to his works." (*Minutes of Some Late Conversations* [May 13, 1746], in *Works* [S], 5:204)

"But does he practice accordingly?" If he does not, we grant all his faith will not save him. And this leads me to show you, in few and plain words, what the practice of a true Protestant is.

I say, *a true Protestant*, for I disclaim all common swearers, Sabbath break-ers, drunkards; all whoremongers, liars, cheats, extortioners; in a word, all that live in open sin. These are no Protestants; they are no Christians at all. Give them their own name; they are open heathens. They are the curse of the nation, the bane of society, the shame of mankind, the scum of the earth. (*A Letter to a Roman Catholic* [July 18, 1749], in Coll. C, 306)

Paul says he [Abraham] was *justified by faith* [Rom. 4:2, etc.]. Yet James does not contradict him, for he does not speak of the same justification. Paul speaks of that which Abraham received many years before Isaac was born [Gen. 15:6]. James, of that which he did not receive till *he had offered up Isaac on the altar.* He was justified, therefore in Paul's sense, that is, accounted righ-teous by *faith* antecedent to his works. He was justified in James's sense, that is, made righteous by *works* consequent to his *faith.* So that James's justifica-tion by *works* is the fruit of Paul's justification by *faith.* (*NT Notes,* 577, comment on James 2:21)

All who expect to be sanctified at all expect to be sanctified by faith. But, meantime, they know that faith will not be given but to them that obey. Remotely, therefore, the blessing depends on our works; although immedi-ately, on simple faith. (Letter to Miss Furly [August 19, 1759], in *Works* [WL], 12:190)

St. Paul speaks of *works* antecedent to justification: St. James of *works* con-sequent upon it. This is the plain, easy, natural way of reconciling the two apostles. (Letter to the Rev. Dr. Horne [March 5, 1762], in *Works,* 13:110)

You want nothing but this—to be filled with the faith that worketh by love. (Letter to Philothea Briggs [January 5, 1772], *Letters* [JT], 5:299)

It is *by works* only that it [faith] can be *made perfect.* (Letter to Mary Bishop [November 30, 1774], *Letters* [JT], 6:127-28)

For seeing no faith avails but that "which worketh by love," which produces both inward and outward good works, to affirm, No man is finally saved without this, is, in effect, to affirm, No man is finally saved without works. . . .

. . . I still hold (as I have done above these forty years) that "by grace we are saved through faith," yet so as not to contradict that other expression of the same apostle, "Without holiness no man shall see the Lord." (*Thoughts on Salvation by Faith* [1779], in *Works* [WL], 11:494-95)

FAITH: BOLD AND CONFIDENT

I have been sometimes afraid you have suffered loss for want of a frank acknowledgment of the truth: . . . If we openly avow what we approve, the fear or shame generally lights on them; but if we are ashamed or afraid, then they pursue and will be apt to rally us both out of our reason and religion. (Letter to Ebenezer Blackwell [January 26, 1747], in *Letters*, 295)

FASTING

The annual fasts in our church are the forty days of Lent, the Ember days at the four seasons, the Rogation days, and the vigils or eves of several solemn festivals: the weekly, all Fridays in the year except Christmas Day. (Quoted in "Of Fasting," chap. 10 in Coll. A, 73)

God hath, in all ages, appointed this to be a means of averting his wrath and obtaining whatever blessings we from time to time stand in need of. How powerful a means this is, to avert the wrath of God, we may learn from the remarkable instance of Ahab (and from other instances cited from the Old Testament).

And it is a means not only of turning away the wrath of God but also of obtaining whatever blessings we stand in need of . . .

In like manner the apostles always joined fasting with prayer when they desired the blessing of God on any important undertaking . . .

Yea, that blessings are to be obtained in the use of this means, which are no otherwise attainable, our Lord expressly declares in his answer to his disciples, asking, "Why could not we cast him out? . . . if ye have faith, nothing shall be impossible unto you. Howbeit this kind goeth not out but by prayer and fasting."

These were the *appointed* means. For it was not merely by the light of reason or of natural conscience (as it is called) that the people of God have been in all ages directed to use fasting as a means to these ends. But they have been from time to time taught it of God himself by clear and open revelations of his will. Such is that remarkable one by the prophet Joel [2:12, etc.] . . .

Now whatever reasons there were to quicken those of old in the zealous and constant discharge of this duty, they are of equal force still to quicken us. But above all these we have a peculiar reason for being "in fastings often," namely, the command of him by whose name we are called. He does not indeed in this place *expressly* enjoin either fasting, giving of alms, or prayer. But his directions how to fast, to give alms, and to pray are of the same force with such injunctions. For the commanding us to do anything *thus* is an unquestionable command to do that thing, seeing it is impossible to perform it *thus*, if it be not performed *at all*. Consequently, the saying, give alms, pray, fast, in *such a manner* is a clear command to *perform* all those duties as well as to perform them in that *manner*, which shall in no wise lose its reward. 'Tis possible either to fast or pray, in such a manner, as to make you much worse than before—more unhappy and more unholy. Yet the fault does not lie in the means itself but in the *manner* of using it. Use it still, but use it in a different manner. Do what God commands *as* he commands it, and then doubtless his promise shall not fail. (Quoted in "Of Fasting," chap. 10 in Coll. A, 69-70)

But *afterwards*, some in *London* carried them [Wednesday and Friday fasts] to excess and fasted so as to impair their health. It was not long before others made this a pretense for not fasting at all. And I fear there are now thousands of Methodists so called, both in England and Ireland, who, following the same bad example, have entirely left off fasting: who are so far from fasting twice in the week that they do not fast twice in the month. Yea, are there not some of you who do not fast one day from the beginning of the year to the end? But what excuse can there be for this? I do not say for those that call themselves members of the Church of England, but for any who profess to believe the Scripture to be the Word of God since, according to this, *the man that never fasts is no more in the way to heaven than the man that never prays.* (Quoted in "Of Fasting," chap. 10 in Coll. A, 73)

FATHERS OF THE CHURCH

But it was not long before Providence brought me to those who showed me a sure rule of interpreting Scripture, [namely], *Consensus veterum: "Quod ab omnibus, quod ubique, quod semper credilum."* At the same time they sufficiently insisted upon a due regard to the one church at all times and in all places.

Nor was it long before I bent the bow too far the other way:

1. By making antiquity a coordinate rather than subordinate rule with Scripture.

2. By admitting several doubtful writings as undoubted evidences of antiquity.

3. By extending antiquity too far, even to the middle or end of the fourth century.

4. By believing more practices to have been universal in the ancient church than ever were so.

5. By not considering that the decrees of one provincial synod could bind only that province; and that the decrees of a general synod, only those provinces whose representatives met therein.

6. By not considering that the most of those decrees were adapted to particular times and occasions; and consequently when those occasions ceased must cease to bind even those provinces. (Journal entry [January 25, 1738], *Works* [B], 18:212n95)

We prove the doctrines we preach by Scripture and reason and, if need be, by antiquity. (*A Farther Appeal to Men of Reason and Religion* [1745], pt. 3, in *Works,* 12:263)

The primitive Fathers: I mean particularly Clemens Romanus, Ignatius, Polycarp, Justin Martyr, Irenaeus, Origen, Clemens Alexandrinus, Cyprian; to whom I would add Macarius and Ephraem Syrus. . . .

. . . I exceedingly reverence them as well as their writings and esteem them very highly in love. I reverence them because they were Christians. . . . And I reverence their writings because they describe true, genuine Christianity and direct us to the strongest evidence of the Christian doctrine. . . .

I reverence these ancient Christians (with all their failings) the more because I see so few Christians now; because I read so little in the writings of later times, and hear so little, of genuine Christianity. (*A Letter to the Rev. Dr. Conyers Middleton Occasioned by His Late "Free Inquiry"* [January 4, 1749], in *Works* [S], 5:761)

The esteeming the writings of the three first centuries, not equally with but next to the Scriptures, never carried any man yet into dangerous errors, nor probably ever will. But it has brought many out of dangerous errors, and particularly out of the errors of popery. (*A Letter to the Rev. Dr. Conyers Middleton Occasioned by His Late "Free Inquiry"* [January 4, 1749], in *Works* [S], 5:715)

The authors of the following collection were contemporaries of the holy apostles; one of them bred under our Lord himself and the others well instructed by those great men whom he commissioned to go forth and teach all nations. We cannot therefore doubt but what they deliver to us is the pure doctrine of the gospel; what Christ and his apostles taught and what these holy men had themselves received from their own mouths.

. . . Nor had they only the advantage of living in the apostolic times, of hearing the holy apostles and conversing with them, but were themselves of a very eminent character in the church—men raised to the highest honor and authority, chosen by the apostles to preside in their several sees and those some of the most eminent then in the world. Such men therefore, we may be well assured, must have been carefully instructed in the mystery of the gospel and have had a most comprehensive and perfect knowledge of the faith as it is in Jesus.

. . . Had they been men of no note, no authority in the church, yet the very age wherein they lived would have rendered their discourses justly venerable to us. But now, having to do with men not only instructed in common by the apostles, with the other Christians of those days, but particularly bred up and instituted by them; having here the writings of men who had attained to so perfect a knowledge of the mystery of godliness as to be judged worthy by the apostles themselves to be overseers of the great churches of Rome, Antioch, and Smyrna; we cannot with any reason doubt of what they deliver to us as the gospel of Christ but ought to receive it, though not with equal veneration, yet with only little less regard than we do the sacred writings of those who were their masters and instructors.

. . . We read in Eusebius, with what a holy zeal Ignatius first and then his fellow disciple St. Polycarp, set themselves against those who taught other doctrines than what the apostles had delivered unto them; what wise directions they gave for the discovery of false teachers, and how earnestly they exhorted all the churches to keep firm to their respective bishops and presbyters, and to the apostolic doctrine derived from them. . . .

. . . Such reason have we to look on the writings of these holy men as containing the pure, uncorrupted doctrine of Christ. But to advance higher yet they were not only thus qualified by these ordinary means to deliver the gospel to us but were likewise endued with the extraordinary assistance of the Holy Spirit.

. . . The plain inference is not only that they were not mistaken in their interpretations of the gospel of Christ but that, in all the necessary parts of it, they were so assisted by the Holy Ghost as to be scarce capable of mistaking. Consequently, we are to look on their writings, though not of equal authority with the Holy Scriptures (because neither were the authors of them called in so extraordinary a way to the writing them, nor endued with so large a portion of the blessed Spirit), yet as worthy of a much greater respect than any composures which have been made since . . . (Preface to the *Epistles of the Apostolical Fathers,* in *Works* [S], 7:526-28)

Can any who spend several years in those seats of learning be excused if they do not add to that of the languages and sciences, the knowledge of the Fathers? the most authentic commentators on Scripture, as being both nearest the fountain and eminently endued with that Spirit by whom all Scripture was given. It will be easily perceived, I speak chiefly of those who wrote before the Council of Nicaea. But who would not likewise desire to have some acquaintance with those that followed them? with St. Chrysostom, Basil, Jerome, Austin [Augustine], and, above all, the man of a broken heart, Ephraem Syrus? . . .

. . . Am I acquainted with the Fathers, at least with those venerable men who lived in the earliest ages of the church? Have I read over and over the golden remains of Clemens Romanus, of Ignatius and Polycarp, and have I given one reading, at least, to the works of Justin Martyr, Tertullian, Origen, Clemens Alexandrinus, and Cyprian? . . .

. . . How much more shall I suffer in my usefulness, if I have wasted the opportunities I once had of acquainting myself with the great lights of antiquity, the ante-Nicene fathers. (*An Address to the Clergy* [February 6, 1756], in Coll. C, 266-67, 277-78)

I regard no authorities but those of the ante-Nicene fathers, nor any of them in opposition to Scripture. (Letter to Joseph Benson [February 22, 1782], in *Works* [S], 7:81)

From a child I was taught to love and reverence the Scripture, the oracles of God, and next to these to esteem the primitive Fathers, the writers of the three first centuries. (*Farther Thoughts on Separation from the Church* [December 11, 1789], in Coll. C, 287)

FREE WILL

If, then, God be just, there cannot, on your scheme, be any judgment to come. We may add, nor any future state, either of reward or punishment. If there be such a state, God will therein "render to every man according to his works. To them who, by patient continuance in well-doing, seek for glory and honour and immortality, eternal life: but to them that do not obey the truth, but obey unrighteousness, indignation and wrath, tribulation and anguish upon every soul of man that doeth evil."

But how is this reconcilable with your scheme? You say, the reprobates cannot but do evil and that the elect, from the day of God's power, cannot but continue in well-doing. You suppose all this is unchangeably decreed, in consequence whereof God acts irresistibly on the one and Satan on the other. Then it is impossible for either one or the other to *help acting* as they do, or rather, to *help* being *acted upon* in the manner wherein they are. For if we speak properly, neither the one nor the other can be said to *act* at all. Can a stone be said to act when it is thrown out of a sling? or a ball, when it is projected from a cannon? No more can a man be said to act if he be only moved by a force he cannot resist. But if the case be thus, you leave no room either for reward or punishment. Shall the stone be rewarded for rising from the sling or punished for falling down? Shall the cannon ball be rewarded for flying toward the sun or punished for receding from it? As incapable of either punishment or reward is the man who is supposed to be impelled by a force he cannot resist. Justice can have no place in rewarding or punishing mere machines, driven to and fro by an external force. So that your supposition of God's ordaining from eternity whatsoever should be done to the end of the world, as well as that of God's acting irresistibly in the elect and Satan's acting irresistibly in the reprobates, utterly overthrows the Scripture doctrine of rewards and punishments, as well as of a judgment to come. (*Predestination Calmly Considered* [1752], in *Works* [T], 9:392-93)

The Assembly of Divines, who met at Westminster in the last century, express very nearly the same sentiment, though placed in a different light. They speak to this effect: "Whatever happens in time was unchangeably determined from all eternity. GOD ordained or ever the world was made all the things that should come to pass therein. The greatest and the smallest events were equally predetermined: in particular all the thoughts, all the words, all the actions of every child of man—all that every man thinks or speaks or does from his birth till his spirit returns to God that gave it." It follows that no man can do either more or less good or more or less evil than he does. None can think, speak, or act any otherwise than he does, not in any the smallest circumstance. In all, he is bound by an invisible but more than adamantine chain. No man can move his head or foot, open or shut his eyes, lift his hand, or stir a finger any otherwise than as GOD determined he should, from all eternity. . . .

F

The Assembly of Divines do as directly ascribe the necessity of human actions to God, in affirming that God has eternally determined whatsoever shall be done in time. So likewise does Mr. [Jonathan] Edwards of New England . . .

. . . If all the actions and passions and tempers of men are quite independent on their own choice, are governed by a principle exterior to themselves, then none of them is either rewardable or punishable, is either praise or blame-worthy. The consequence is undeniable: I cannot praise the sun for warming nor blame the stone for wounding me, because neither the sun nor the stone acts from choice but from necessity. Therefore neither does the latter deserve blame, nor the former deserve praise. Neither is the one capable of reward, nor the other of punishment. And if a man does good as necessarily as the sun, he is no more praise-worthy than that. If he does evil as necessarily as the stone, he is no more blame-worthy. The dying to save your country is no way rewardable if you are compelled thereto. And the betraying your country is no way punishable if you are necessitated to do it. (*Thoughts upon Necessity* [May 14, 1774], in *Works* [T], 9:459, 462-63)

Whoever asserts the predetermination of all human actions, a doctrine totally inconsistent with the scriptural doctrines of a future judgment, heaven and hell, strikes hereby at the very foundation of Scripture, which must necessarily stand or fall with them. (*Thoughts upon Necessity* [May 14, 1774], in *Works* [T], 9:465)

FRIDAY ABSTINENCE

The Annual fasts in our church are, . . . all Fridays in the year except Christmas Day. (Quoted in "Of Fasting," chap. 10 in Coll. A, 73)

While we were at Oxford, the rule of every Methodist was (unless in case of sickness) to fast every Wednesday and Friday in the year, in imitation of the primitive church, for which we had the highest reverence. Now this practice of the primitive church is universally allowed: "Who does not know (says Epiphanius, an ancient writer) that the fasts of the fourth and sixth days of the week (Wednesday and Friday) are observed by the Christians throughout the whole world?" So they were by the Methodists for several years; by them all, without any exception. (Quoted in "Of Fasting," chap. 10 in Coll. A, 73)

F

GIFTS, EXTRAORDINARY: CESSATION OF

It does not appear that these extraordinary gifts of the Holy Ghost were common in the church for more than two or three centuries. . . . From this time they almost totally ceased; very few instances of the kind were found. The cause of this was not (as has been vulgarly supposed) "because there was no more occasion for them," because all the world was become Christians. . . . The real cause was, "the love of many," almost of all Christians, so called, was "waxed cold." The Christians had no more of the Spirit of Christ than the other heathens. The Son of man, when he came to examine his church, could hardly "find faith upon earth." This was a real cause, why the extraordinary gifts of the Holy Ghost were no longer to be found in the Christian church; because the Christians were turned heathens again and had only a dead form left. ("The More Excellent Way" [July—August 1787], sermon, in Coll. C, 92-93)

GOD

"Which art in heaven": high and lifted up; God over all, blessed forever. Who, sitting on the circle of the heavens, beholdeth all things both in heaven and earth. Whose eye pervades the whole sphere of created being; yea, and of uncreated night; unto whom "are known all his works" and all the works of every creature, not only "from the beginning of the world" (a poor, low, weak translation) but . . . from all *eternity,* from everlasting to everlasting. Who constrains the host of heaven, as well as the children of men, to cry out with wonder and amazement, O the depth! "The depth of the riches, both of the wisdom and of the knowledge of God!" "Which art in heaven": the Lord and ruler of all, superintending and disposing all things; who art the King of kings and Lord of lords, the blessed and only Potentate; who art strong and girded about with power, doing whatsoever pleaseth thee! The Almighty, for whensoever thou willest to do, is present with thee. "In heaven": eminently there. Heaven is thy throne, "the place where thine honour" particularly "dwelleth." But not there alone, for thou fillest heaven and earth, the whole expanse of space. "Heaven and earth are full of thy glory. Glory be to thee, O Lord, most high!"

Therefore should we "serve the Lord with fear, and rejoice unto him with reverence." Therefore should we think, speak, and act as continually under the eye, in the immediate presence of the Lord the King.

. . . "Hallowed be thy name": This is the first of the six petitions whereof the prayer itself is composed. The name of God is God himself; the nature of God, so far as it can be discovered to man. It means, therefore, together with his existence, all his attributes or perfections; his eternity, particularly signified by his great and incommunicable name, JEHOVAH, as the Apostle John translates it: . . . "the Alpha and Omega, the beginning and the end; he which is, and which was, and which is to come"; his *fullness of being,* denoted by his other great name, *I AM THAT I AM!* his omnipresence; his omnipotence; who is indeed the only agent in the material world; all matter being essentially dull and inactive and moving only as it is moved by the finger of God; and he is the spring of action in every creature, visible and invisible, which could neither act nor exist without the continual influx and agency of his almighty power. His wisdom, clearly deduced from the things that are seen, from the goodly order of the universe. His trinity in unity and unity in trinity discovered to us in the very first line of his written word, [*bara' 'elohim*]: literally, *the Gods created,* a plural noun joined with a verb of the singular number; as well as in every part of his subsequent revelations, given by the mouth of all his holy prophets and apostles. His essential purity and holiness and, above all, his love, which is the very brightness of his glory.

In praying that God, or his name, may "be hallowed" or glorified, we pray that he may be known, such as he is, by all that are capable thereof, by all intelligent beings and with affections suitable to that knowledge; that he may be duly honored and feared and loved by all in heaven above and in the earth beneath; by all angels and men whom for that end he has made capable of knowing and loving him to eternity. (Meditation on the Lord's Prayer from "On Our Lord's Sermon on the Mount: Discourse 6" [1748], Sermon 28, in *Works* [T], 5:284-85)

He is happy in knowing there is a God, an intelligent cause and Lord of all, and that he is not the produce either of blind chance or inexorable necessity. He is happy in the full assurance he has that this Creator and end of all things is a being of boundless wisdom, of infinite power to execute all the designs of his wisdom, and of no less infinite goodness to direct all his power to the advantage of all his creatures. Nay, even the consideration of his immutable justice, rendering to all their due—of his unspotted holiness, of his all-sufficiency in himself, and of that immense ocean of all perfections which center in God from eternity to eternity—is a continual addition to the happiness of a Christian. (*A Plain Account of Genuine Christianity* [1749], in Coll. C, 317)

GOD: ALL-HOLY

Holiness is another of the attributes of the almighty, all-wise God. He is infinitely distant from every touch of evil. He "is light; and in him is no darkness at all." He is a God of unblemished justice and truth, but above all is his mercy. This we may easily learn from that beautiful passage in the thirty-third and thirty-fourth chapters of Exodus: "And Moses said, I beseech thee, show me thy glory. And the Lord descended in the cloud, and proclaimed the name of the Lord, The Lord, the Lord God, merciful and gracious, longsuffering, and abundant in goodness and truth; keeping mercy for thousands, and forgiving iniquity and transgression and sin." (Quoted in "Of God," chap. 3 in Coll. D, 39-40)

GOD: ETERNITY OF

A second essential attribute of God is eternity. He existed before all time. Perhaps we might more properly say, he *does exist* from everlasting to everlasting. But what is eternity? A celebrated author says that the divine eternity is . . . "The at once entire and perfect possession of never-ending life." But how much wiser are we for this definition? We know just as much of it as we did before. . . . Who can conceive what this means? (Quoted in "Of God," chap. 3 in Coll. D, 38-39)

GOD: HIS PROVIDENCE

"There is a great difference between particular providences and such extraordinary interpositions." Pray, Sir, show me what this difference is. It is a subject that deserves your coolest thoughts. "I know no ground—to hope or pray for such immediate reliefs. These things must be represented either as common accidents or as miracles." I do not thoroughly understand your terms. What is a common *accident*? That a sparrow falls to the ground? Or something more inconsiderable than the hairs of your head? Is there no medium between accident and miracle? If there be, what is that medium? (*The Principles of a Methodist Farther Explained* [1746], in *Works*, 12:372)

[A Christian] takes knowledge of the invisible things of God, even his eternal power and wisdom in the things that are seen, the heavens, the earth, the fowls of the air, the lilies of the field. How much more, while rejoicing in the constant care which he still takes of the work of his own hand, he breaks out in a transport of love and praise, "O Lord, our Governor! How excellent is thy name in all the earth! Thou that hast set thy glory above the heavens!" While he, as it were, sees the Lord sitting upon his throne and ruling all things well: while he observes the general providence of God coextended with his whole creation and surveys all the effects of it in the heavens and the earth as a well-pleased spectator; while he sees the wisdom and goodness of his general government descending to every particular; so presiding over the whole universe, as over a single person, so watching over every single person as if he were the whole universe: how does he exult, when he reviews the various traces of the almighty goodness, in what has befallen himself in the several circumstances and changes of his own life! All which he now sees have been allotted to him and dealt out in number, weight, and measure. With what triumph of soul, in surveying either the general or particular providence of God, does he observe every line pointing out a hereafter, every scene opening into eternity. (*A Letter to the Rev. Dr. Conyers Middleton Occasioned by His Late "Free Inquiry"* [January 4, 1749], in *Works* [S], 5:755)

God will do his own work in his own manner, and exceeding variously in different persons. It matters not whether it be wrought in a more pleasing or painful manner, so it is wrought; so nature is subdued, pride and self-will dethroned, and the will of God done in us and by us. Therefore, trouble not yourself about the experience of others; God knows you, and let him do with you as he sees best. (Letter to Miss Furly [October 21, 1757], in *Works* [WL], 12:186)

By a various train of providences you have been led to the very place where God intended you should be. And you have reason to praise him, that he has not suffered your labor there to be in vain. (Letter to the Rev. Lawrence Coughlan [August 1768], in *Letters*, 238)

There is frequently something very mysterious in the ways of divine providence. A little of them we may understand, but much more is beyond our comprehension; and we must be content to say, "What thou doest I know not now, but I shall know hereafter." At present, it is sufficient for me to know that all his ways are mercy and truth to them that love him. (Letter to Miss Jane Hilton [November 13, 1778], in *Works* [S], 7:46)

It is a great step toward Christian resignation to be thoroughly convinced of that great truth, that there is no such thing as chance in the world; that fortune is only another name for providence; only it is covered providence. An event, the cause of which does not appear, we commonly say, comes by chance. Oh, no; it is guided by an unerring hand; it is the result of infinite wisdom and goodness. Such are all the afflictive circumstances that have followed you in a constant succession, almost from your childhood. He that made the captain of your salvation perfect through sufferings has called you to walk in the same path and for the same end; namely, that you may learn obedience, a more perfect conformity to his death, by the things that you suffer. (Letter to Miss Nancy Bolton [January 2, 1781], in *Letters*, 368)

Equally conspicuous is the wisdom of God in the government of nations, of states, and kingdoms; yea, rather more conspicuous if infinite can be allowed to admit of any degrees. For the whole inanimate creation, being totally passive and inert, can make no opposition to his will. Therefore, in the natural world, all things roll on in an even, uninterrupted course. But it is far otherwise in the moral world. Here evil men and evil spirits continually oppose the divine will and create numberless irregularities. Here, therefore, is full scope for the exercise of all the riches both of the wisdom and knowledge of God, in counteracting all the wickedness and folly of men and all the subtlety of Satan, to carry on his own glorious design—the salvation of lost mankind. Indeed, were he to do this by an absolute decree and by his own irresistible power, it would imply no wisdom at all. But his wisdom is shown by saving man in such a manner as not to destroy his nature, nor to take away the liberty which he has given him. (Quoted in "Of God," chap. 3 in Coll. D, 28-29)

But they [the pagans] had no conception of his having a regard to the least things as well as the greatest, of his presiding over all that he has made and governing atoms as well as worlds. This we could not have known, unless it had pleased God to reveal it unto us himself. Had he not himself told us so, we should not have dared to think that "not a sparrow falleth to the ground without the will of our Father which is in heaven" and much less affirm that "even the very hairs of our head are all numbered!" (Quoted in "Of God," chap. 3 in Coll. D, 32)

GOD: JUST JUDGE

He will "judge the world in righteousness," and every man therein, according to the strictest justice. He will punish no man for doing anything which he could not possibly avoid, neither for omitting anything which he could not possibly do. Every punishment supposes the offender might have avoided the offense for which he is punished. Otherwise, to punish him would be palpably unjust and inconsistent with the character of God our Governor. (*Thoughts upon God's Sovereignty,* in *Works* [T], 9:473)

GOD: OMNIPOTENCE OF

And he is omnipotent as well as omnipresent: there can be no more bounds to his power than to his presence. He "hath a mighty arm: strong is his hand, and high is his right hand." He doeth whatsoever pleaseth him in the heavens, the earth, the sea, and in all deep places. With men, we know, many things are impossible; "but not with God: with him all things are possible." Whensoever he willeth, to do is present with him. ("The Unity of the Divine Being" [April 9, 1789], Sermon 119, in *Works* [S], 2:429-30)

GOD: OMNIPRESENCE OF

This subject is far too vast to be comprehended by the narrow limits of human understanding. We can only say, The great God, the eternal, the almighty Spirit, is as unbounded in his presence as in his duration and power. In condescension, indeed, to our weak understanding, he is said to dwell in heaven: but, strictly speaking, the heaven of heavens cannot contain him; but he is in every part of his dominion. The universal God dwelleth in universal space . . .

If we may dare attempt the illustrating this a little farther: What is the space occupied by a grain of sand, compared to that space which is occupied by the starry heavens? It is as a cipher; it is nothing; it vanishes away in the comparison. What is it then to the whole expanse of space, to which the whole creation is infinitely less than a grain of sand! And yet this space, to all the whole creation bears no proportion to all; is infinitely less in comparison of the great God than a grain of sand, yea, a millionth part of it, bears to that whole space.

This seems to be the plain meaning of those solemn words, which God speaks of himself: "Do not I fill heaven and earth?" And these sufficiently prove his omnipresence, which may be farther proved from this consideration: God acts everywhere and therefore is everywhere, for it is an utter impossibility that any being, created or uncreated, should work where it is not. . . .

This comfortable truth, that "God filleth heaven and earth," we learn also from the Psalmist above recited: "If I climb up into heaven, thou art there; if I go down to hell, thou art there also. If I take the wings of the morning and remain in the uttermost parts of the sea, even there thy hand shall lead me." The plain meaning is, If I remove to any distance whatever, thou art there; thou still besettest me and layest thine hand upon me. Let me flee to any conceivable or inconceivable distance; above, beneath, or on any side; it makes no difference; thou art still equally there; in thee I still "live, and move, and have my being."

And where no creature is, still God is there. The presence or absence of any or all creatures makes no difference with regard to him. He is equally in all or without all. Many have been the disputes among philosophers, whether there be any such thing as empty space in the universe; and it is now generally supposed that all space is full. Perhaps it cannot be proved, that all space is filled with matter. But the heathen himself will bear us witness, *Jovis omnia plena*: "All things are full of God." Yea, and whatever space exists beyond the bounds of creation (for creation must have bounds; seeing nothing is boundless, nothing can be but the great Creator), even that space cannot exclude him who fills the heaven and the earth.

Just equivalent to this is the expression of the apostle [Eph. 1:23] (not as some have strangely supposed, concerning the church, but concerning the head of it), "The fulness of him that filleth all in all," . . . literally . . . *all things in all things*: the strongest expression of universality which can possibly be conceived. It necessarily includes the least and the greatest of all things that exist. So that if any expression could be stronger, it would be stronger than even that, the "filling heaven and earth."

Indeed, this very expression, "Do not I fill heaven and earth?" (the question being equal to the strongest affirmation), implies the clearest assertion of God's being present everywhere and filling all space: for it is well known, the Hebrew phrase "heaven and earth" includes the whole universe, the whole extent of space, created or uncreated, and all that is therein. (Quoted in "Of God," chap. 3 in Coll. D, 31-34)

GOD: OMNISCIENCE OF

The omnipresent God sees and knows all the properties of the beings that he hath made. He knows all the connections, dependencies, and relations, and all the ways wherein one of them can affect another. In particular, he saw all the inanimate parts of the creation, whether in heaven above or in the earth beneath. He knows how the stars, comets, or planets above influence the inhabitants of the earth beneath; what influence the lower heavens, with their magazines of fire, hail, snow, and vapors, winds, and storms, have on our planet, and what effects may be produced in the bowels of the earth by fire, air, or water; what exhalations may be raised therefrom, and what changes wrought thereby; what effects every mineral or vegetable may have upon the children of men: all these lie naked and open to the eye of the Creator and Preserver of the universe!

He knows all the animals of the lower world, whether beasts, birds, fishes, reptiles, or insects. He knows all the qualities and powers he hath given them, from the highest to the lowest. He knows every good angel and every evil angel in every part of his dominions and looks from heaven upon the children of men over the whole face of the earth. He knows all the hearts of the sons of men and understands all their thoughts; he sees what any angel, any devil, any man either thinks or speaks or does, yea, and all they feel. He sees all their sufferings, with every circumstance of them. (Quoted in "Of God," chap. 3 in Coll. D, 36-37)

GOD: OUTSIDE OF TIME

The almighty, all-wise God sees and knows, from everlasting to everlasting, all that is, that was, and that is to come, through one eternal now. With him nothing is either past or future, but all things equally present. He has, therefore, if we speak according to the truth of things, no foreknowledge, no after-knowledge. This would be ill-consistent with the apostle's words, "With him is no variableness or shadow of turning," and with the account he gives of himself by the prophet, "I the Lord change not." Yet when he speaks to us, knowing whereof we are made, knowing the scantiness of our understanding, he lets himself down to our capacity and speaks of himself after the manner of men. Thus, in condescension to our weakness, he speaks of his own purpose, counsel, plan, foreknowledge. Not that God has any need of counsel, of purpose, or of planning his work beforehand. Far be it from us to impute these to the Most High, to measure him by ourselves! It is merely in compassion to us that he speaks thus of himself as foreknowing the things in heaven or earth and as predestinating or foreordaining them. (Quoted in "Of God," chap. 3 in Coll. D, 29-30)

GOD: SOVEREIGNTY OF

I believe this Father of all not only to be able to do whatsoever pleaseth him but also to have an eternal right of making what and when and how he pleaseth, and of possessing and disposing of all that he has made, and that he of his own goodness created heaven and earth and all that is therein. (*A Letter to a Roman Catholic* [July 18, 1749], in Coll. C, 304)

The sovereignty of God appears, (1) in fixing from eternity that decree touching the sons of men, "He that believeth shall be saved; he that believeth not shall be damned"; (2) in all the general circumstances of creation—in the time, the place, the manner of creating all things—in appointing the number and kinds of creatures, visible and invisible; (3) in allotting the natural endowments of men, these to one and those to another; (4) in disposing the time, place, and other outward circumstances (as parents, relations) attending the birth of everyone; (5) in dispensing the various gifts of the Spirit for the edification of his church; (6) in ordering all temporal things (as health, fortune, friends), everything short of eternity. But in disposing the eternal states of men (allowing only what was observed under the first article), it is clear that not sovereignty alone, but justice, mercy, and truth hold the reins. (*Predestination Calmly Considered* [1752], in *Works* [T], 9:401)

GOD: SUSTAINER OF CREATION

If by affirming, "All this is purely natural," you mean, it is not providential, or that God has nothing to do with it, this is not true, that is, supposing the Bible to be true. For supposing this, you may descant ever so long on the natural causes of murrain, winds, thunder, lightning, and yet you are altogether wide of the mark, you prove nothing at all, unless you can prove that God never works in or by natural causes. But this you cannot prove; nay, none can doubt of his so working, who allows the Scripture to be of God. . . . allowing there are natural causes of all these, they are still under the direction of the Lord of nature: Nay, what is nature itself, but the art of God or God's method of acting in the material world? True philosophy therefore ascribes all to God. (*Serious Thoughts Occasioned by the Late Earthquake at Lisbon* [1755], in *Works* [WL], 11:6-7)

Let us even dare to own we believe there is a God; nay, and not a lazy, indolent, epicurean deity who sits at ease upon the circle of the heavens and neither knows nor cares what is done below; but one who, as he created heaven and earth and all the armies of them, as he sustains them all by the word of his power, so cannot neglect the work of his own hands. With pleasure we own there is such a God, whose eye pervades the whole sphere of created beings, who knoweth the number of the stars and calleth them all by their names; a God whose wisdom is as the great abyss, deep and wide as eternity. (*Serious Thoughts Occasioned by the Late Earthquake at Lisbon* [1755], in *Works* [WL], 11:10)

As this wisdom appears even to shortsighted men (and much more to spirits of a higher order) in the creation and disposition of the whole universe and every part of it, so it equally appears in their preservation, in his "upholding all things by the word of his power." And it no less eminently appears in the permanent government of all that he has created. How admirably does his wisdom direct the motions of the heavenly bodies! of all the stars in the firmament, whether those that are fixed or those that wander, though never out of their several orbits! of the sun in the midst of heaven! of those amazing bodies, the comets, that shoot in every direction through the immeasurable fields of ether! How does he superintend all the parts of this lower world, this "speck of creation," the earth! So that all things are still as they were at the beginning, "beautiful in their seasons," and summer and winter, seedtime and harvest, regularly follow each other. (Quoted in "Of God," chap. 3 in Coll. D, 27-28)

God acts in heaven, in earth, and under the earth—throughout the whole compass of his creation—by sustaining all things, without which everything would in an instant sink into its primitive nothing; by governing all, every moment superintending everything that he has made; strongly and sweetly influencing all and yet without destroying the liberty of his rational creatures. The very heathens acknowledge that the great God governs the large and conspicuous parts of the universe; that he regulates the motions of the heavenly bodies, of the sun, moon, and stars. (Quoted in "Of God," chap. 3 in Coll. D, 32)

And as this all-wise, all-gracious being created all things, so he sustains all things. He is the Preserver as well as the Creator of everything that exists. "He upholdeth all things by the word of his power," that is, by his powerful word. Now it must be that he knows everything he has made and everything that he preserves from moment to moment; otherwise, he could not preserve it; he could not continue to it the being which he has given it. (Quoted in "Of God," chap. 3 in Coll. D, 35-36)

GOD: WILL OF

Perhaps some may ask, "Ought we not then to inquire, What is the will of God in all things? And ought not his will to be the rule of our practice?" Unquestionably it ought. But how is a sober Christian to make this inquiry? To know what is the will of God? Not by waiting for supernatural dreams. Not by expecting God to reveal it in visions. Not by looking for any *particular impressions* or sudden impulses on his mind. No, but by consulting the oracles of God. "To the law and to the testimony." This is the general method of knowing what is "the holy and acceptable will of God."

. . . "But how shall I know what is the will of God, in such and such a particular case? The thing proposed is, in itself, of an indifferent nature, and so left undetermined in Scripture." I answer, the Scripture itself gives you a general rule applicable to all particular cases. ("The Nature of Enthusiasm" [1750], Sermon 39, in *Works* [T], 5:395)

GOSPEL

The gospel (that is, good tidings, good news for guilty, helpless sinners), in the largest sense of the word, means the whole revelation made to man by Jesus Christ, and sometimes the whole account of what our Lord did and suffered, while he tabernacled among men. The substance of all is, "Jesus Christ came into the world to save sinners." Or, "God so loved the world, that he gave his only begotten Son, to the end we might not perish, but have everlasting life." Or, "he was bruised for our transgressions, he was wounded for our iniquities: the chastisement of our peace was upon him, and with his stripes we are healed."

. . . Believe this, and the kingdom of God is thine. By faith thou attainest the promise. "He pardoneth and absolveth all that truly repent, and unfeignedly believe his holy gospel." As soon as ever God hath spoken to thy heart, "Be of good cheer, thy sins are forgiven thee," his kingdom comes; thou hast righteousness and peace and joy in the Holy Ghost. ("The Way to the Kingdom" [June 6, 1742], Sermon 7, in *Works* [T], 5:71)

But of all preaching, what is usually called gospel preaching is the most useless, if not the most mischievous—a dull, yea, or lively harangue on the sufferings of Christ or salvation by faith without strongly inculcating holiness. I see, more and more, that this naturally tends to drive holiness out of the world. (Letter to Charles Wesley [November 4, 1772], in *Works* [WL], 12:130)

I find more profit in sermons on either good tempers or good works than in what are vulgarly called *gospel sermons*. That term has now become a mere cant word; I wish none of our society would use it. It has no determinate meaning. Let but a pert, self-sufficient animal that has neither sense nor grace bawl out something about Christ or his blood or justification by faith and his hearers cry out, "What a fine gospel sermon!" Surely the Methodists have not so learned Christ! We know no gospel without salvation from sin. (Letter to Miss Bishop [1778], quoted in Coll. C, 260n†)

GOSSIP

Of all gossiping, religious gossiping is the worst; it adds hypocrisy to uncharitableness and effectually does the work of the devil in the name of the Lord. (Letter to a young disciple [June 20, 1772], in *Works* [S], 7:92)

GOVERNMENT

It is my religion which obliges me "to put men in mind to be subject to principalities and powers." Loyalty is with me an essential branch of religion, and which I am sorry any Methodist should forget. There is the closest connection, therefore, between my religious and my political conduct; the self-same authority enjoining me to "fear God" and to "honor the king." (Letter to Walter Churchey [June 25, 1777], in *Works* [S], 7:84)

GOVERNMENT: CHURCH

Q. . . . Is Episcopal, Presbyterian, or Independent church government most agreeable to reason?

A. The plain origin of church government seems to be this: Christ sends forth a person to preach the gospel; some of those who hear him repent, and believe in Christ; they then desire him to watch over them, to build them up in faith, and to guide their souls in the paths of righteousness.

Here, then, is an Independent congregation, subject to no pastor but their own; neither liable to be controlled, in things spiritual, by any other man or body of men whatsoever.

But soon after, some from other parts, who were occasionally present whilst he was speaking in the name of the Lord, beseech him to come over and help them also. He complies; yet not till he confers with the wisest and holiest of his congregation; and with their consent appoints one who has gifts and grace to watch over his flock in his absence.

If it please God to raise another flock in the new place, before he leaves them, he does the same thing, appointing one whom God hath fitted for the work to watch over these souls also. In like manner, in every place where it pleases God to gather a little flock by his word, he appoints one in his absence to take the oversight of the rest, to assist them as of the ability which God giveth. These are deacons, or servants of the church; and they look upon their first pastor as the common father of all these congregations and regard him in the same light and esteem him still as the shepherd of their souls.

These congregations are not strictly independent, as they depend upon one pastor, though not upon each other.

As these congregations increase, and the deacons grow in years and grace, they need other subordinate deacons, or helpers, in respect of whom they may be called Presbyters or elders, as their father in the Lord may be called the bishop or overseer of them all. (Minutes of the Methodist Conference at Bristol, August 3, 1745, in *Minutes*, 26-27)

Q. . . . Does a church in the New Testament always mean "a single congregation"?

A. We believe it does; we do not recollect any instance to the contrary.

Q. . . . What instance or ground is there then in the New Testament for a *national* church?

A. We know none at all; we apprehend it to be a merely political institution.

Q. . . . Are the three orders of bishops, priests, and deacons plainly described in the New Testament?

A. We think they are and believe they generally obtained in the church of the apostolic age.

Q. . . . But are you assured that God designed the same plan should obtain in all churches, throughout all ages?

A. We are not assured of it, because we do not know it is asserted in holy writ. . . .

Q. . . . Must there not be numberless accidental variations in the government of various churches?

A. There must, in the nature of things. As God variously dispenses his gifts of nature, providence, and grace, both the offices themselves and the officers in each ought to be varied from time to time.

Q. . . . Why is it that there is no determinate plan of church government appointed in Scripture?

A. Without doubt because the wisdom of God had a regard to that necessary variety. (Minutes of the Methodist Conference, June 15, 1747, in *Minutes*, 36)

I believe the Episcopal form of church government to be scriptural and apostolic. If you think the Presbyterian or Independent is better, think so still, and act accordingly. ("Catholic Spirit" [1750], Sermon 41, in *Works* [T], 5:416)

As to my own judgment, I still believe "the episcopal form of church government to be scriptural and apostolical." I mean, well agreeing with the practice and writings of the apostles. But that it is *prescribed* in Scripture, I do not believe. This opinion, which I once zealously espoused, I have been heartily ashamed of ever since I read Bishop Stillingfleet's *Irenicon*. I think he has unanswerably proved, that "neither Christ nor his apostles *prescribe* any particular form of church government; and that the plea of *divine right* for diocesan episcopacy was never heard of in the primitive church." (Letter to the Rev. Mr. Clarke [July 3, 1756], in *Works*, 16:26)

Concerning diocesan episcopacy, there are several questions I should be glad to have answered: (1) Where is it prescribed in Scripture? (2) How does it appear that the apostles "settled it in all the churches they planted"? (3) How does it appear that they so settled it in any, as to make it of perpetual obligation? It is allowed, "Christ and his apostles did put the churches under some form of government or other." But, (1) Did they put all churches under the same precise form? If they did, (2) Can we prove this to have been the very same which now remains in the Church of England? (Second letter to the Rev. Mr. Clarke [September 10, 1756], in *Works* [S], 7:285-86)

As long as I live, the people shall have no share in choosing either stewards or leaders among the Methodists. We have not, and never had, any such custom. We are no republicans and never intend to be. (Letter to Mr. John Mason [January 13, 1790], in Coll. C, 367-68)

GRACE

All the blessings which God hath bestowed upon man are of his mere grace, bounty, or favor; his free, undeserved favor; favor altogether undeserved; man having no claim to the least of his mercies. . . . whatever righteousness may be found in man, this is also the gift of God. ("Salvation by Faith" [June 18, 1738], sermon, in Coll. C, 17)

In every state we need Christ in the following respects: (1) Whatever grace we receive, it is a free gift from him. (2) We receive it as his purchase, merely in consideration of the price he paid. (3) We have this grace, not only *from* Christ, but *in* him. For our perfection is not like that of a tree, which flourishes by the sap derived from its own root, but . . . like that of a branch which, united to the vine, bears fruit, but, severed from it, *is dried up and withered*. (4) All our blessings—temporal, spiritual, and eternal—depend on his intercession for us, which is one branch of his priestly office, whereof therefore we have always equal need. (*A Plain Account of Christian Perfection* [1767; rev. 1777], in *Works* [WL], 11:395-96)

The holiest of men still need Christ, as their Prophet, as *the light of the world.* For he does not give them light, but from moment to moment: The instant he withdraws, all is darkness. They still need Christ as their King, for God does not give them a stock of holiness. But unless they receive a supply every moment, nothing but unholiness would remain. They still need Christ as their Priest, to make atonement for their holy things. Even perfect holiness is acceptable to God only through Jesus Christ. (*A Plain Account of Christian Perfection* [1767; rev. 1777], in *Works* [WL], 11:417)

The grace or love of God, whence cometh our salvation, is *free in all* and *free for all.*
    First, it is free *in all* to whom it is given. It does not depend on any power or merit in man, no, not in any degree, neither in whole nor in part. It does not in any wise depend either on the good works or righteousness of the receiver, not on anything he has done or anything he is. It does not depend on his endeavors. It does not depend on his good tempers or good desires or good purposes and intentions, for all these flow from the free grace of God; they are the streams only, not the fountain. They are the fruits of free grace and not the root. They are not the cause but the effects of it. Whatsoever good is in man or is done by man, God is the author and doer of it. Thus is his grace free in all; that is, no way depending on any power or merit in

man, but on God alone, who freely gave us his own Son and "with him freely giveth us all things." (Quoted in "Of God, chap. 3 in Coll. D, 52-53)

GRACE: DEGREES OR GREATER MEASURE OF

Everyone must be entirely sanctified in the article of death. . . . till then a believer daily grows in grace, comes nearer and nearer to perfection. (*A Plain Account of Christian Perfection* [1767; rev. 1777], in *Works* [WL], 11:388)

You seem to think I allow no degrees in grace and that I make no distinction between the full assurance of faith and a low or common measure of it. (Letter to Mr. Richard Tompson [February 5, 1756], in Coll. B, 208)

But is there not a repentance consequent upon as well as a repentance previous to justification? And is it not incumbent on all that are justified to be *zealous of good works*? Yea, are not these so necessary that if a man willingly neglect them he cannot reasonably expect that he shall ever be sanctified in the full sense, that is, *perfected in love*? Nay, can he *grow* at all *in the grace, in the* loving *knowledge of our Lord Jesus Christ*? Yea, can he retain the grace which God has already given him? Can he continue in the faith which he has received or in the favor of God? ("The Scripture Way of Salvation" [1765], Sermon 22, in *Works* [T], 5:211)

Can those who are perfect grow in grace? . . . Undoubtedly they can, and that not only while they are in the body but to all eternity. (*A Plain Account of Christian Perfection* [1767; rev. 1777], in *Works* [WL], 11:426)

Sometimes there is painful conviction of sin, preparatory to full sanctification; sometimes a conviction that has far more pleasure than pain, being mixed with joyful expectation. Always there should be a gradual growth in grace, which need never be intermitted from the time we are justified. Do not wait therefore for pain or anything else but simply for all-conquering faith. (Letter to Miss Bishop [November 5, 1770], in Coll. B, 533)

GRACE: FALLING AWAY FROM (APOSTASY)

And, no doubt, a true believer in Christ may lose the light of faith. And so far as this is lost, he may, for a time, fall again into condemnation. But this is not the case of them who now "are in Christ Jesus," who now believe in his name. For so long as they believe and walk after the Spirit, neither God condemns them nor their own heart. ("The First Fruits of the Spirit" [1746], Sermon 8, in *Works* [T], 5:75)

I believe a saint may fall away, that one who is holy or righteous in the judgment of God himself may nevertheless so fall from God as to perish everlastingly.

. . . For thus saith the Lord, "When the righteous turneth away from his righteousness, and committeth iniquity, [. . .] in his trespass that he hath trespassed, and in his sin that he hath sinned, in them shall he die" [Ezek. 18:24].

That this is to be understood of eternal death appears from the 26th verse: "When a righteous man turneth away from his righteousness, and committeth iniquity, and dieth in them; *[here is temporal death]* for his iniquity that he hath done he shall die": *here is death eternal.*

It appears farther, from the whole scope of the chapter, which is to prove, "The soul that sinneth, it shall die" [v. 4]. If you say, "The soul here means the body," I answer, that will die whether you sin or not.

Again, thus saith the Lord, "When I shall say to the righteous, that he shall surely live: if he trust to his own righteousness" [yea, or to that promise as absolute and unconditional] "and committeth iniquity, all his righteousness shall not be remembered; but for the iniquity that he hath committed shall he die" [33:13].

Again, "When the righteous turneth from his righteousness and committeth iniquity, he shall even die thereby" [v. 18]. Therefore, one who is holy and righteous in the judgment of God himself may yet so fall as to perish everlastingly. (*Serious Thoughts upon the Perseverance of the Saints* [1751], in *Works* [T], 9:439-40)

But how can this be reconciled with the words of our Lord, "He that believeth shall be saved?"

Do you think these words mean, *He that believeth* at this moment *shall* certainly and inevitably *be saved*? If this interpretation be good, then by all the rules of speech, the other part of the sentence must mean, *He that does not believe* at this moment *shall* certainly and inevitably *be damned.* Therefore that interpretation cannot be good. The plain meaning then of the whole sentence is, *He that believeth*, if he continue in faith, *shall be saved; he that believeth not*, if he continue in unbelief, *shall be damned.* (*Serious Thoughts upon the Perseverance of the Saints* [1751], in *Works* [T], 9:442)

That one who is endued with the faith which produces a good conscience may, nevertheless, finally fall, appears from the words of St. Paul to Timothy [1 Tim. 1:18-19]. "War a good warfare, holding faith and a good conscience, which some having put away concerning faith have made shipwreck."

Observe, (1) These men had once the faith that produces a *good conscience*, which they once had or they could not have *put it away.*

Observe, (2) They *made shipwreck* of the faith, which necessarily implies the total and final loss of it.

You object, "Nay, the *putting away* a good conscience does not suppose they had it but rather that they had it not."

This is really surprising. But how do you prove it? "Why by Acts [13:46], where St. Paul says to the Jews, 'It was necessary that the word of God should first have been spoken to you. But seeing ye put it from you—lo, we turn to the Gentiles.' Here you see the Jews, who never had the gospel, are said to *put it away.*"

How! are you sure they "never had what they are here said *to put away?*" Not so; what they put away, it is undeniable they had till they *put it away*: namely, *the word of God spoken* by Paul and Barnabas. This instance, therefore, makes full against you. It proves just the reverse of what you cited it for. . . .

. . . Those who are grafted into the good olive tree—the spiritual, invisible church—may nevertheless finally fall. For thus saith the apostle, "Some of the branches are broken off, and thou art grafted in among them, and with them partakest of the root and fatness of the olive tree. Be not highminded, but fear: if God spared not the natural branches, take heed lest he spare not thee. Behold the goodness and severity of God! on them which fell, severity, but toward thee, goodness, if thou continue in his goodness; otherwise thou shalt be cut off" [Rom. 11:17-22]. (*Predestination Calmly Considered* [1752], in *Works* [T], 9:408)

Those who are branches of Christ, the true vine, may yet finally fall from grace. For thus saith our blessed Lord himself, "I am the true vine, and my Father is the husbandman. Every branch in me that beareth not fruit he taketh away. [. . .] I am the vine, ye are the branches. [. . .] If a man abide not in me, he is cast forth as a branch, and is withered; and men gather them, and cast them into the fire, and they are burned" [John 15:1-2, 5-6].

Here we may observe,

1. The persons spoken of were *in Christ, branches of the true vine.*

2. Some of these *branches abide not* in Christ, but "the Father taketh them away."

3. The *branches* which *abide not* are *cast forth*, cast out from Christ and his church.

4. They are not only *cast forth* but *withered*, consequently never grafted in again.

5. They are not only *cast forth* and *withered* but also *cast into* the *fire*. And,

6. *They are burned.* It is not possible for words more strongly to declare that those who are branches of the true Vine may finally fall. . . .

. . . Those who so effectually know Christ, as by that knowledge to have escaped the pollutions of the world, may yet fall back into those pollutions and perish everlastingly. For thus saith the Apostle Peter, "If after they have escaped the pollutions of the world through the knowledge of the Lord and Saviour Jesus Christ" (the only possible way of escaping them), "they are entangled again therein and overcome, the latter end is worse with them than the beginning" [2 Pet. 2:20]. (*Predestination Calmly Considered* [1752], in *Works* [T], 9:409-10)

If you imagine these texts are not sufficient to prove that a true believer may finally fall, I will offer a few more to your consideration, which I would beg you to weigh farther at your leisure.

[Matt. 5:13], "Ye (Christians) are the salt of the earth. But if the salt have lost its savour, wherewith shall it be salted? It is henceforth good for nothing but to be cast out, and trodden under foot of men."

[12:43-45], "When the unclean spirit goeth out of a man" (as he doth out of every true believer), "he walketh through dry places, seeking rest, and findeth none. Then he saith, I will return, [. . .] and he taketh with him seven other spirits, [. . .] and they enter in and dwell there. And the last state of that man is worse than the first."

[24:10, 12-13], "And then shall many be offended, [. . .] and the love" (toward God and man) "of many shall wax cold. But he that shall endure to the end, the same shall be saved."

[Vv. 45, 49-51], "Who, then, is a faithful and wise servant, whom his Lord hath made ruler over his household? [. . .] But if that evil servant" (wise and faithful as he was once) "shall begin to smite his fellowservants, [. . .] the Lord shall cut him asunder, and appoint him his portion with the hypocrites," apostates being no better than they.

[Luke 21:34], "Take heed to yourselves" (ye that believe) "lest at any time your heart be overcharged with the cares of this life, and so that day come upon you unawares." Plainly implying that otherwise they would not be "accounted worthy to stand before the Son of Man."

[John 5:14], "Sin no more, lest a worse thing" (than any temporal evil) "come unto thee."

[John 8:31-32], "If ye continue in my word, then are ye my disciples indeed. And ye shall know the truth, and the truth shall make you free."

[1 Cor. 9:27], "I keep my body under, [. . .] lest, by any means, when I have preached to others, I myself should be a castaway."

[1 Cor. 10:3-6, 12], "Our fathers did all eat the same spiritual meat, and did all drink the same spiritual drink: for they drank of that spiritual Rock that followed them: and that Rock was Christ. But with many of them God was not well pleased" for they were overthrown in the wilderness. Now these things were our examples, [. . .] Wherefore let him that thinketh he standeth take heed lest he fall."

[2 Cor. 6:1], "We, therefore, as workers together with him, beseech you that ye receive not the grace of God in vain." But this were impossible, if none that ever had it could perish.

[Gal. 5:4], "Ye are fallen from grace" [6:9], "We shall reap, if we faint not." Therefore, we shall not reap if we do.

[Heb. 3:14], "We are made partakers of Christ, if we hold the beginning of our confidence steadfast unto the end."

[2 Pet. 3:17], "Beware, lest ye also, being led away with the error of the wicked, fall from your own steadfastness."

2 John 8, "Look to yourselves, that we lose not the things which we have wrought."

[Rev. 3:11], "Hold that fast which thou hast, that no man take thy crown."

And to conclude, "So likewise shall my heavenly Father do also unto you, if ye from your hearts forgive not every one his brother their trespasses" [Matt. 18:35]. So! How? He will retract the pardon he had given and deliver you to the tormentors. (*Predestination Calmly Considered* [1752], in *Works* [T], 9:415-16)

Certainly some years ago you [were] alive to God. You experienced the life and power of religion. And does not God intend that the trials you meet with should bring you back to this? You cannot stand still; you know this is impossible. You must go forward or backward. Either you must recover that power and be a Christian altogether, or in a while you will have neither power nor form, inside nor outside. (Letter to Mr. John Trembath [August 17, 1760], in Coll. C, 355)

Q. . . . Can they fall from [grace]?

A. I am well assured they can; matter of fact puts this beyond dispute. Formerly we thought one saved from sin could not fall; now we know the contrary. We are surrounded with instances of those who lately experienced all that I mean by perfection. They had both the fruit of the Spirit and the witness, but they have now lost both. Neither does anyone stand by virtue of anything that is implied in the nature of the state. There is no such height or strength of holiness as it is impossible to fall from. If there be any that cannot fall, this wholly depends on the promise of God.

Q. . . . Can those who fall from this state recover it?

A. Why not? We have many instances of this also. Nay, it is an exceeding common thing for persons to lose it more than once, before they are established therein.

It is therefore to guard them who are saved from sin, from every occasion of stumbling, that I give the following advices. (*A Plain Account of Christian Perfection* [1767; rev. 1777], in *Works* [WL], 11:426-27)

Two things are certain: the one, that it is possible to lose even the pure love of God; the other, that it is not necessary, it is not unavoidable; it may be lost, but it may be kept. Accordingly, we have some, in every part of the kingdom, who have never been moved from their steadfastness. And from this moment you need never be moved; his grace is sufficient for you. But you must continue to grow if you continue to stand, for no one can stand still. (Letter to Mrs. Jane Barton [May 8, 1770], in *Works* [S], 7:43)

GRACE: IRRESISTIBLE (FALSITY OF)

But, say some, "If Christ died for all, why are not all saved?"

I answer, "Because they believe not in the name of the only begotten Son of God." Because God "called, and they refused to answer; he stretched out his hand, and they regarded not; he counseled them, but they would hear none of his counsels"; he reproved them, but they set at naught all his reproofs; "they followed after lying vanities and forsook their own mercies"; they "denied the Lord that bought them and so brought upon themselves swift destruction"; and "because they received not the love of the truth, that they might be saved, therefore" (if you would know wherefore) "God gave them up to believe a lie" and to be damned. "How often" (saith our Lord) "would I have gathered you together, and ye would not!" *Ye would not.* Here is the plain reason why all men are not saved. For God promiseth no man salvation, whether he will or not, but leaveth them to everlasting destruction who will not *believe and obey the gospel.* (*The Scripture Doctrine Concerning Predestination, Election, and Reprobation* [1741], in *Works* [T], 9:428)

With regard to [. . .] irresistible grace, I believe,

That the grace which brings faith and thereby salvation into the soul is irresistible at that moment.

That most believers may remember some time when God did irresistibly convince them of sin.

That most believers do, at some other times, find God irresistibly acting upon their souls.

Yet I believe that the grace of God, both before and after those moments, may be and hath been resisted, and

That, in general, it does not act irresistibly, but we may comply therewith, or may not.

And I do not deny,

That in those eminently styled, "the elect" (if such there be), the grace of God is so far irresistible that they cannot but believe and be finally saved.

But I cannot believe,

That all those must be damned in whom it does not thus irresistibly work, or

That there is one soul on earth who has not, and never had, any other grace than such as does, in fact, increase his damnation and was designed of God so to do. ("Calvinistic Controversy," in *Works* [S], 7:480-81)

"Nay, but God must work *irresistibly* in me, or I shall never be saved." Hold! consider that word. You are again advancing a doctrine which has not one plain, clear text to support it. I allow, God *may* possibly at *some times* work irresistibly in *some* souls. I believe he *does*. But can you infer from hence that he *always* works thus in all that are saved? Alas, my brother, what kind of conclusion is this? And by what scripture will you prove it? Where, I pray, is it written that none are saved but by irresistible grace? By almighty grace, I grant, by that power alone, to which all things are possible. But show me any one plain scripture for this, that "all saving grace is irresistible."

. . . But this doctrine is not only unsupported by Scripture, it is flatly contrary thereto. How will you reconcile it, to instance in a very few, with the following texts?

[Matt. 22:3], "He sent to call them, and they would not come."

[Mark 6:5-6], "He could do no mighty works there, [. . .] because of their unbelief."

[Luke 5:17], "There were Pharisees, [. . .] and the power of the Lord was present to heal them." Nevertheless they were not healed in fact, as the words immediately following show. [7:30], "The Pharisees and lawyers made void the counsel of God against themselves." [13:34], "O Jerusalem, Jerusalem, how often would I have gathered thy children, and ye would not."

[John 6:63-64], "It is the spirit that quickeneth; the words that I speak unto you, they are spirit. But there are some of you that believe not." Therefore that Spirit did not work irresistibly.

[Acts 7:51], "Ye do always resist the Holy Ghost: as your fathers did, so do ye." [13:46], "Ye put it from you, and judge yourselves unworthy of eternal life."

[Heb. 3:8], "While it is called to-day, harden not your heart." [V. 12], "Take heed lest there be in any of you an evil heart of unbelief, in departing from a living God." [12:25], "See that ye refuse not him that speaketh." (*Predestination Calmly Considered* [1752], in *Works* [T], 9:416-17)

G

GRACE: MEANS OF

But are there any *ordinances* now, since life and immortality were brought to light by the gospel? Are there under the Christian dispensation any *means* ordained of God as the usual channels of his grace? This question could never have been proposed in the apostolic church, unless by one who openly avowed himself to be a heathen, the whole body of Christians being agreed that Christ had ordained certain outward means for conveying his grace into the souls of men. Their constant practice set this beyond all dispute, for so long as "all that believed were together, and had all things common" [Acts 2:44]: "they continued steadfastly in the teaching of the apostles, and in breaking of bread, and in prayers" [v. 42]. . . .

The chief of these means are prayer, whether in secret or with the great congregation; searching the Scriptures (which implies reading, hearing, and meditating thereon), and receiving the Lord's Supper, eating bread and drinking wine in remembrance of him; and these we believe to be ordained of God as the ordinary channels of conveying his grace to the souls of men. ("The Means of Grace" [November 15, 1739], Sermon 16, in *Works* [T], 5:150, 152)

I earnestly besought them all to stand in the old paths: to go to church; to communicate; to fast; to use as much private prayer as they can; to read the Scripture: Because I believe these are *means of grace*, [that is], do ordinarily convey God's grace to unbelievers [who have not the faith "that overcometh"]. (Quoted in "Of Justification by Faith," chap. 11 in Coll. A, 75)

Although this expression of our [Anglican] Church, "means of grace," be not found in Scripture, yet if the sense of it undeniably is, to cavil at the term, is a mere strife of words.

But the sense of it is undeniably found in Scripture. For God hath in Scripture ordained prayer, reading or hearing, and the receiving the Lord's Supper, as the ordinary means of conveying his grace to man. (*Journal*, April 25, 1740)

Not only in this, and many other parts of the Journals, but in a sermon written professedly on the subject, I contend that all the ordinances of God are the stated channels of his grace to man and that it is our bounden duty to use them all at all possible opportunities. So that to charge the Methodists in general, or me in particular, with undervaluing or disparaging them shows just as much regard for justice and truth as if you were to charge us with Mahometanism. (*A Second Letter to the Author of* The Enthusiasm of Methodists

and Papists Compared [November 27, 1750], in *Works,* 13:57)

GRACE: PREVENIENT

I believe,

1. There are degrees in faith and that a man may have some degree of it before all things in him are become new; before he has the full assurance of faith, the abiding witness of the Spirit, or the clear perception that Christ dwelleth in him.

2. Accordingly, I believe there is a degree of justifying faith (and, consequently, a state of justification) short of, and commonly antecedent to, this. (*Journal,* December 31, 1739)

It is allowed, also, that repentance and "fruits meet for repentance" go before faith [Mark 1:15; Matt. 3:8]. Repentance absolutely must go before faith; fruits meet for it, if there be opportunity. By repentance I mean conviction of sin producing real desires and sincere resolutions of amendment; and by "fruits meet for repentance," forgiving our brother [Matt. 6:14-15], ceasing from evil, doing good [Luke 3:4, 9, etc.], using the ordinances of God, and in general obeying him according to the measure of grace which we have received [Matt. 7:7; 25:29]. But these I cannot as yet term good works, because they do not spring from faith and the love of God. (*Conditions of Justification* [1744], in Coll. B, 178)

Do by nature—That is, without an outward rule; though this also, strictly speaking, is by preventing grace. *The things contained in the law*—The ten commandments being only the substance of the law of nature. *These, not having the written law, are a law unto themselves*—That is, what the law is to the Jews, they are, by the grace of God, to themselves; namely, a rule of life. (*NT Notes,* 362, comment on Rom. 2:14)

One of Mr. Fletcher's Checks considers at large the Calvinistic supposition "that a natural man is as dead as a stone" and shows the utter falseness and absurdity of it: seeing no man living is without some preventing grace; and every degree of grace is a degree of life. (Letter to John Mason [November 21, 1776], in *Works* [S], 7:97)

A gradual work of grace constantly precedes the instantaneous work both of justification and sanctification. But the work itself (of sanctification as well as justification) is undoubtedly instantaneous. As after a gradual conviction of the guilt and power of sin you [were] justified in a moment, so after a gradually increasing conviction of inbred sin you will be sanctified in a moment. (Letter to Arthur Keene [June 21, 1784], *Letters* [JT], 7:222)

G

Salvation begins with what is usually termed (and very properly) preventing grace: including the first wish to please God; the first dawn of light concerning his will; and the first slight transient conviction of having sinned against him. All these imply some tendency toward life; some degree of salvation; the beginning of a deliverance from a blind, unfeeling heart, quite insensible of God and the things of God. (Quoted in "Of Sanctification and Christian Perfection," chap. 12 in Coll. D, 209)

Yet this is no excuse for those who continue in sin, and lay the blame upon their Maker, by saying, "It is God only that must quicken us, for we cannot quicken our own souls." For allowing that all the souls of men are dead in sin by *nature*, this excuses none, seeing there is no man that is in a state of mere nature; there is no man, unless he has quenched the Spirit, that is wholly void of the grace of God. No man living is entirely destitute of what is vulgarly called *natural conscience*. But this is not natural; it is more properly termed *preventing grace*. Every man has a greater or less measure of this, which waiteth not for the call of man. Everyone has, sooner or later, good desires; although the generality of men stifle them before they can strike deep root or produce any considerable fruit. Everyone has some measure of that light, some faint glimmering ray, which sooner or later, more or less, enlightens every man that cometh into the world. And everyone, unless he be one of the small number whose conscience is seared as with a hot iron, feels more or less uneasy when he acts contrary to the light of his own conscience. So that no man sins because he has not grace but because he does not use the grace which he hath. ("On Working Out Our Own Salvation" [October 1785], Sermon 90, in *Works* [S], 2:237-38)

HADES; SHEOL; PARADISE; INTERMEDIATE STATE

Even in paradise, in the intermediate state between death and the resurrection, we shall learn more concerning these in an hour than we could in an age during our stay in the body. We cannot tell, indeed, how we shall then exist or what kind of organs we shall have; the soul will not be encumbered with flesh and blood, but probably it will have some sort of ethereal vehicle even before God clothes us "with our nobler house of empyrean light." (Letter to Miss Bosanquet [December 21, 1776], in Coll. B, 548)

But as happy as the souls in paradise are, they are preparing for far greater happiness. For paradise is only the porch of heaven; and it is there the spirits of just men are made perfect. It is in heaven only that there is the fullness of joy; the pleasures that are at God's right hand forevermore. (Quoted in "Of a Future State," chap. 17 in Coll. D, 328)

St. Paul teaches that it is in heaven we are to be joined with "the spirits of just men made perfect," in such a sense as we cannot be on earth or even in paradise. In paradise the souls of good men rest from their labors and are with Christ from death to the resurrection. This bears no resemblance at all to the popish purgatory, wherein wicked men are supposed to be tormented in purging fire till they are sufficiently purified to have a place in heaven. But we believe (as did the ancient church) that none suffer after death but those who suffer eternally. We believe that we are to be *here* saved from sin and enabled to love God with all our heart. (Letter to George Blackall [February 25, 1783], in *Works* [S], 7:227)

"The beggar died . . . and was carried by angels"—nobler servants than any that attended the rich man—"into Abraham's bosom." So the Jews commonly termed what our blessed Lord styles paradise—the place "where the wicked cease from troubling and where the weary are at rest," the receptacle of holy souls from death to the resurrection. It is, indeed, very generally supposed that the souls of good men, as soon as they are discharged from the body, go directly to heaven, but this opinion has not the least foundation in the oracles of God. On the contrary, our Lord says to Mary, after the resurrection, "Touch me not: for I am not yet ascended to my Father," in heaven. But he had been in paradise, according to his promise to the penitent thief, "This day shalt thou be with me in paradise." Hence, it is plain that paradise is not heaven. It is, indeed (if we may be allowed the expression), the antechamber of heaven where the souls of the righteous remain till, after the general Judgment, they are received into glory. ("The Rich Man and Lazarus" [March 25, 1788], Sermon 48, in *Works* [T], 6:52-53)

H

Hades, namely, the invisible world. Accordingly, by Christ descending into hell, they meant his body remained in the grave, his soul remained in Hades (which is the receptacle of separate spirits) from death to the resurrection. Here we cannot doubt but the spirits of the righteous are inexpressibly happy. They are, as St. Paul expresses it, "with the Lord" [and] favored with so intimate a communion with him as "is far better" than whatever the chief of the apostles experienced while in this world. On the other hand, we learn from our Lord's own account of Dives and Lazarus that the rich man, from the moment he left the world, entered into a state of torment. And "there is a great gulf fixed" in Hades between the place of holy and that of the unholy spirits which it is impossible for either the one or the other to pass over. Indeed a gentleman of great learning, the Honorable Mr. Campbell, in his account of the Middle State published not many years ago, seems to suppose that wicked souls may amend in Hades and then remove to a happier mansion. He has great hopes that "the rich man" mentioned by our Lord, in particular, might be purified by that penal fire till, in process of time, he might be qualified for a better abode. But who can reconcile this with Abraham's assertion that none can pass over the "great gulf"?

I cannot therefore but think that all those who are with the rich man in the unhappy division of Hades will remain there, howling and blaspheming, cursing and looking upwards, till they are cast into "The everlasting fire, prepared for the devil and his angels." And, on the other hand, can we reasonably doubt but that those who are now in paradise, in Abraham's bosom, all those holy souls who have been discharged from the body from the beginning of the world unto this day will be continually ripening for heaven; will be perpetually holier and happier till they are received into the "kingdom prepared for them from the foundation of the world"?

But who can inform us in what part of the universe Hades is situated? This abode of both happy and unhappy spirits till they are reunited to their bodies? (Quoted in "Of Man," chap. 7 in Coll. D, 150-52)

HAPPINESS

As there is but one God in heaven above and in the earth beneath, so there is only one happiness for created spirits, either in heaven or earth. This one God made our heart for himself, and it cannot rest till it resteth in him. It is true that while we are in the vigor of youth and health—while our blood dances in our veins, while the world smiles upon us and we have all the conveniences, yea, and superfluities of life—we frequently have pleasing dreams and enjoy a kind of happiness. But it cannot continue; it flies away like a shadow. And even while it does, it is not solid or substantial; it does not satisfy the soul. We still pant after something else, something which we have not. . . .

That *something* is neither more nor less than the knowledge and love of God, without which no spirit can be happy either in heaven or earth.

This happy knowledge of the true God is only another name for religion; I mean Christian religion which indeed is the only one that deserves the name. . . .

None but a Christian is happy; none but a real inward Christian. A glutton, a drunkard, a gamester may be *merry*, but he cannot be happy. The beau, the belle, may eat and drink and rise up to play, but still they feel they are not happy. Men or women may adorn their own dear persons with all the colors of the rainbow. They may dance and sing and hurry to and fro and flutter hither and thither. They may roll up and down in their splendid carriages and talk insipidly to each other. They may hasten from one diversion to another, but happiness is not there. . . .

Every Christian is happy, and he who is not happy is not a Christian. . . .

And it is equally certain, on the other hand, that he who is not happy is not a Christian, seeing if he was a real Christian he could not but be happy.

(Quoted in "Of Religion," chap. 2 in Coll. D, 20-23)

HARDENING OF THE HEART

We read, "When Pharaoh saw that there was respite" (after he was delivered from the plague of frogs) "he hardened his heart, and hearkened not unto them" [Exod. 8:15]. So after the plague of flies, "Pharaoh hardened his heart at this time also, neither would he let the people go" [v. 32]. Again, "When Pharaoh saw that the rain and the hail were ceased he sinned yet more, and hardened his heart, he and his servants" [Exod. 9:34]. After God had given him all this space to repent and had expostulated with him for his obstinate impenitence in those solemn words: "How long wilt thou refuse to humble thyself before me?" [10:3]. What wonder is it, if God then *hardened his heart*, that is, permitted Satan to harden it? if he at length wholly withdrew his softening grace and "gave him up to a reprobate mind"? (*Predestination Calmly Considered* [1752], in *Works* [T], 9:402)

HEALING, MIRACULOUS

I do not believe the case of Averel Spencer was natural, yet when I kneeled down by her bedside I had no thought at all of God's then giving any "attestation to my ministry." But I asked of God to deliver an afflicted soul, and he did deliver her. (Letter to John Smith [probably one of the archbishops of Canterbury, Thomas Herring or Thomas Secker] [December 30, 1745], in *Works* [WL], 12:64)

My horse was so exceedingly lame that I was afraid I must have lain by too. We could not discern what it was that was amiss, and yet he would scarcely set his foot to the ground. By riding thus seven miles, I was thoroughly tired, and my head ached more than it had done for some months. (What I here aver is the naked fact; let every man account for it as he sees good.) I then thought, "Cannot God heal either man or beast by any means or without any?" Immediately my weariness and headache ceased, and my horse's lameness in the same instant. Nor did he halt any more either that day or the next. A very odd accident this also! (*Journal*, March 17, 1746)

As it can be proved by abundance of witnesses that these cures were frequently (indeed almost always) the *instantaneous* consequences of prayer, your inference is just. I cannot, dare not affirm that they were purely *natural*. I believe they were not. I believe many of them were wrought by the *supernatural* power of God. That of John Haydon [a cured demoniac] in particular (I fix on this and will join issue with you upon it when you please), and yet this is not *barefaced enthusiasm*. Nor can you prove it any enthusiasm at all, unless you can prove that this is *falsely* ascribed to a *supernatural* power. (*The Principles of a Methodist Farther Explained* [1746], in *Works*, 12:378)

I acknowledge that I have seen with my eyes and heard with my ears several things which, to the best of my judgment, cannot be accounted for by the ordinary course of natural causes and which I therefore believe ought to be *ascribed to the extraordinary interposition of God*. If any man choose to style these *miracles*, I reclaim not. I have diligently inquired into the facts. I have weighed the preceding and following circumstances. I have strove to account for them in a *natural* way. I could not without doing violence to my reason. Not to go far back, I am clearly persuaded that the sudden deliverance of John Haydon was one instance of this kind and my own recovery on May the 10th another. I cannot account for either of these in a *natural* way. Therefore I believe they were both *supernatural*.

I must, secondly, observe that the truth of these facts is supported by the same kind of proof as that of all other facts is wont to be, namely, the testimony of competent witnesses; and that the testimony here is in as high a degree as any reasonable man can desire. Those witnesses were many in number; they could not be deceived themselves, for the facts in question they saw with their own eyes and heard with their own ears. Nor is it credible that so many of them would combine together with a view of deceiving others, the greater part being men that feared God, as appeared by the general tenor of their lives. Thus, in the case of John Haydon, this thing was not contrived and executed in a corner and in the presence of his own family only or three or four persons prepared for the purpose. No; it was in an open street of the city of Bristol, at one or two in the afternoon. And the doors being all open from the beginning, not only many of the neighbors from every side, but several others (indeed whosoever desired it), went in till the house could contain no more. Nor yet does the account of my own illness and recovery *depend*, as you suppose, *on my bare word*. There were many witnesses both of my disorder on Friday and Saturday and of my lying down most part of Sunday (a thing which they were well satisfied could not be the effect of a slight indisposition). And all who saw me that evening plainly discerned (what I could not wholly conceal) that I was in pain, about two hundred of whom were present when I was seized with that cough, which cut me short so that I could speak no more till I cried out aloud, "Lord, increase my faith; Lord, confirm the word of thy grace." The same persons saw and heard that at that instant I changed my posture and broke out into thanksgiving, that quickly after I stood upright (which I could not before) and showed no more sign either of sickness or pain.

Yet I must desire you well to observe, thirdly, that my will or choice or desire had no place either in this or any case of this kind that has ever fallen under my notice. Five minutes before, I had no thought of this. I expected nothing less. I was willing to wait for a gradual recovery, in the ordinary use of outward means. I did not look for any other cure till the moment before I found it. And it is my belief that the case was always the same, with regard to the most *real and undoubted miracles*. I believe God never interposed his miraculous power but according to his own sovereign will—not according to the will of man, neither of him by whom he wrought, nor of any other man whatsoever. The wisdom as well as the power are his, nor can I find that ever, from the beginning of the world, he lodged this power in any mere man to be used whenever that man saw good. . . .

. . . I cannot but think there have been already so many plain interpositions of divine power as will shortly leave you without excuse if you either deny or despise them. We desire no favor but the justice that diligent inquiry may be made concerning them. We are ready to name the persons on whom that power was shown, which belongeth to none but God (not one or two or ten or twelve only) to point out their places of abode, and we engage they shall answer every pertinent question fairly and directly and, if required, shall give all those answers upon oath before any who are empowered so to receive them. It is our particular request that the circumstances which went before, which accompanied, and which followed after the facts under consideration may be thoroughly examined and punctually noted down. . . . We have no fear, that any reasonable man should scruple to say, *This hath God wrought!* (*The Principles of a Methodist Farther Explained* [1746], in *Works*, 12:381-83)

HEARTFELT CONVERSION; WHOLEHEARTED DEVOTION TO GOD

Here, then, is the sum of the perfect law, this is the true *Circumcision of the Heart.* Let the spirit return to God that gave it, with the whole train of its affections. . . . Other sacrifices from us he would not, but the living sacrifice of the heart he hath chosen. Let it be continually offered up to God through Christ, in flames of holy love. . . . "Set your heart firm on him and on other things only as they are in and from him. Let your soul be filled with so entire a love of him that you may love nothing but for his sake." "Have a pure intention of heart, a steadfast regard to his glory in all your actions." ("The Circumcision of the Heart" [January 1, 1733], Sermon 17, in *Works* [T], 5:170)

But true religion, or a heart right toward God and man, implies happiness as well as holiness. For it is not only *righteousness* but also "peace and joy in the Holy Ghost." ("The Way to the Kingdom" [1746], Sermon 7, in *Works* [T], 5:67)

Perfection does not consist in any outward state whatever, but in an absolute devotion of all our heart and all our life to God. (*Thoughts on a Single Life* [1743], in *Works* [WL], 11:463)

The great end of religion is to renew our hearts in the image of God, to repair that total loss of righteousness and true holiness which we sustained by the sin of our first parents. (Quoted in "Of Religion," chap. 2 in Coll. D, 20)

In terming either faith or hope or love supernatural I only mean that they are not the effect of any or all of our natural faculties but are wrought in us (be it swiftly or slowly) by the Spirit of God. But I would rather say, Faith is "productive of all Christian holiness" than "of all Christian practice," because men are so exceeding apt to rest in practice, so called, I mean, in outside religion, whereas true religion is eminently seated in the heart, renewed in the image of him that created us. (Letter to John Smith [probably one of the archbishops of Canterbury, Thomas Herring or Thomas Secker] [December 30, 1745], in *Works* [WL], 12:67)

Abundance of those who bear the name of Christians put a part of religion for the whole, generally some outward work or form of worship; . . . whatever is thus put for the whole of religion (in particular, where it is used to supersede or commute for the religion of the heart), it is no longer a part of it, it is gross irreligion, it is mere mockery of God. (Letter to John Smith [probably one of the archbishops of Canterbury, Thomas Herring or Thomas Secker] [March 25, 1747], in *Works* [WL], 12:81)

H

A Christian . . . has a continual sense of his dependence on the Parent of good for his being and all the blessings that attend it. To him he refers every natural and every moral endowment with all that is commonly ascribed either to fortune or to the wisdom, courage, or merit of the possessor. And hence he acquiesces in whatsoever appears to be his will, not only with patience, but with thankfulness. He willingly resigns all he is, all he has, to his wise and gracious disposal. The ruling temper of his heart is the most absolute submission and the tenderest gratitude to his sovereign Benefactor. And this grateful love creates filial fear, an awful reverence toward him, and an earnest care not to give place to any disposition, not to admit an action, word, or thought, which might in any degree displease that indulgent power to whom he owes his life, breath, and all things. (*A Plain Account of Genuine Christianity* [1749], in Coll. C, 312-13)

They know this religion is too superficial. It is but, as it were, skin deep. Therefore it is not Christianity, for that lies in the heart; it is worshipping God in spirit and in truth. It is no other than "the kingdom of God within us"; it is "the Life of God" in the soul of man; it is "the mind which was in Christ Jesus"; it is "righteousness, and peace, and joy in the Holy Ghost." (*A Blow at the Root* [1762], in *Works* [T], 9:454)

Still I cannot but remember the clear light you had with regard to the nature of real, scriptural Christianity. You saw what heart religion meant, and the gate of it, *justification*. You had earnest desires to be a partaker of the whole gospel blessing, and you discovered the sincerity of those desires by the steps you took in your family. So that in everything you were hastening to be, not almost, but altogether a Christian.

Where is that light now? Do you now see that true religion is not a negative or an external thing, but the life of God in the soul of man? The image of God stamped upon the heart? Do you now see that, in order to this, we are justified freely through the redemption which is in Christ Jesus? (Letter to Mr. Knox [May 30, 1765], in *Works*, 16:97)

In the year 1729 I began not only to read but to *study* the Bible as the one, the only standard of truth and the only model of pure religion. Hence I saw, in a clearer and clearer light, the indispensable necessity of having *the mind which was in Christ* and of *walking as Christ also walked*; even of having, not *some part* only, but all the mind which was in him; and of walking as he walked, not only in *many* or in *most* respects, but in *all* things. And this was the light wherein at this time I generally considered religion, as a *uniform* following of Christ, an *entire* inward and outward conformity to our Master. (*A Plain Account of Christian Perfection* [1767; rev. 1777], in *Works* [WL], 11:367)

On January 1, 1733, I preached before the university [Oxford] in St. Mary's church on *the Circumcision of the Heart* . . .

I concluded in these words: "Here is the sum of *the perfect law*, the circumcision of the heart. Let the spirit return to God that gave it, with the whole train of its affections. Other sacrifices from us he would not, but the living sacrifice of the heart hath he chosen. . . . 'Have a *pure intention* of heart, a steadfast regard to his glory in all your actions.' For then, and not till then, is that 'mind in us, which was also in Christ Jesus,' when in *every* motion of our heart, in *every* word of our tongue, in *every* work of our hands, we 'pursue nothing but in relation to him, and in subordination to his pleasure.'" (*A Plain Account of Christian Perfection* [1767; rev. 1777], in *Works* [WL], 11:367-68)

It is devoutly to be wished for that we may rejoice evermore, and it is certain the inward kingdom of God implies not only righteousness and peace but joy in the Holy Ghost. You have, therefore, reason to ask for and expect the whole gospel blessing. Yet it cannot be denied that many times joy is withheld, even from them that walk uprightly. The great point of all is a heart and a life entirely devoted to God. Keep only this and let all the rest go; give him your heart and it sufficeth. (Letter to Miss Bosanquet [December 21, 1776], in Coll. B, 547-48)

I do not mean external religion, but the religion of the heart—the religion which Kempis, Pascal, Fénelon enjoyed—that life of God in the soul of man, the walking with God and having fellowship with the Father and the Son. . . .

. . . Christ in you the hope of glory, Christ reigning in your heart and subduing all things to himself. (Letter to Samuel Wesley Jr. [April 29, 1790], *Letters* [JT], 8:218)

HEATHENS AND SALVATION

Inasmuch as to them little is given, of them little will be required. As to the ancient heathens, millions of them likewise were savages. No more, therefore, will be expected of them than the living up to the light they had. But many of them, especially in the civilized nations, we have great reason to hope, although they lived among heathens, yet were quite of another spirit; being taught of God by his inward voice all the essentials of true religion. (Quoted in "Of Faith," chap. 9 in Coll. D, 177)

HEAVEN

The just shall enjoy inconceivable happiness in the presence of God to all eternity. (*A Letter to a Roman Catholic* [July 18, 1749], in Coll. C, 306)

All holiness must precede our entering into glory. (Letter to the Rev. Dr. Horne [1762], in *Works,* 13:108)

I do not know whether the usual question be well stated, "Is heaven a state or a place?" There is no opposition between these two; it is both the one and the other. It is the *place* where God more immediately dwells with those saints who are in a glorified *state.* Homer could only conceive of the place that it was *paved with brass.* Milton, in one place, makes *heaven's pavement beaten gold*; in another he defines it more sublimely, "The house of God, *star-paved.*" . . .

"But what is the essential part of heaven?" Undoubtedly, it is to see God, to know God, to love God. We shall then know both his nature and his works of creation and providence and of redemption. (Letter to Mary Bishop [April 17, 1776], *Letters* [JT], 6:213-14)

HELL

I entirely agree that hell was designed only for stubborn, impenitent sinners and, consequently, that it would be absurd to "threaten damnation to any merely for differing from me in speculations." But it is an absurdity which I have nothing to do with, for it never yet entered into my thoughts. (Letter to John Smith [probably one of the archbishops of Canterbury, Thomas Herring or Thomas Secker] [March 22, 1748], in *Works* [WL], 12:96)

The unjust shall, after their resurrection, be tormented in hell forever. (*A Letter to a Roman Catholic* [July 18, 1749], in Coll. C, 306)

Consider the *Poena Damni*, the punishment of loss. This commences in that very moment wherein the soul is separated from the body; in that instant, the soul loses all those pleasures, the enjoyment of which depends on the outward senses. The smell, the taste, the touch, delight no more; the organs that ministered to them are spoiled, and the objects that used to gratify them are removed far away. In the dreary regions of the dead, all these things are forgotten or, if remembered, are only remembered with pain, seeing they are gone forever. All the pleasures of the imagination are at an end. There is no grandeur in the infernal regions; there is nothing beautiful in those dark abodes; no light but that of livid flames. And nothing new, but one unvaried scene of horror upon horror! There is no music but that of groans and shrieks; of weeping, wailing, and gnashing of teeth; of curses and blasphemies against God, or cutting reproaches of one another. Nor is there anything to gratify the sense of honor. No; they are the heirs of shame and everlasting contempt.

Thus are they totally separated from all the things they were fond of in the present world. At the same instant will commence another loss, that of all the *persons* whom they loved. They are torn away from their nearest and dearest relations—their wives, husbands, parents, children—and (what to some will be worse than all this) the friend which was as their own soul. All the pleasure they ever enjoyed in these is lost, gone, vanished away, for there is no friendship in hell. . . .

But they will then be sensible of a greater loss than all they have enjoyed on earth. They have lost their place in Abraham's bosom, in the paradise of God. Hitherto, indeed, it hath not entered into their hearts to conceive what holy souls enjoy in the garden of God, in the society of angels, and of the wisest and best men that have lived from the beginning of the world (not to mention the immense increase of knowledge which they will then, undoubtedly, receive); but they will then fully understand the value of what they have vilely cast away.

. . . They will then know and feel that God alone is the center of all created spirits and, consequently, that a spirit made for God can have no rest out of him. It seems that the apostle had this in his view when he spoke of those "who shall be punished with everlasting destruction from the presence of the Lord." Banishment from the presence of the Lord is the very essence of destruction to a spirit that was made for God. And if that banishment last forever, it is "everlasting destruction."

Such is the loss sustained by those miserable creatures on whom that awful sentence will be pronounced, "Depart from me, ye cursed." What an unspeakable curse, if there were no other! But, alas! this is far from being the whole, for to the punishment of loss will be added the punishment of sense. What they lose implies unspeakable misery which yet is inferior to what they feel. This it is which our Lord expresses in those emphatic words, "Where their worm dieth not, and the fire is not quenched." (Quoted in "Of a Future State," chap. 17 in Coll. D, 327-29)

HENRY VIII (AND HIS DESTRUCTION OF CHURCH BUILDINGS)

Walsingham . . . I walked over what is left of the famous Abbey. We then went to the Friary; the Cloisters and Chapel whereof are almost entire. Had there been a grain of virtue or public spirit in Henry the VIIIth, these noble buildings need not have run to ruin. (Quoted in "Of Honor Where Honor Is Due," chap. 16 in Coll. A, 120)

HOLINESS

And what is Christian liberty but another word for holiness? . . . Holiness is the love of God and man, or the mind which was in Christ. Now, I trust, the love of God is shed abroad in your heart by the Holy Ghost which is given unto you. And if you are holy, is not that mind in you which was also in Christ Jesus? (Letter to Joseph Benson [October 5, 1770], in Coll. B, 533)

HOLY DAYS

Sunday, Nov. 1. Being All Saints' Day (a festival I dearly love) I could not but observe the admirable propriety with which the Collect, Epistle, and Gospel for the day are suited to each other. (Quoted in "Of Honor Where Honor Is Due," chap. 16 in Coll. A, 119)

HOLY SPIRIT

I believe the infinite and eternal Spirit of God, equal with the Father and the Son, to be not only perfectly holy in himself but the immediate cause of all holiness in us; enlightening our understandings, rectifying our wills and affections, renewing our natures, uniting our persons to Christ, assuring us of the adoption of sons, leading us in our actions; purifying and sanctifying our souls and bodies, to a full and eternal enjoyment of God. (*A Letter to a Roman Catholic* [July 18, 1749], in Coll. C, 305)

HOLY SPIRIT: BEING FILLED WITH

Mr. Hall, Kinchin, Ingham, Whitefield, Hutchins, and my brother Charles were present at our love feast in Fetter Lane, with about sixty of our brethren. About three in the morning, as we were continuing instant in prayer, the power of God came mightily upon us, insomuch that many cried out for exceeding joy and many fell to the ground. As soon as we were recovered a little from that awe and amazement at the presence of his Majesty, we broke out with one voice, "We praise thee, O God; we acknowledge thee to be the Lord!" (*Journal,* January 1, 1739)

I do not mean that Christians now receive the Holy Ghost in order to work miracles, but they do doubtless now "receive," yea, are "filled with the Holy Ghost" in order to be filled with the fruits of that blessed Spirit. And he inspires into all true believers now a degree of the same peace and joy and love which the apostles felt in themselves on that day when they were first "filled with the Holy Ghost." (*Operations of the Holy Ghost* [1744], in Coll. B, 194)

It was, therefore, for a more excellent purpose than this that "they were all filled with the Holy Ghost."

It was to give them (what none can deny to be essential to all Christians in all ages) the mind which was in Christ, those holy fruits of the Spirit which whosoever hath not is none of his; to fill them with "love, joy, peace, long suffering, gentleness, goodness" [Gal. 5:22-24]; to endue them with faith (perhaps it might be rendered, *fidelity*), with meekness and temperance; to enable them to crucify the flesh with its affections and lusts, its passions and desires, and, in consequence of that inward change, to fulfill all outward righteousness, to "walk as Christ also walked," "in the work of faith, in the patience of hope, the labour of love" [1 Thess. 1:3]. ("Scriptural Christianity" [August 24, 1744], sermon, in Coll. C, 138)

That we "must be baptized with the Holy Ghost," implies this and no more, that we cannot be "renewed in righteousness and true holiness," any otherwise than by being overshadowed, quickened, and animated by that blessed Spirit. (*An Extract of a Letter to the Rev. Mr. Law* [January 6, 1756], in *Works,* 13:373)

And with all zeal and diligence confirm the brethren, (1) in holding fast that whereto they have attained; namely, the remission of all their sins by faith in a bleeding Lord; (2) in expecting a second change whereby they shall be saved from all sin and perfected in love.

If they like to call this "receiving the Holy Ghost," they may; only the phrase, in that sense, is not scriptural and not quite proper; for they all "received the Holy Ghost" when they were justified. God then "sent forth the Spirit of his Son into their hearts, crying, Abba Father." (Letter to Joseph Benson [December 28, 1770], in *Works* [S], 7:71)

HOLY SPIRIT: INDWELLING OF

From . . . [reading the authoritative documents of the Anglican Church] it may sufficiently appear for what purposes every Christian, according to the doctrine of the Church of England, does now "receive the Holy Ghost." . . . the reader may likewise observe a plain, rational sense of God's revealing himself to us, of the inspiration of the Holy Ghost, and of a believer's feeling in himself "the mighty working" of the Spirit of Christ. . . .

. . . Every true Christian now "receives the Holy Ghost" as the Paraclete or Comforter promised by our Lord [John 14:16]; secondly, that every Christian receives him as "the Spirit of truth" (promised John [John 16]) to "teach him all things"; and, thirdly, that "the anointing," mentioned in the First Epistle of St. John, "abides in every Christian." . . .

Every good gift is from God and is given to man by the Holy Ghost. By nature there is in us no good thing, and there can be none but so far as it is wrought in us by that good Spirit. Have we any true knowledge of what is good? This is not the result of our natural understanding. "The natural man discerneth not the things of the Spirit of God," so that we never can discern them until God "reveals them unto us by his Spirit." *Reveals*, that is, unveils, uncovers; gives us to know what we did not know before. Have we love? It "is shed abroad in our hearts by the Holy Ghost which is given unto us." He *inspires*, breathes, infuses into our soul, what of ourselves we could not have. Does our spirit rejoice in God our Savior? It is "joy in" or by "the Holy Ghost." Have we true inward peace! It is "the peace of God" wrought in us by the same Spirit. Faith, peace, joy, love are all his fruits. And as we are figuratively said to *see* the light of faith, so, by a like figure of speech, we are said to *feel* this peace and joy and love; that is, we have an inward experience of them which we cannot find any fitter word to express. (*Operations of the Holy Ghost* [1744], in Coll. B, 190-91, 193)

"If ye love me, keep my commandments. And I will pray the Father, and he shall give you another Comforter, that he may abide with you for ever; even the Spirit of truth; whom the world cannot receive, because it seeth him not, neither knoweth him" [John 14:15-17]. . . . the text must be interpreted of the ordinary operations of the Spirit, in all future ages of the church . . . And indeed that the promise in this text belongs to all Christians, evidently appears . . . from the text itself, for who can deny that this Comforter, or Paraclete, is now given to all them that believe? (*A Farther Appeal to Men of Reason and Religion* [1745], pt. 1, in *Works*, 12:86-87)

H

HOLY SPIRIT: TESTIMONY AND WITNESS OF

None is truly "led by the Spirit" unless that "Spirit bear witness with his spirit, that he is a child of God." ("The Circumcision of the Heart" [January 1, 1733], Sermon 17, in *Works* [T], 5:169)

This witness of the Spirit is the private testimony given to our own consciences which, consequently, all sober Christians may claim without any danger of enthusiasm. (*A Farther Appeal to Men of Reason and Religion* [1745], pt. 1, in *Works*, 12:93)

"Infallible testimony" was your word, not mine: I never use it; I do not like it. But I did not object to your using that phrase, because I would not fight about words. If, then, the question be repeated, "In what sense is that attestation of the Spirit infallible?" any one has my free leave to answer, In no sense at all. And yet, though I allow that some may fancy they have it, when in truth they have it not; I cannot allow that any fancy they have it not, at the time when they really have. I know no instance of this. When they have this faith, they cannot possibly doubt of their having it; although it is very possible, when they have it not, they may doubt whether ever they had it or no. (Letter to John Smith [probably one of the archbishops of Canterbury, Thomas Herring or Thomas Secker] [December 30, 1745], in *Works* [WL], 12:65-66)

We must be holy of heart and holy in life before we can be conscious that we are so, before we can have the testimony of our spirit that we are inwardly and outwardly holy. But we must love God before we can be holy at all, this being the root of all holiness. Now we cannot love God till we know he loves us. "We love him, because he first loved us." And we cannot know his pardoning love to us till his Spirit witnesses it to our spirit. Since, therefore, this testimony of his Spirit must precede the love of God and all holiness, of consequence it must precede our inward consciousness thereof or the testimony of our spirit concerning them.

Then, and not till then—when the Spirit of God beareth that witness to our spirit, "God hath loved thee, and given his own Son to be the propitiation for thy sins; the Son of God hath loved thee, and hath washed thee from thy sins in his blood"; "we love God, because he first loved us"; and, for his sake, we love our brother also. And of this we cannot but be conscious to ourselves: we "know the things that are freely given to us of God." We know that we love God and keep his commandments; and "hereby also we know that we are of God." This is that testimony of our own spirit which, so long as we continue to love God and keep his commandments, continues joined with the testimony of God's Spirit, "that we are the children of God." (Quoted in "Of the Holy Ghost," chap. 5 in Coll. D, 83-84)

The sum of all this is: the testimony of the Spirit is an inward impression on the souls of believers whereby the Spirit of God directly testifies to their spirit that they are children of God. And it is not questioned whether there is a testimony of the Spirit but whether there is any *direct* testimony? Whether there is any other than that which arises from a consciousness of the fruit of the Spirit? We believe there is because this is the plain natural meaning of the text, illustrated both by the preceding words and by the parallel passage in the Epistle to the Galatians; because, in the nature of the thing, the testimony must precede the fruit which springs from it; and, because this plain meaning of the Word of God is confirmed by the experience of innumerable children of God; yea, and by the experience of all who are convinced of sin, who can never rest till they have a direct witness; and even of the children of the world, who, not having the witness in themselves, one and all declare none can *know* his sins forgiven.

And whereas it is objected that experience is not sufficient to prove a doctrine unsupported by Scripture; that madmen and enthusiasts of every kind have imagined such a witness; that the design of that witness is to prove our profession genuine, which design it does not answer; that the Scripture says, "The tree is known by its fruit," "examine yourselves: prove your own selves"; and, meantime, the direct witness is never referred to in all the Book of God; that it does not secure us from the greatest delusions; and, lastly, that the change wrought in us is a sufficient testimony unless in such trials as Christ alone suffered. We answer, (1) experience is sufficient to *confirm* a doctrine which is grounded on Scripture; (2) though many fancy they experience what they do not, this is no prejudice to real experience; (3) the design of that witness is to assure us we are children of God, and this design it does answer; (4) the true witness of the Spirit is known by its fruit, "love, peace, joy," not indeed preceding, but following it; (5) it cannot be proved that the direct as well as the indirect witness is not referred to in that very text, "Know ye not your own selves, that Jesus Christ is in you?" (6) the Spirit of God, witnessing with our spirit, does secure us from all delusion. And, lastly, we are all liable to trials, wherein the testimony of our own spirit is not sufficient; wherein nothing less than the direct testimony of God's Spirit can assure us that we are his children. (Quoted in "Of the Holy Ghost," chap. 5 in Coll. D, 86-88)

JESUS CHRIST

I believe that Jesus of Nazareth was the Savior of the world, the Messiah so long foretold; that, being anointed with the Holy Ghost, he was a Prophet, revealing to us the whole will of God; that he was a Priest, who gave himself a sacrifice for sin and still makes intercession for transgressors; that he is a King, who has all power in heaven and in earth and will reign till he has subdued all things to himself.

I believe he is the proper, natural Son of God, God of God, very God of very God, and that he is the Lord of all, having absolute, supreme, universal dominion over all things, but more peculiarly our Lord, who believe in him, both by conquest, purchase, and voluntary obligation.

I believe that he was made man, joining the human nature with the divine in one person; being conceived by the singular operation of the Holy Ghost and born of the blessed Virgin Mary, who, as well after as before she brought him forth continued a pure and unspotted virgin.

I believe he suffered inexpressible pains both of body and soul, and at last, death, even the death of the cross, at the time that Pontius Pilate governed Judea, under the Roman emperor; that his body was then laid in the grave and his soul went to the place of separate spirits; that the third day he rose again from the dead; that he ascended into heaven; where he remains in the midst of the throne of God, in the highest power and glory, as Mediator till the end of the world, as God to all eternity; that, in the end, he will come down from heaven to judge every man according to his works; both those who shall be then alive and all who have died before that day. (*A Letter to a Roman Catholic* [July 18, 1749], in Coll. C, 304-5)

JESUS CHRIST: CREATOR

He is the true God, the only Cause, the sole Creator of all things. "By him," saith the Apostle Paul, "were created all things that are in heaven, and that are on earth." . . . So St. John: "All things were made by him, and without him was not anything made that was made." And accordingly St. Paul applies to him those strong words of the Psalmist: "Thou, Lord, in the beginning, hast laid the foundation of the earth, and the heavens are the work of thy hands." (Quoted in "Of Christ," chap. 4 in Coll. D, 68-69)

JESUS CHRIST: DIVINITY OF

He is "God over all, blessed forever." "He was with God," with God the Father, "from the beginning"; from eternity; "and was God." "He and the Father are one"; and consequently, "he thought it not robbery to be equal with God." Accordingly, the inspired writers give him all the titles of the Most High God. They call him over and over by the incommunicable name *Jehovah*, never given to any creature. They ascribe to him all the attributes and all the works of God. So that we need not scruple to pronounce him "God of God, Light of Light, very God of very God: in glory equal with the Father, in Majesty co-eternal." (Quoted in "Of Christ," chap. 4 in Coll. D, 68)

J

JESUS CHRIST: SAVIOR AND REDEEMER

In this state we were, even all mankind, when "God so loved the world, that he gave his only begotten Son, to the end we might not perish, but have everlasting life." In the fullness of time he was made man, another common head of mankind, a second general parent and representative of the whole human race. And as such it was that "he bore our griefs," "the Lord laying upon him the iniquities of us all." Then was he "wounded for our transgressions, and bruised for our iniquities." "He made his soul an offering for sin"; he poured out his blood for the transgressors; he "bare our sins in his own body on the tree," that by his stripes we might be healed—and by that one oblation of himself, once offered, he hath redeemed me and all mankind, having thereby "made a full, perfect, and sufficient sacrifice and satisfaction for the sins of the whole world."

In consideration of this, that the Son of God hath "tasted death for every man," God hath now "reconciled the world to himself, not imputing to them their former trespasses." And thus, "as by the offence of one, judgment came upon all men to condemnation, even so by the righteousness of one, the free gift came upon all men unto justification." So that for the sake of his well-beloved Son, of what he hath done and suffered for us, God now vouchsafes, on one only condition (which himself also enables us to perform), both to remit the punishment due to our sins, to reinstate us in his favor, and to restore our dead souls to spiritual life, as the earnest of life eternal.

This, therefore, is the general ground of the whole doctrine of justification. By the sin of the first Adam, who was not only the father but likewise the representative of us all, we all fell short of the favor of God; we all became children of wrath or, as the apostle expresses it, "judgment came upon all men to condemnation." Even so, for the sacrifice for sin made by the second Adam, as the representative of us all, God is so far reconciled to all the world that he hath given them a new covenant; the plain condition whereof being once fulfilled, "there is no more condemnation" for us, but "we are justified freely by his grace, through the redemption that is in Jesus Christ." (Quoted in "Of Christ," chap. 4 in Coll. D, 74-76)

The Methodists always held, and have declared a thousand times, the death of Christ is the meritorious cause of our salvation, that is, of pardon, holiness, and glory; loving, obedient faith is the condition of glory. (Letter to Mrs. Elizabeth Bennis [May 2, 1774], in *Works* [S], 7:60)

JESUS CHRIST: SUSTAINER OF CREATION

And as the true God, he is also the Supporter of all the things that he hath made. He beareth, upholdeth, sustaineth all created things by the word of his power, by the same powerful word which brought them out of nothing. As this was absolutely necessary for the beginning of their existence, it is equally so for the continuance of it; were his almighty influence withdrawn they could not subsist a moment longer. Hold up a stone in the air; the moment you withdraw your hand, it naturally falls to the ground. In like manner, were he to withdraw his hand for a moment, the creation would fall into nothing.

As the true God, he is likewise the Preserver of all things. He not only keeps them in being but preserves them in that degree of well-being which is suitable to their several natures. He preserves them in their several relations, connections, and dependencies, so as to compose one system of beings, to form one entire universe according to the counsel of his will. . . . "By whom all things consist"; or, more literally, "By and in him are all things compacted into one system." He is not only the support but also the cement of the whole universe. (Quoted in "Of Christ," chap. 4 in Coll. D, 69)

JEWS AND SALVATION

It is not so easy to pass any judgment concerning the faith of our modern Jews. It is plain "the veil is still upon their hearts," when Moses and the Prophets are read. The god of this world still hardens their hearts and still blinds their eyes, "lest at any time the light of the glorious gospel" should break in upon them. So that we may say of this people, as the Holy Ghost said to their forefathers, "the heart of this people is waxed gross, and their ears are dull of hearing, and their eyes have they closed; lest they should see with their eyes, and hear with their ears, and understand with their hearts, and should be converted, and I should heal them" [Acts 28:27]. Yet it is not our part to pass sentence upon them, but to leave them to their own Master. (Quoted in "Of Faith," chap. 9 in Coll. D, 178)

JOY

With this peace of God, wherever it is fixed in the soul, there is also "joy in the Holy Ghost"; joy wrought in the heart by the Holy Ghost, by the ever-blessed Spirit of God. He it is that worketh in us that calm, humble rejoicing in God, through Christ Jesus, "by whom we have now received the atonement," . . . the reconciliation with God; and that enables us boldly to confirm the truth of the royal Psalmist's declaration, "Blessed is the man (or rather *happy*) . . . whose unrighteousness is forgiven and whose sin is covered." He it is that inspires the Christian soul with that even, solid joy which arises from the testimony of the Spirit that he is a child of God; and that gives him to "rejoice with joy unspeakable, in hope of the glory of God"; hope both of the glorious image of God which is in part and shall be fully "revealed in him" and of that crown of glory which fadeth not away, reserved in heaven for him. ("The Way to the Kingdom" [1746], Sermon 7, in *Works* [T], 5:67)

You never learned, either from my conversation or preaching or writings that "holiness consisted in a flow of joy." I constantly told you quite the contrary. I told you it was love—the love of God and of our neighbor, the image of God stamped on the heart, the life of God in the soul of man, the mind that was in Christ enabling us to walk as Christ also walked. . . . It is true that joy is one part of "the fruit of the Spirit," of the kingdom of God within us. But this is first "righteousness," then "peace" and "joy in the Holy Ghost." It is true further that if you love God "with all your heart" you may "rejoice evermore." Nay, it is true still further that many serious, humble, sober-minded believers who do feel the love of God sometimes and do then rejoice in God their Savior cannot be content with this, but pray continually that he would enable them to love, and "rejoice in the Lord always." (Letter to the Rev. Lawrence Coughlan [August 1768], in *Letters*, 239)

Rapturous joy, such as is frequently given in the beginning of justification or of entire sanctification is a great blessing, but it seldom continues long before it subsides into calm, peaceful love. (Letter to Mrs. Jane Barton [July 29, 1777], in *Works* [S], 7:46)

JUDGMENT OF NATIONS

The universal corruption of all orders and degrees of men loudly calls for the vengeance of God. Inasmuch as all other nations are equally corrupt, it seems God will punish us by one another. What can prevent this but a universal or, at least, a general repentance? Otherwise we have great reason to fear God will soon say, "Sword, go through that land and destroy it." (Letter to Thomas Rankin [July 28, 1775], in *Letters,* 258)

JUSTIFICATION

The plain scriptural notion of justification is pardon, the forgiveness of sins. It is that act of God the Father whereby, for the sake of the propitiation made by the blood of his Son, he "showeth forth his righteousness (or mercy) by the remission of the sins that are past." This is the easy, natural account of it given by St. Paul, throughout this whole epistle. So he explains it himself, more particularly in this and in the following chapter. Thus, in the next verses but one to the text, "Blessed are they," saith he, "whose iniquities are forgiven, and whose sins are covered. Blessed is the man to whom the Lord will not impute sin." To him that is justified or forgiven, God "will not impute sin" to his condemnation. He will not condemn him on that account, either in this world or in that which is to come. His sins, all his past sins, in thought, word, and deed, are covered, are blotted out, shall not be remembered or mentioned against him, any more than if they had not been. God will not inflict on that sinner what he deserved to suffer, because the Son of his love hath suffered for him. And from the time we are "accepted through the Beloved," "reconciled to God through his blood," he loves and blesses and watches over us for good, even as if we had never sinned. ("Justification by Faith" [1746], Sermon 5, in *Works* [T], 5:49)

The nature of justification. It sometimes means our acquittal at the last day [Matt. 12:37]. But this is altogether out of the present question; that justification whereof our articles and homilies speak meaning present forgiveness, pardon of sins, and, consequently, acceptance with God; who therein "declares his righteousness" (or mercy, by or) "for the remission of the sins that are past," saying, "I will be merciful to thy unrighteousness, and thine iniquities I will remember no more" [Rom. 3:25; Heb. 8:12].

I believe the condition of this is faith [Rom. 5:5, etc.]; I mean not only that without faith we cannot be justified but also that as soon as anyone has true faith, in that moment he is justified.

Good works follow this faith but cannot go before it [Luke 6:43]; much less can sanctification, which implies a continued course of good works springing from holiness of heart. But it is allowed that entire sanctification goes before our justification at the last day [Heb. 12:14]. (*Conditions of Justification* [1744], in Coll. B, 177-78)

Q. (1) What is it to be justified? A. To be pardoned and received into God's favor; into such a state, that if we continue therein, we shall be finally saved. (*Minutes of Some Late Conversations* [June 25, 1744], *Works* [S], 5:194)

Q. (1) What is it to be justified? A. To be pardoned. Q. (2) Is faith the condition of justification? A. Yes. Q. (3) But must not repentance and works meet for repentance go before this faith? A. Without doubt: if by repentance you mean conviction of sin; and by works meet for repentance, obeying God as far as we can, forgiving our brother, leaving off from evil, doing good, and using his ordinances according to the power we have received. (Quoted in "Of Justification by Faith," chap. 11 in Coll. A, 77)

To the first of these propositions you object, "That justification is not only twofold but manifold. For a man may possibly sin many times and as many times be justified or forgiven."

I grant it. I grant also that justification sometimes means a *state* of acceptance with God. But all this does not in the least affect my assertion that "*that justification* which is spoken of by St. Paul to the Romans, and by our [Anglican] Church in the 11th, 12th, and 13th articles, is not *our acquittal* at the last day but the *present remission* of our sins." (*Answer to the Rev. Mr. Church's "Remarks on the Rev. Mr. Wesley's Last Journal"* [February 2, 1745], in *Works*, 12:302)

Justification is another word for pardon. It is the forgiveness of all our sins and, what is necessarily implied therein, our acceptance with God. The price whereby this hath been procured for us (commonly termed the meritorious cause of our justification) is the blood and righteousness of Christ or, to express it a little more clearly, all that Christ hath done and suffered for us till he "poured out his soul for the transgressors." The immediate effects of justification are the peace of God, a "peace that passeth all understanding," and a "rejoicing in hope of the glory of God" "with joy unspeakable and full of glory." (Quoted in "Of Justification," chap. 10 in Coll. D, 191)

J

I think on justification just as I have done any time these seven and twenty years and just as Mr. Calvin does. In this respect, I do not differ from him a hair's breadth. (Letter to John Newton, in *Journal*, May 14, 1765)

I do not insist on the term *impression*. I say again, I will thank anyone that will find a better, be it *discovery, manifestation, deep sense*, or whatever it may. That *some consciousness* of our being in favor with God is joined with Christian faith, I cannot doubt, but it is not the essence of it. A consciousness of pardon cannot be the condition of pardon. (Letter to Joseph Benson [May 21, 1781], in *Works* [S], 7:80)

JUSTIFICATION AND ABSOLUTE ASSURANCE OF PARDON; FIDUCIAL FAITH

Q. Is an assurance of God's pardoning love absolutely necessary to our being in his favor? Or may there possibly be some exempt cases?

A. We dare not positively say there are not. (Letter to Mr. Richard Tompson [February 5, 1756], in Coll. B, 208)

Is justifying faith a sense of pardon? It is denied (by *justifying faith* I mean that faith which whosoever hath not is under the wrath and the curse of God; by *a sense of pardon* I mean a distinct explicit assurance that my sins are forgiven). I cannot allow that justifying faith is such an assurance or *necessarily connected* therewith. Because, if justifying faith necessarily implies such an explicit assurance of pardon, then everyone who has it not, and everyone so long as he has it not, is under the wrath and under the curse of God. But this is a supposition contrary to Scripture [Isa. 50:10; Acts 10:34]. Contrary to experience, for J. R. [and others] had peace with God before they had that sense of pardon, and so have I frequently had. Contrary to reason, [yea,] flatly absurd, for how can a sense of our having received pardon be the condition of our receiving it? . . . Everyone is deeply concerned to understand this question well, but preachers most of all, lest they either make them *sad* whom God hath not made sad or encourage them to say *Peace* where there is no peace. (Quoted in "Of Justification by Faith," chap. 11 in Coll. A, 78)

I agree with you that justifying faith cannot be a conviction that I am justified, and that a man who is not assured that his sins are forgiven may yet have a kind or degree of faith which distinguishes him not only from a devil but also from a heathen, and on which I may admit him to the Lord's Supper. But still I believe the proper Christian faith which purifies the heart implies such a conviction. (Letter to Mr. Richard Tompson [July 25, 1755], in Coll. B, 206)

You think "full assurance excludes all doubt." I think so too. But there may be faith without *full assurance*. And these lower degrees of faith do not exclude doubts which frequently mingle therewith, more or less. But this you cannot allow. You say it cannot be shaken without being overthrown and trust I shall be "convinced upon reflection that the distinction between *shaken* and *destroyed* is *absolutely* without a difference." Hark! The wind rises, the house *shakes*; but it is not *overthrown*. It *totters*, but it is not *destroyed*. . . .

Your next remark is, "The Spirit's witnessing that we are accepted cannot be the faith whereby we are accepted." I allow it. A conviction that we are justified cannot be implied in justifying faith. (Letter to Mr. Richard Tompson [February 5, 1756], in Coll. B, 209)

JUSTIFICATION AND BEING "BORN AGAIN"

We allow that at the very moment of justification we are *born again*: in that instant we experience that inward change from "darkness into marvellous light," from the image of the brute and the devil into the image of God, from the earthly, sensual, devilish mind to the mind which was in Christ Jesus. But are we then *entirely* changed? Are we *wholly* transformed into the image of him that created us? Far from it; we still retain a depth of sin, and it is the consciousness of this which constrains us to groan for a full deliverance to him that is mighty to save. ("The Repentance of Believers" [April 24, 1767], Sermon 14, in *Works* [T], 5:137)

J

JUSTIFICATION AND NEW BIRTH

If any doctrine within the whole compass of Christianity may be properly termed fundamental, they are, doubtless, these two—the doctrine of justification and that of the new birth: the former relating to that great work which God does *for us* in forgiving our sins; the latter, to the great work which God does *in us* in renewing our fallen nature. In order of time, neither of these is before the other: in the moment we are justified by the grace of God, through the redemption that is in Jesus, we are also *born of the Spirit*; but in order of thinking, as it is termed, justification precedes the new birth. We first conceive his wrath to be turned away and then his Spirit to work in our hearts. ("On the New Birth" [1760], Sermon 21, in *Works* [T], 5:197)

JUSTIFICATION AND PRESENT ASSURANCE

A divine conviction of my being reconciled to God is, I think, directly implied (not in a divine evidence or conviction of something else but) in a divine conviction that Christ loved *me* and gave himself for *me*, and still more clearly in the Spirit's bearing witness with my spirit that I am a child of God.

. . . the same compassion which moves God to pardon a mourning, brokenhearted sinner moves him to comfort that mourner by witnessing to his spirit that his sins are pardoned.

. . . I contend only for this, that every true Christian believer has "a sure trust and confidence in God that through the merits of Christ he is reconciled to God" and that, in consequence of this, he is able to say, "The life which I now live I live by faith in the Son of God, who loved me, and gave himself for me." (Letter to Mr. Richard Tompson [February 5, 1756], in Coll. B, 209-10)

JUSTIFICATION AND "RECEIVING THE HOLY SPIRIT"

If they like to call this "receiving the Holy Ghost," they may; only the phrase in that sense is not scriptural and not quite proper, for they all "received the Holy Ghost" when they were justified. God then "sent forth the Spirit of his Son into their hearts, crying, Abba, Father." (Letter to Joseph Benson [December 28, 1770], in *Works* [S], 7:71)

JUSTIFICATION AND REGENERATION

To put this out of dispute, you go on, "Thus faith and being born of God are said to be an instantaneous work, at once, and in a moment, as lightning. Justification, the same as regeneration, and having a lively faith, this always in a moment" . . . I know not which to admire most, the English or the sense, which you here father upon me; but in truth it is all your own. I do not thus confound "*faith* and being *born* of God." I always speak of them as different things; it is you that thus jumble them together. It is you who discover "*justification*" also to be the "same as *regeneration* and having a lively faith." I take them to be three different things; so different as not ever to come under one *genus*. And yet it is true that each of these "as far as I know" is at first experienced suddenly, although two of them (I leave you to find out which) gradually increase from that hour. (*A Letter to the Author of* The Enthusiasm of Methodists and Papists Compared [1750], in *Works*, 13:9)

JUSTIFICATION AND SANCTIFICATION

As earnestly therefore as our [Anglican] Church inculcates justification by faith alone, she nevertheless supposes repentance to be previous to faith and *fruits meet for repentance*: yea, and universal holiness to be previous to final justification. (*A Farther Appeal to Men of Reason and Religion* [1745], pt. 1, in *Works*, 12:54)

Both inward and outward holiness are consequent on this faith and are the ordinary, stated condition of final justification.
. . . I not only allow but vehemently contend that none shall ever enter into glory who is not holy on earth, as well in heart, as in all manner of conversation. (*A Farther Appeal to Men of Reason and Religion* [1745], pt. 1, in *Works*, 12:58)

J

We grant, (1) That many of those who have died in the faith, yea, the greater part of those we have known, were not perfected in love till a little before their death. (2) That the term *sanctified* is continually applied by St. Paul to all that were justified. (3) That by this term alone he rarely, if ever, means "saved from all sin." (4) That, consequently, it is not proper to use it in that sense, without adding the word *wholly, entirely,* or the like. (5) That the inspired writers almost continually speak of or to those who were justified but very rarely of or to those who were wholly sanctified. (6) That, consequently, it behooves us to speak almost continually of the state of justification; but more rarely, "at least in full and explicit terms, concerning entire sanctification." (*A Plain Account of Christian Perfection* [1767; rev. 1777], in *Works* [WL], 11:388)

They know, indeed, that at the same time a man is justified, sanctification properly begins. For when he is justified, he is "born again," "born from above," "born of the Spirit" which, although it is not (as some suppose) the whole process of sanctification, is doubtless the gate of it. Of this, likewise, God has given them a full view. They know the new birth implies as great a change in the soul in him that is "born of the Spirit" as was wrought in his body when he was born of a woman. Not an outward change only, as from drunkenness to sobriety, from robbery or theft to honesty (this is the poor, dry, miserable conceit of those that know nothing of real religion) but an inward change from all unholy to all holy tempers—from pride to humility, from passionateness to meekness, from peevishness and discontent to patience and resignation; in a word, from an earthly, sensual, devilish mind to the mind that was in Christ Jesus.

. . . It is, then, a great blessing given to this people that as they do not think or speak of justification so as to supersede sanctification, so neither do they think or speak of sanctification so as to supersede justification. They take care to keep each in its own place, laying equal stress on one and the other. They know God has joined these together, and it is not for man to put them asunder. Therefore they maintain, with equal zeal and diligence, the doctrine of free, full, present justification, on the one hand, and of entire sanctification both of heart and life, on the other; being as tenacious of inward holiness as any mystic, and of outward, as any Pharisee. ("On God's Vineyard" [October 17, 1787], Sermon 107, in *Works* [WL], 7:205)

JUSTIFICATION BY FAITH

I am firmly persuaded that every man of the offspring of Adam is very far gone from original righteousness and is of his own nature inclined to evil; that this corruption of our nature in every person born in the world deserves God's wrath and damnation; that, therefore, if ever we receive the remission of our sins and are accounted righteous before God, it must be only for the merit of Christ, by faith and not for our own works or deservings of any kind. Nay, I am persuaded that all works done before justification have in them the nature of sin and that, consequently, till he is justified a man has no power to do any work which is pleasing and acceptable to God.

. . . I believe that "conversion," meaning thereby justification, is an instantaneous work and that the moment a man has living faith in Christ he is converted or justified, which faith he cannot have without knowing that he has it.

I believe the moment a man is justified he has peace with God, which he cannot have without knowing that he has it. (*The Principles of a Methodist* [1743], in Coll. B, 41, 46)

When I say, faith alone is the condition of present salvation, what I would assert is this: (1) That without faith no man can be saved from his sins, can be either inwardly or outwardly holy. And, (2) That at what time soever faith is given, holiness commences in the soul. For that instant, the love of God (which is the source of holiness) is shed abroad in the heart. (*A Farther Appeal to Men of Reason and Religion* [1745], pt. 1, in *Works*, 12:73)

J

But to him that worketh not—It being impossible he should without faith. *But believeth* [. . .], *his faith is imputed to him for righteousness*—Therefore God's affirming of Abraham, that *faith was imputed to him for righteousness*, plainly shows that he *worked not* or, in other words, that he was not justified by works, but by faith only. Hence we see plainly how groundless that opinion is, that holiness or sanctification is previous to our justification. For the sinner, being first convinced of his sin and danger by the Spirit of God, stands trembling before the awful tribunal of divine justice and has nothing to plead but his own guilt and the merits of a Mediator. Christ here interposes; justice is satisfied; the sin is remitted, and pardon is applied to the soul, by a divine faith wrought by the Holy Ghost, who then begins the great work of inward sanctification. Thus God *justifies the ungodly* and yet remains just and true to all his attributes! But let none hence presume to "continue in sin," for to the impenitent God "is a consuming fire." *On him that justifieth the ungodly*—If a man could possibly be made holy before he was justified, it would entirely set his justification aside, seeing he could not, in the very nature of the thing, be justified if he were not at that very time ungodly. (*NT Notes*, 367, comment on Rom. 4:5)

By faith we mean *the evidence of things not seen*, by justifying faith, a divine evidence or conviction that Christ *loved me and gave himself for me*. St. Paul affirms that a man is justified by *this faith*, which James never denies but only asserts, that a man cannot be justified by a *dead faith*. And this St. Paul never affirms. (Letter to the Rev. Dr. Free [May 2, 1758], in *Works*, 13:84-85)

JUSTIFICATION BY GRACE ALONE

At the same time we are convinced that we are not sufficient of ourselves to help ourselves, that without the Spirit of God we can do nothing but add sin to sin, that it is he alone *who worketh in us by* his almighty power either *to will or do* that which is good, it being as impossible for us even to think a good thought without the supernatural assistance of his Spirit as to create ourselves or to renew our whole souls in righteousness and true holiness. ("The Circumcision of the Heart" [January 1, 1733], Sermon 17, in *Works* [T], 5:164)

I believe justification by faith alone. But *let it be observed*, the *true sense* of those words, "We are justified by faith in Christ only," is not that this our own act to believe in Christ or this our faith which is within us justifies us (for that were to account ourselves to be justified by some act or virtue that is within us), but that although we have faith, hope, and love within us and do never so many good works, yet we must renounce the merit of all, of faith, hope, love, and all other virtues and good works, which we either have done, shall do, or can do, as far too weak to deserve our justification: for which therefore we must trust only in God's mercy and the merits of Christ. For it is he alone that taketh away our sins. To him alone are we to go for this, forsaking all other virtues, good words, thoughts, and works and putting our trust in Christ only. In strictness therefore, neither our faith nor our works justify us, [that is], deserve the remission of our sins. But God himself justifies us of his own mercy, through the merits of his Son only. Nevertheless, because by faith we embrace the promise of God's mercy and of the remission of our sins, therefore the Scripture says that faith does justify, yea, faith without works. And it is all one to say, faith without works, and faith alone justifies us, therefore the ancient fathers from time to time speak thus, Faith alone justifies us. (Quoted in "Of Justification by Faith," chap. 11 in Coll. A, 74-75)

If you ask, "Why then have not all men this faith? all, at least, who conceive it to be so happy a thing? Why do they not believe immediately?"

We answer (on the Scripture hypothesis), "It is the gift of God." No man is able to work it in himself. It is a work of omnipotence. It requires no less power thus to quicken a dead soul than to raise a body that lies in the grave. It is a new creation, and none can create a soul anew but he who at first created the heavens and the earth.

May not your own experience teach you this? Can you give yourself this faith? . . .

. . . You not only do not but cannot, by your own strength, thus believe. The more you labor so to do, the more you will be convinced "it is the gift of God."

It is the free gift of God which he bestows not on those who are worthy of his favor, not on such as are previously holy and so fit to be crowned with all the blessings of his goodness, but on the ungodly and unholy, on those who till that hour were fit only for everlasting destruction . . . No merit, no goodness in man precedes the forgiving love of God. (*An Earnest Appeal to Men of Reason and Religion* [1743], in Coll. C, 212-13)

The author of faith and salvation is God alone. It is he that works in us both to will and to do. He is the sole giver of every good gift and the sole author of every good work. There is no more of power than of merit in man; but as all merit is in the Son of God, in what he has done and suffered for us, so all power is in the Spirit of God. And therefore every man, in order to believe unto salvation, must receive the Holy Ghost. This is essentially necessary to every Christian, not in order to his working miracles, but in order to faith, peace, joy, and love—the ordinary fruits of the Spirit.

. . . However it be expressed, it is certain all true faith, and the whole work of salvation, every good thought, word, and work, is altogether by the operation of the Spirit of God. (*Conditions of Justification* [1744], in Coll. B, 179-80)

Although therefore our [Anglican] Church does frequently assert that we ought to repent and bring forth fruits meet for repentance, if ever we would attain to that faith whereby alone we are justified, yet she never asserts (and here the hinge of the question turns) that these are good works, so long as they are previous to justification. Nay, she expressly asserts the direct contrary, [namely], that they have all the nature of sin. (*A Farther Appeal to Men of Reason and Religion* [1745], pt. 1, in *Works*, 12:56)

We have no trust or confidence but in the alone merit of our Lord and Savior Jesus Christ for justification or salvation, either in life, death, or the day of judgment.

. . . That we are justified by faith alone is spoken to take away clearly all merit of our works and wholly to ascribe the merit and deserving of our justification to Christ only. (Quoted in "Of Justification by Faith," chap. 11 in Coll. A, 80-81)

JUSTIFICATION: IMPUTED

Least of all does justification imply that God is deceived in those whom he justifies, that he thinks them to be what, in fact, they are not, that he accounts them to be otherwise than they are. It does by no means imply that God judges concerning us contrary to the real nature of things, that he esteems us better than we really are or believes us righteous when we are unrighteous. Surely no. The judgment of the all-wise God is always according to truth. Neither can it ever consist with his unerring wisdom to think that I am innocent, to judge that I am righteous or holy, because another is so. He can no more, in this manner, confound me with Christ than with David or Abraham. Let any man to whom God hath given understanding weigh this without prejudice, and he cannot but perceive that such a notion of justification is neither reconcilable to reason nor Scripture. ("Justification by Faith" [1746], Sermon 5, in *Works* [T], 5:49)

We do not find it expressly affirmed in Scripture that God imputes the righteousness of Christ to any. Although we do find that faith is imputed to us for righteousness. (*Minutes of Some Late Conversations* [June 25, 1744], *Works* [S], 5:196)

But in what sense is this righteousness imputed to believers? In this: all believers are forgiven and accepted, not for the sake of anything in them or of anything that ever was, that is, or ever can be done by them, but wholly and solely for the sake of what Christ hath done and suffered for them. I say again, not for the sake of anything in them or done by them of their own righteousness or works: "Not for works of righteousness which we have done, but of his own mercy he saved us." "By grace ye are saved through faith, [. . .] not of works, lest any man should boast" but wholly and solely for the sake of what Christ hath done and suffered for us. We are "justified freely by his grace through the redemption that is in Jesus Christ." ("The Lord Our Righteousness" [November 24, 1765], Sermon 64, in *Works* [T], 6:246)

Frequent mention is made in Scripture of "faith counted for righteousness." So [Gen. 15:6]: "He (Abraham) believed in the Lord, and he counted it to him for righteousness"—a text repeated, with but little variation, over and over in the New Testament. [Rom. 4:5]: "To him that worketh not, but believeth on him who justifieth the ungodly, his faith is counted for righteousness." Thus it was that "Noah became heir of the righteousness," the justification, "which is by faith" [Heb. 11:7]. Thus also "the Gentiles," when the Jews fell short, "attained to righteousness, even the righteousness which is by faith" [Rom. 9:30]. But that expression, *the righteousness of Christ*, does not occur in any of these texts.

. . . We are all agreed as to the *meaning* but not as to the *expression*, the *imputing the righteousness of Christ*, which I still say, I dare not insist upon, neither require anyone to use; because I cannot find it in the Bible. If anyone can, he has better eyes than I, and I wish he would show me where it is.

. . . Now, if by the righteousness of Christ we mean anything which the Scripture does not mean, it is certain we put darkness for light. If we mean

J

the same which the Scripture means by different expressions, why do we prefer this expression to the scriptural? Is not this correcting the wisdom of the Holy Ghost and opposing our own to the perfect knowledge of God?

. . . I am myself the more sparing in the use of it, because it has been so frequently and so dreadfully abused and because the Antinomians use it at this day to justify the grossest abominations. And it is great pity those who love, who preach, and follow after holiness should, under the notion of honoring Christ, give any countenance to those who continually make him *the minister of sin*, and so build on his righteousness, as to live in such ungodliness and unrighteousness as is scarcely named even among the heathens. (*Thoughts on the Imputed Righteousness of Christ* [April 5, 1762], in *Works* [T], 9:451-52)

I continually affirm: to them that believe, *faith is imputed for righteousness*. And I do not contradict this, in still denying that *phrase*, the *imputed righteousness of Christ*, to be in the Bible . . .

. . . The doctrine which I believe has done immense hurt is that of the imputed righteousness of Christ in the Antinomian sense. The doctrine which I have constantly held and preached is that faith is imputed for righteousness. (*Some Remarks on Mr. Hill's Farrago Double-Distilled* [March 14, 1773], in *Works* [T], 9:516-17)

J

JUSTIFICATION: INFUSED

I believe God implants righteousness in everyone to whom he has imputed it. I believe "Jesus Christ is made of God unto us sanctification" as well as "righteousness" or that God sanctifies as well as justifies all them that believe in him. They to whom the righteousness of Christ is imputed are made righteous by the Spirit of Christ, are renewed in the image of God, "after the likeness wherein they were created, in righteousness and true holiness." (Quoted in "Of Christ," chap. 4 in Coll. D, 81)

"Know ye not," whoever teacheth you otherwise, "that the unrighteous shall not inherit the kingdom of God?" . . . as the Lord liveth, "Neither fornicators, nor idolaters, nor adulterers, nor effeminate, nor sodomites, nor thieves, nor covetous, nor drunkards, nor revilers, nor extortioners, shall inherit the kingdom of God." Such indeed "were some of you. But ye are washed, but ye are sanctified, as well as justified, in the name of the Lord Jesus, and by the Spirit of our God." You are really changed; you are not only accounted but actually made righteous. "The law," the inward power, "of the Spirit of Life in Christ Jesus, hath made you free," really, actually free "from the law (or *power*) of sin and death." This is liberty, true gospel liberty, experienced by every believer: not freedom from the law of God or the works of God but from the law of sin and the works òf the devil. See that ye "stand fast" in this real, not imaginary "liberty, wherewith Christ hath made you free." And take heed ye be not "entangled again," by means of these vain boasters, "in the yoke" of that vile "bondage" to sin from which ye are now clean escaped. I testify unto you that if you still continue in sin, Christ shall profit you nothing, that Christ is no Savior to you unless he saves you from your sins, and that unless it purify your heart, faith shall profit you nothing. [Oh,] when will ye understand that to oppose either inward or outward holiness, under color of exalting Christ, is directly to act the part of Judas, to "betray the Son of Man with a kiss"? Repent, repent! lest he cut you in sunder with the two-edged sword that cometh out of his mouth! It is you yourselves that, by opposing the very end of his coming into the world, are "crucifying the Son of God afresh, and putting him to an open shame." It is you that by expecting to see the Lord without holiness, through the righteousness of Christ, "make the blood of the covenant an unholy thing," keeping those unholy that so trust in it.

[Oh,] beware! for evil is before you! If those who name not the name of Christ and die in their sins shall be punished sevenfold, surely you who thus make Christ "a minister of sin" shall be punished seventy and seven fold. What! make Christ destroy his own kingdom! Make Christ a factor for Satan! Set Christ against holiness! Talk of Christ as "saving his people in their sins"! It is no better than to say he saves them from the guilt and not from the power of sin. Will you make the righteousness of Christ such a cover for the unrighteousness of man? So that by this mean the unrighteous of every kind shall inherit the kingdom of God! . . . [Oh,] come back to the true, the pure, the old gospel! That which ye received in the beginning. Come back to Christ, who died to make you a holy people, "zealous of good works." "Remember from whence you are fallen, and repent and do the first works." Your "Father worketh hitherto"; do ye work, else your faith is vain. For "wilt thou know, O vain," O empty "man, that faith without works is dead?" Wilt thou know, that "though I have all faith, so as to remove mountains, and have not love, I am nothing"? Wilt thou know that all the blood and righteousness of Christ, unless that "mind be in thee which was in" him, and thou likewise "walk as Christ walked," will only increase thy damnation? . . . Do not stupidly and senselessly call this *legal*, a silly, unmeaning word. Be not afraid of being "under the law of God" but of being "under the law of sin." Love the strictest preaching best, that which most searches the heart and shows you wherein you are unlike Christ and that which presses you most to love him with all your heart and serve him with all your strength. (*A Blow at the Root* [1762], in *Works* [T], 9:455-56)

KINGDOM OF HEAVEN

This holiness and happiness joined in one are sometimes styled in the inspired writings, the *kingdom of God* (as by our Lord in the text) and sometimes *the kingdom of heaven*. It is termed *the kingdom of God* because it is the immediate fruit of God's reigning in the soul. So soon as ever he takes unto himself his mighty power and sets up his throne in our hearts, they are instantly filled with this "righteousness, and peace, and joy in the Holy Ghost." It is called *the kingdom of heaven* because it is (in a degree) heaven opened in the soul. ("The Way to the Kingdom" [June 6, 1742], Sermon 7, in *Works* [T], 5:67-68)

KNEELING AND BOWING

"It is not lawful for Christians to kneel or bow the body, or uncover the head to any man." If this is not lawful, then some law of God forbids it. Can you show me that law? If you cannot, then the scrupling this is another plain instance of superstition, not Christianity. (*A Letter to a Person Lately Joined to the People Called Quakers* [February 2, 1748], in *Works* [T], 9:117)

LATITUDINARIANISM

Well, how blind was I! I always supposed, till the very hour I read these words, that when I was charged with differing from the [Anglican] Church, I was charged with differing from the articles or homilies. And for the compilers of these, I can sincerely profess great deference and veneration. But I cannot honestly profess any veneration at all for those pastors of the present age who solemnly subscribe to those articles and homilies which they do not believe in their hearts. Nay, I think, unless I differ from these men (be they bishops, priests, or deacons) just as widely as they do from those articles and homilies, I am no true Church of England man. (Letter to John Smith [probably one of the archbishops of Canterbury, Thomas Herring or Thomas Secker] [September 28, 1745], in *Works* [WL], 12:63)

A catholic spirit is not *speculative* latitudinarianism. It is not an indifference to all opinions. This is the spawn of hell, not the offspring of heaven. This unsettledness of thought, this being "driven to and fro, and tossed about with every wind of doctrine," is a great curse, not a blessing; an irreconcilable enemy, not a friend to true catholicism. A man of a true catholic spirit has not now his religion to seek. He is fixed as the sun in his judgment concerning the main branches of Christian doctrine. It is true, he is always ready to hear and weigh whatsoever can be offered against his principles. But as this does not show any wavering in his own mind, so neither does it occasion any. He does not halt between two opinions, nor vainly endeavor to blend them into one. Observe this, you who know not what spirit ye are of who call yourselves men of a Catholic spirit only because you are of a muddy understanding, because your mind is all in a mist, because you have no settled, consistent principles but are for jumbling all opinions together. Be convinced that you have quite missed your way; you know not where you are. You think you are got into the very Spirit of Christ when, in truth, you are nearer the spirit of antichrist. Go first and learn the first elements of the gospel of Christ, and then shall you learn to be of a truly catholic spirit. ("Catholic Spirit" [1750], Sermon 41, in *Works* [T], 5:418)

LAW AND GOSPEL

The moral law, contained in the Ten Commandments and enforced by the prophets, Christ did not take away. It was not the design of his coming to revoke any part of this. This is a law which never can be broken, which "stands fast as the faithful witness in heaven." The moral stands on an entirely different foundation from the ceremonial or ritual law, which was only designed for a temporary restraint upon a disobedient and stiff-necked people, whereas this was from the beginning of the world being "written, not on tables of stone" but on the hearts of all the children of men, when they came out of the hands of the Creator. And, however, the letters once wrote by the finger of God are now in a great measure defaced by sin, yet cannot they wholly be blotted out while we have any consciousness of good and evil. Every part of this law must remain in force upon all mankind and in all ages, as not depending either on time or place or any other circumstances liable to change, but on the nature of God and the nature of man and their unchangeable relation to each other.

"I am not come to destroy but to fulfill." . . . Without question, his meaning in this place is (consistently with all that goes before and follows after)—I am come to establish it in its fullness, in spite of all the glosses of men. I am come to place in a full and clear view whatsoever was dark or obscure therein. I am come to declare the true and full import of every part of it, to show the length and breadth, the entire extent of every commandment contained therein, and the height and depth, the inconceivable purity and spirituality of it in all its branches. (Quoted in "Of the Divine Law," chap. 6 in Coll. D, 108-9)

From all this we may learn that there is no contrariety at all between the law and the gospel, that there is no need for the law to pass away in order to the establishing the gospel. Indeed neither of them supersedes the other, but they agree perfectly well together. Yea, the very same words considered in different respects are parts both of the law and of the gospel: if they are considered as commandments, they are parts of the law; if as promises, of the gospel. Thus, "thou shalt love the Lord thy God with all thy heart," when considered as a commandment is a branch of the law; when regarded as a promise is an essential part of the gospel—the gospel being no other than the commands of the law proposed by way of promise. Accordingly, poverty of spirit, purity of heart, and whatever else is enjoined in the holy law of God are no other, when viewed in a gospel light, than so many great and precious promises.

There is, therefore, the closest connection that can be conceived between the law and the gospel. On the one hand, the law continually makes way for and points us to the gospel; on the other, the gospel continually leads us to a more exact fulfilling of the law. The law, for instance, requires us to love God, to love our neighbor, to be meek, humble, or holy. We feel that we are not sufficient for these things, yea, that "with man this is impossible." But we see a promise of God to give us that love and to make us humble, meek, and holy. We lay hold of this gospel, of these glad tidings; it is done unto us according to our faith, and "the righteousness of the law is fulfilled in us" through faith which is in Christ Jesus. (Quoted in "Of the Divine Law," chap. 6 in Coll. D, 107-8)

LAW: GOD'S

It is indeed, in the highest degree, pure, chaste, clean, holy. Otherwise it could not be the immediate offspring and much less the express resemblance of God, who is essential holiness. It is pure from all sin, clean and unspotted from any touch of evil. It is a chaste virgin, incapable of any defilement, of any mixture with that which is unclean or unholy. It has no fellowship with sin of any kind, for "what communion hath light with darkness?" As sin is in its very nature enmity to God, so his law is enmity to sin.

Therefore it is that the apostle rejects with such abhorrence that blasphemous supposition that the law of God is either sin itself or the cause of sin. God forbid that we should suppose it is the cause of sin because it is the discoverer of it, because it detects the hidden things of darkness and drags them out into open day. . . . It is true that "sin worketh death by that which is good," which in itself is pure and holy. When it is dragged out to light, it rages the more; when it is restrained, it bursts out with greater violence. Thus the apostle (speaking in the person of one who was convinced of sin but not yet delivered from it), "Sin taking occasion by the commandment," detecting and endeavoring to restrain it, disdained the restraint and so much the more "wrought in me all manner of concupiscence" [Rom. 7:8], all manner of foolish and hurtful desire which that commandment sought to restrain. Thus, "when the commandment came, sin revived" [v. 9]; it fretted and raged the more. But this is no stain on the commandment. Though it is abused, it cannot be defiled. This only proves that "the heart of man is desperately wicked." But the law of God is holy still.

And it is, secondly, just; it renders to all their due. It prescribes exactly what is right, precisely what ought to be done, said, or thought, both with regard to the author of our being, with regard to ourselves, and with regard to every creature which he has made. (Quoted in "Of the Divine Law," chap. 6 in Coll. D, 97-98)

LENT

In every parish where I have been curate yet, I have observed the rubrics with a scrupulous exactness, not for wrath but for conscience sake. And this, . . . I do now. . . . The forty days of Lent. (Quoted in "Of Obedience to Church Authority," chap. 17 in Coll. A, 121)

The annual fasts in our church are the forty days of Lent . . . (Quoted in "Of Fasting," chap. 10 in Coll. A, 73)

L

LOTS, CASTING OF

I come now to what you expatiate upon at large, as the two grand instances of enthusiasm. The first is plainly this. At some rare times when I have been in great distress of soul or in utter uncertainty how to act in an important case which required a speedy determination, after using all other means that occurred, I have cast lots or opened the Bible. And by this means I have been relieved from that distress or directed in that uncertainty. . . .

. . . You allow, indeed, there are "instances of this in Scripture" [see, e.g., Josh. 18:8, 10; Acts 1:26] but affirm these "were miraculous: nor can we without presumption" (a species of enthusiasm) "apply this method." I want proof of this; bring one plain text of Scripture, and I am satisfied. (*The Principles of a Methodist Farther Explained* [1746], in *Works*, 12:368, 370)

LOVE

It nothing avails that I declare again and again, "Love is the fulfilling of the law." I believe this love is given in a moment. But about this I contend not. Have this love, and it is enough. For this I will contend till my spirit returns to God. Whether I am singular or no, in thinking this love is instantaneously given, this is not my "most beloved opinion." . . . I want, I value, I preach the love of God and man. These are my "favorite tenets" (if you will have the word) "more insisted on" by me ten times over, both in preaching and writing, than any or all other subjects that ever were in the world.

. . . in my general tenor of preaching, I teach nothing as the substance of religion more singular than the love of God and man. And it was for preaching this very doctrine (before I preached or knew salvation by faith) that several of the clergy forbade me their pulpits. (Letter to John Smith [probably one of the archbishops of Canterbury, Thomas Herring or Thomas Secker] [September 28, 1745], in *Works* [WL], 12:62)

I regard even faith itself not as an end but a means only. The end of the commandment is love, of every command, of the whole Christian dispensation. Let this love be attained by whatever means and I am content; I desire no more. All is well if we love the Lord our God with all our heart and our neighbor as ourselves. (Letter to John Smith [probably one of the archbishops of Canterbury, Thomas Herring or Thomas Secker] [June 25, 1746], in *Works* [WL], 12:77)

LUTHER, MARTIN

I finished the translation of Martin Luther's Life. Doubtless he was a man highly favored of God and a blessed instrument in his hand. But [oh]! what pity that he had no faithful friend! None that would, at all hazards, rebuke him plainly and sharply for his rough, untractable spirit and bitter zeal for opinions so greatly obstructive of the work of God! (*Journal,* July 19, 1749)

It has been frequently observed that very few were clear in their judgment both with regard to justification and sanctification. Many who have spoken and written admirably well concerning justification had no clear conception, nay, were totally ignorant of the doctrine of sanctification. Who has written more ably than Martin Luther on justification by faith alone? And who was more ignorant of the doctrine of sanctification or more confused in his conceptions of it? In order to be thoroughly convinced of this, of his total ignorance with regard to sanctification, there needs no more than to read over, without prejudice, his celebrated comment on the Epistle to the Galatians. ("On God's Vineyard" [October 17, 1787], Sermon 107, in *Works* [WL], 7:204)

MAN: PURPOSE OF

For what end is life bestowed upon the children of men? Why were we sent into the world? For one sole end and for no other, to prepare for eternity. For this alone we live. For this and no other purpose is our life either given or continued. It pleased the all-wise God, at the season which he saw best, to arise in the greatness of his strength and create the heavens and the earth and all things that are therein. Having prepared all things for him, "he created man in his own image after his own likeness." And what was the end of his creation? It was one and no other—that he might know and love and enjoy and serve his great Creator to all eternity. (Quoted in "Of Man," chap. 7 in Coll. D, 136)

MARRIAGE: NOT A SACRAMENT

In one sense it may be so. For St. Austin [Augustine] says, "Signs, when applied to religious things, are called sacraments." In this large sense he calls the sign of the cross a sacrament, and others give this name to washing the feet. But it is not a sacrament according to the Romish definition of the word, for it no more "confers grace" than washing the feet or signing with the cross. (*Popery Calmly Considered* [1779], in *Works,* 15:193)

MARY

We honor the blessed Virgin as the mother of the holy Jesus and as a person of eminent piety. (*Popery Calmly Considered* [1779], in *Works,* 15:184-85)

MARY: PERPETUAL VIRGINITY OF

The blessed Virgin Mary who, as well after as before she brought him forth, continued a pure and unspotted virgin. (*A Letter to a Roman Catholic* [July 18, 1749], in Coll. C, 305)

MERIT

I do not use the word *merit.* I never did, neither do now, contend for the use of it. But I ask you, or any other, a plain question: And do not cry, Murder, but give me an answer. What is the difference between *mereri* and *to deserve?* or between *deserving* and *meritum?* I say still, I cannot tell. Can you? . . . In asking this question, I neither plead for merit, nor against it. I have nothing to do with it. I have declared a thousand times, There is no goodness in man till he is justified—no merit either before or after, that is, taking the word in its proper sense. For in a loose sense, *meritorious* means no more than *rewardable.* (Letter to Charles Wesley [August 3, 1771], in *Works* [WL], 12:127)

M

Take the word *merit* in a *strict* sense, and I utterly renounce it. Take it in a *looser* sense [God rewarding grace-produced works], and though I never use it, yet I do not condemn it. (*Some Remarks on Mr. Hill's Review of All the Doctrines Taught by Mr. John Wesley* [September 9, 1772], in *Works* [T], 9:490)

METHODISM

The distinguishing marks of a Methodist are not his opinions of any sort. His assenting to this or that scheme of religion, his embracing any particular set of notions, his espousing the judgment of one man or of another are all quite wide of the point. Whosoever, therefore, imagines that a Methodist is a man of such or such an opinion is grossly ignorant of the whole affair; he mistakes the truth totally. We believe, indeed, that "all Scripture is given by the inspiration of God," and herein we are distinguished from Jews, Turks, and infidels. We believe the written word of God to be the only and sufficient rule both of Christian faith and practice, and herein we are fundamentally distinguished from those of the Romish Church. We believe Christ to be the eternal, supreme God, and herein we are distinguished from the Socinians and Arians. But as to all opinions which do not strike at the root of Christianity, we think and let think. So that, whatsoever they are, whether right or wrong, they are no distinguishing marks of a Methodist. (*The Character of a Methodist* [1742], in Coll. C, 292-93)

I would to God both thou and all men knew that I and all who follow my judgment do vehemently refuse to be distinguished from other men by any but the common principles of Christianity—the plain, old Christianity that I teach, renouncing and detesting all other marks of distinction. And whosoever is what I preach (let him be called what he will, for names change not the nature of things), he is a Christian, not in name only but in heart and in life. He is inwardly and outwardly conformed to the will of God as revealed in the written Word. He thinks, speaks, and lives according to the method laid down in the revelation of Jesus Christ. His soul is renewed after the image of God, in righteousness and in all true holiness. And having the mind that was in Christ, he so walks as Christ also walked.

By these marks, by these fruits of a living faith do we labor to distinguish ourselves from the unbelieving world, from all those whose minds or lives are not according to the gospel of Christ. But from real Christians, of whatsoever denomination they be, we earnestly desire not to be distinguished at all, not from any who sincerely follow after what they know they have not yet attained. No, "Whosoever doeth the will of my Father which is in heaven, the same is my brother, and sister, and mother." (*The Character of a Methodist* [1742], in Coll. C, 301-2)

By Methodists I mean a people who profess to pursue (in whatsoever measure they have attained) holiness of heart and life, inward and outward conformity in all things to the revealed will of God; who place religion in a uniform resemblance of the great object of it, in a steady imitation of him they worship, in all his imitable perfections, more particularly in justice, mercy, and truth, or universal love filling the heart and governing the life.

. . . Perhaps not one in a hundred of those who use the term *Methodist* have any ideas of what it means. (*Advice to the People Called Methodists* [October 10, 1745], in Coll. B, 47, 50)

Therefore the distinguishing doctrines on which I do insist in all my writings and in all my preaching will lie in a very narrow compass. You sum them all up in perceptible inspiration. For this I earnestly contend, and so do all who are called Methodist preachers. But be pleased to observe what we mean thereby. We mean that inspiration of God's Holy Spirit whereby he fills us with righteousness, peace, and joy, with love to him and to all mankind. And we believe it cannot be, in the nature of things, that a man should be filled with this peace and joy and love by the inspiration of the Holy Spirit without perceiving it as clearly as he does the light of the sun.

This is (so far as I understand them) the main doctrine of the Methodists. This is the substance of what we all preach. And I will still believe none is a true Christian till he experiences it; and, consequently, "that people, at all hazards, must be convinced of this; yea, though that conviction at first unhinge them ever so much, though it should in a manner distract them for a season. For it is better that they should be perplexed and terrified now than that they should sleep on and awake in hell."

I do not therefore, I will not, shift the question, though I know many who desire I should. I know the proposition I have to prove, and I will not move a hair's breadth from it. It is this: "No man can be a true Christian without such an inspiration of the Holy Ghost as fills his heart with peace and joy and love, which he who perceives not has it not." This is the point for which alone I contend, and this I take to be the very foundation of Christianity. (Letter to John Smith [probably one of the archbishops of Canterbury, Thomas Herring or Thomas Secker] [December 30, 1745], in *Works* [WL], 12:69)

[A Methodist is] one that lives according to the method laid down in the Bible. (*Note to* The Complete English Dictionary [1753], quoted in Coll. C, 295n)

Afterward I met the society and explained to them at large the original design of the Methodists, [namely], not to be a distinct party but to stir up all parties, Christians or heathens, to worship God in spirit and in truth; but the Church of England in particular, to which they belonged from the beginning. With this view I have uniformly gone on for fifty years, never varying from the doctrine of the Church at all; nor from her discipline, of choice, but of necessity. So, in a course of years, necessity was laid upon me (as I have proved elsewhere) (1) to preach in the open air; (2) to pray extempore; (3) to form Societies; (4) to accept of the assistance of lay preachers; and, in a few other instances, to use such means as occurred to prevent or remove evils that we either felt or feared. (*Journal*, April 12, 1789)

The Methodists in general, my Lord, are members of the Church of England. They hold all her doctrines, attend her service, and partake of her sacraments. (Letter to Bishop Dr. Pretyman Tomline [June 26, 1790], in *Letters*, 133-34)

METHODISM: AMERICAN

Dear brethren,

1. By a very uncommon train of providences many of the provinces of North America are totally disjoined from their mother country and erected into independent states. The English government has no authority over

them, either civil or ecclesiastical, any more than over the states of Holland. A civil authority is exercised over them, partly, by the Congress, partly by the provincial Assemblies. But no one either exercises or claims any ecclesiastical authority at all. In this peculiar situation some thousands of the inhabitants of the States desire my advice; and in compliance with their desire I have drawn up a little sketch.

2. Lord King's *Account of the Primitive Church* convinced me many years ago [in January 1746, per his *Journal*] that bishops and presbyters are the same order and consequently have the same rights to ordain. For many years I have been importuned, from time to time, to exercise this right by ordaining part of our traveling preachers. But I have still refused, not only for peace' sake, but because I was determined as little as possible to violate the established order of the national Church to which I belonged.

3. But the case is widely different between England and North America. Here there are bishops who have a legal jurisdiction; in America there are none, neither any parish ministers. So that for some hundred miles together there is none either to baptize or to administer the Lord's Supper. Here, therefore, my scruples are at an end; and I conceive myself at full liberty, as I violate no order and invade no man's right by appointing and sending laborers into the harvest.

M

4. I have accordingly appointed Dr. Coke and Mr. Francis Asbury to be joint superintendents [rather than bishops] over our brethren in North America, as also Richard Whatcoat and Thomas Vasey to act as elders among them by baptizing and administering the Lord's Supper. And I have prepared a liturgy, little differing from that of the Church of England (I think the best constituted national Church in the world), which I advise all the traveling preachers to use on the Lord's Day in all the congregations, reading the litany only on Wednesdays and Fridays and praying extempore on all other days. I also advise the elders to administer the Supper of the Lord on every Lord's Day.

5. If anyone will point out a more rational and scriptural way of feeding and guiding these poor sheep in the wilderness, I will gladly embrace it. At present I cannot see any better method than that I have taken.

6. It has, indeed, been proposed to desire the English bishops to ordain part of our preachers for America. But to this I object. (1) I desired the bishop of London to ordain only one but could not prevail. (2) If they consented, we know the slowness of their proceedings, but the matter admits of no delay. (3) If they would ordain them now, they would likewise expect to govern them. And how grievously would this entangle us! (4) As our American brethren are now totally disentangled both from the state and from the English hierarchy, we dare not entangle them again, either with the one or

the other. They are now at full liberty simply to follow the Scriptures and the primitive church. And we judge it best that they should stand fast in that liberty wherewith God has so strangely made them free. (Letter to Dr. Coke, Mr. Asbury, and our Brethren in North America [September 10, 1784], in *Letters*, 263-65. Note: In 1787 Wesley wrote to Joshua Keighley: "I am quite undetermined whether I shall ever ordain again. I know not but I have already gone too far." His brother Charles wrote on April 28, 1785: "I can scarcely yet believe it, that . . . my brother . . . should have assumed the episcopal character, ordained elders, consecrated a bishop. . . . My brother does not and will not see that he has renounced the principles and practice of his whole life; that he has acted contrary to all his declarations, protestations, and writings.")

METHODISM: DANGER OF LIBERALISM AND NOMINALISM

We had been speaking in the conference on that very head—the means of preventing spiritual religion from degenerating into formality. It is continually needful to guard against this, as it strikes at the root of the whole work of God. (Letter to Miss Penelope Newman [August 9, 1776], in *Works* [WL], 12:490-91)

I am not afraid that the people called Methodists should ever cease to exist, . . . but I am afraid, lest they should only exist as a dead sect. . . . And this undoubtedly will be the case, unless they hold fast both the doctrine, spirit, and discipline with which they first set out. . . .

. . . For the Methodists in every place grow diligent and frugal; consequently, they increase in goods. Hence they proportionately increase in pride, in anger, in the desire of the flesh, the desire of the eyes, and the pride of life. So, although the form of religion remains, the spirit is swiftly vanishing away.

Is there no way to prevent this? this continual declension of pure religion? (*Thoughts upon Methodism* [August 4, 1786], in *Works* [S], 7:315, 317)

"METHODIST" (TITLE)

I say those who are called Methodists, for let it be well observed that this is not a name which they take to themselves but one fixed upon them by way of reproach without their approbation or consent. It was first given to three or four young men at Oxford, by a student of Christ Church; . . . from their observing a more regular *method* of study and behavior than was usual with those of their age and station.

I should rejoice (so little ambitious am I to be at the head of any sect or party) if the very name might never be mentioned more, but be buried in eternal oblivion. But if that cannot be, at least let those who will use it know the meaning of the word they use. Let us not always be fighting in the dark. Come, and let us look one another in the face. And perhaps some of you who hate what I am *called* may love what I *am* by the grace of God. (*The Character of a Methodist* [1742], in Coll. C, 291-92)

MIRACLES

You add, "I shall give but one account more, and this is, what you give of yourself." The sum whereof is, "At two several times, being ill and in violent pain, I prayed to God and found immediate ease." I did so. I assert the fact still. "Now if these" (you say) "are not miraculous cures, all this is rank *enthusiasm*."

I will put your argument in form:

He that believes those are miraculous cures which are not so, is a rank enthusiast:

But you believe those to be miraculous cures which are not so:

Therefore, you are a rank enthusiast.

Before I answer, I must know what you mean by miraculous? If you term everything so which is not strictly to be accounted for by the ordinary course of natural causes, then I deny the latter part of the minor proposition. And unless you can make this good, unless you can prove the effects in question may strictly be accounted for, by the *ordinary course* of natural causes, your argument is nothing worth. (*Answer to the Rev. Mr. Church's "Remarks on the Rev. Mr. Wesley's Last Journal"* [February 2, 1745], in *Works*, 12:325-26)

"But if you can work miracles when you please, is not this the surest way of proving them? This would put the matter out of dispute at once and supersede all other proof."

You seem to lie under an entire mistake, both as to the nature and use of miracles. It may reasonably be questioned whether there ever was that man living upon earth, except the man Christ Jesus, that could work miracles when he pleased. God only, when he pleased, exerted that power and by whomsoever it pleased him. But if a man could work miracles when he pleased, yet is there no Scripture authority nor even example for doing it in order to satisfy such a demand as this. I do not read that either our Lord or any of his apostles wrought any miracle on such an occasion. Nay, how sharply does our Lord rebuke those who made a demand of this kind? When "certain of the scribes and Pharisees answered, saying, Master, we would see a sign from thee" (observe, this was their method of answering the strong reasons whereby he had just proved the works in question to be of God!), "He answered and said to them, An evil and adulterous generation seeketh after a sign. But there shall no sign be given to it, but the sign of the prophet Jonas" [Matt. 12:38-39]. "An evil and adulterous generation!" Else they would not have needed such a kind of proof. Had they been willing to do his will, they would, without this, have known that the doctrine was of God.

Miracles, therefore, are quite needless in such a case. Nor are they so conclusive a proof as you imagine. If a man could and did work them, in defense of any doctrine, yet this would not supersede other proof. For there may be . . . lying wonders, miracles wrought in support of falsehood. Still therefore this doctrine would remain to be proved, from the proper topics of Scripture and reason. And these even without miracles are sufficient. But miracles without these are not. Accordingly our Savior and all his apostles, in the midst of their greatest miracles, never failed to prove every doctrine they taught, by clear Scripture and cogent reason. (*A Farther Appeal to Men of Reason and Religion* [1745], pt. 3, in *Works,* 12:264-65)

I have seen many things which I believe were miraculous, yet I desire none to believe my words any further than they are confirmed by Scripture and reason. And thus far I disclaim miracles. (Letter to John Smith [probably one of the archbishops of Canterbury, Thomas Herring or Thomas Secker] [June 25, 1746], in *Works* [WL], 12:73)

That "the conversion of sinners to this holiness is no miracle at all" is new doctrine indeed! So new to me that I never heard it before, either among Protestants or Papists. I think a miracle is a work of omnipotence wrought by the supernatural power of God. Now, if the conversion of sinners to holiness is not such a work, I cannot tell what is. (Letter to John Smith [probably one of the archbishops of Canterbury, Thomas Herring or Thomas Secker] [March 22, 1748], in *Works* [WL], 12:99)

You will naturally ask, "Why do you stop there? What reason can you give for this? If you allow miracles before the empire became Christian, why not afterward too?" . . . This very reason St. Chrysostom himself gave in the words you have afterward cited; "There are some who ask, Why are not miracles performed still? Why are there no persons who raise the dead and cure diseases?" To which he replies that it was owing to the want of faith and virtue and piety in those times. (*A Letter to the Rev. Dr. Conyers Middleton Occasioned by His Late "Free Inquiry"* [January 4, 1749], in *Works* [S], 5:706)

MIRACLES: CESSATION (FALSITY OF)

Yet I do not know that God hath any way precluded himself from thus exerting his sovereign power, from working miracles in any kind or degree, in any age to the end of the world. I do not recollect any scripture wherein we are taught that miracles were to be confined within the limits either of the apostolic or Cyprianic age or of any period of time, longer or shorter, even till the restitution of all things. I have not observed, either in the Old Testament or the New, any intimation at all of this kind. St. Paul says indeed once, concerning two of the miraculous gifts of the Spirit (so I think, that text is usually understood), "whether there be prophecies, they shall fail, whether there be tongues, they shall cease." But he does not say either that these or any other miracles shall cease till faith and hope shall cease also, till they all be swallowed up in the vision of God and love be all in all. (*The Principles of a Methodist Farther Explained* [1746], in *Works*, 12:387)

MIRACLES: DEMONIC

I presume you will allow there is one kind of miracles (loosely speaking) which are not ceased, namely, . . . *lying wonders*, diabolical miracles or works beyond the virtue of natural causes wrought by the power of evil spirits. Nor can you easily conceive that these will cease as long as the father of lies is the prince of this world. And why should you think that the God of truth is less active than he or that he will not have his miracles also? Only not as man wills, neither when he wills, but according to his own excellent wisdom and greatness. (*The Principles of a Methodist Farther Explained* [1746], in *Works*, 12:387)

MIRACLES: UNREASONABLE DEMAND FOR, AS PROOF OF METHODISM

What is it you would have us prove by miracles? That the doctrines we preach are true? This is not the way to prove that . . .

What else is it then we are to prove by miracles? Is it (1) that *A. B.* was for many years without God in the world, a common swearer, a drunkard, a Sabbath breaker? Or, (2) that he is not so now? Or, (3) that he continued so till he heard us preach, and from that time was another man?

Not so. The proper way to prove these facts is by the testimony of competent witnesses, and these witnesses are ready, whenever required, to give full evidence of them.

Or would you have us prove by miracles (4) that this was not done by our own power or holiness? That God only is able to raise the dead, those who are dead in trespasses and sins? Nay, if you hear not Moses and the prophets and apostles on this head, neither would you believe though one rose from the dead. It is therefore utterly unreasonable and absurd to require or expect the proof of miracles in questions of such a kind, as are always decided by proofs of quite a contrary nature.

. . . "But you relate them yourself." I relate just what I saw, from time to time: and this is true, that some of those circumstances seem to go beyond the ordinary course of nature. But I do not peremptorily determine whether they were supernatural or not. Much less do I rest upon them either the proof of other facts or of those doctrines which I preach. I prove these in the ordinary way, the one by Testimony, the other by Scripture and reason.

. . . I presume by this time you may perceive the gross absurdity of demanding miracles in the present case, seeing one of the propositions in question (over and above our general doctrines), [namely], "That sinners are reformed," can only be proved by testimony, and the other, "This cannot be done but by the power of God," needs no proof, being self-evident. (*A Farther Appeal to Men of Reason and Religion* [1745], pt. 3, in *Works*, 12:263-65)

No truly *wise* or *sober* man can possibly desire or expect miracles to prove either (1) that these *doctrines* are true; this must be decided by Scripture and reason; or, (2) that these *facts* are true: this can only be proved by testimony; or, (3) that to *change* sinners from darkness to light is the *Work of God* alone only using what instruments he pleases; this is glaringly self-evident; or, (4) that such a change wrought in so many notorious sinners, within so short a time, is a *great* and *extraordinary* work of God. This also carries its own evidence. What then is it which remains to be proved by miracles? Perhaps you will say, it is this: "That God hath *called* or *sent* you to do this." Nay, this is implied in the third of the foregoing propositions. If God has actually *used* us therein, if *his work* hath in fact prospered in our hands, then he hath *called* or *sent* us to do this. I entreat reasonable men to weigh this thoroughly, whether the *fact* does not plainly prove the *call*; whether he who *enables* us thus to save souls alive does not *commission* us so to do? Whether by *giving* us the *power* to pluck these brands out of the burning, he does not *authorize* us to exert it?

[Oh,] that it were possible for you to consider calmly whether the *success* of the gospel of Jesus Christ, even as it is preached by us, the least of his servants, be not itself a *miracle* never to be forgotten! One which cannot be denied as being visible at this day, not in one but a hundred places; one which cannot be accounted for by the ordinary course of any *natural cause* whatsoever; one which cannot be ascribed with any color of reason to *diabolical* agency; and, lastly, one which will bear the infallible test, the trial of the written Word. (*The Principles of a Methodist Farther Explained* [1746], in *Works*, 12:389-90)

There are at least as many pretenders to the love of God as there are to the witness of his Spirit. But does this give me a right, if a man asserts he loves God, to demand his proving that assertion by miracles? Not so, but by their fruits I shall know a real and a pretended love of God. And in the same manner may I know him that has the witness of God's love, from an enthusiastic pretender to it. But if a man disclaims it, he sets himself out of the question. It is beyond dispute that he has it not.

Neither do I want miracles in order to determine my judgment with regard to scriptures variously interpreted. I would not say, in this case,

"Show me a sign" but "Bring forth your strong reasons," and according to these, weighed in an even, impartial scale, would I incline to one side or the other. (Letter to John Smith [probably one of the archbishops of Canterbury, Thomas Herring or Thomas Secker] [July 10, 1747], in *Works* [WL], 12:95-96)

MORAVIANS

As yet I dare in no wise join with the Moravians, (1) Because their whole scheme is mystical, not scriptural, refined in every point above what is written—immeasurably beyond the plain doctrine of the gospel. (2) Because there is darkness and closeness in all their behavior and guile in almost all their words. (3) Because they not only do not practice but utterly despise every self-denial and the daily cross. (4) Because they, upon principle, conform to the world in wearing gold and gay or costly apparel. (5) Because they extend Christian liberty in this and many other respects beyond what is warranted by Holy Writ. (6) Because they are by no means zealous of good works or at least only to their own people; and, lastly, because they make inward religion swallow up outward in general. For these reasons (chiefly) I will rather, God being my helper, stand quite alone than join with them; I mean till I have full assurance that they will spread none of these errors among the little flock committed to my charge. (Letter to Charles Wesley [April 21, 1741], in *Letters,* 74)

I am still afraid their whole church is tainted with quietism, universal salvation, and antinomianism . . .

. . . I still think, (1) that God has some thousands in our own church who have the faith and love which is among them without those errors either of judgment or practice; (2) that next to these, *the body* of the *Moravian* church, however *mistaken some of them* are, are *in the main,* of all whom I have seen, the *best Christians* in the world. (*Answer to the Rev. Mr. Church's "Remarks on the Rev. Mr. Wesley's Last Journal"* [February 2, 1745], in *Works,* 12:285-86)

MUSIC (SUPERIORITY OF MELODY TO HARMONY)

But why is it that modern music, in general, [does not arouse the passions of] . . . the hearers? The grand reason seems to be no other than this—the whole nature and design of music is altered. The ancient composers studied melody alone; the due arrangement of single notes; and it was by melody alone that they wrought such wonderful effects. And as this music was directly calculated to move the passions, so they designed it for this very end. But the modern composers study harmony which, in the present sense of the word, is quite another thing; namely, a contrast of various notes opposite to and yet blended with each other . . .

Dr. Gregory says, "This harmony has been known in the world little more than two hundred years." Be that as it may, ever since it was introduced, ever since counterpoint has been invented, as it has altered the grand design of music, so it has well nigh destroyed its effects. . . .

And as the nature of music is thus changed, so is likewise the design of it. Our composers do not aim at moving the passions, but at quite another thing; at varying and contrasting the notes a thousand different ways. What has counterpoint to do with the passions? It is applied to a quite different faculty of the mind; not to our joy or hope or fear but merely to the ear, to the imagination, or internal sense. And the pleasure it gives is not upon this principle, not by raising any passion whatever. It no more affects the passions than the judgment; both the one and the other lie quite out of its province.

Need we any other and can we have any stronger proof of this than those modern overtures, voluntaries, or concertos which consist altogether of artificial sounds without any words at all? What have any of the passions to do with these? What has judgment, reason, common sense? Just nothing at all. All these are utterly excluded by delicate, unmeaning sound!

In this respect, the modern music has no connection with common sense, any more than with the passions. . . .

It is true, the modern music has been sometimes observed to have as powerful an effect as the ancient; so that frequently single persons and sometimes numerous assemblies have been seen in a flood of tears. But when was this? Generally, if not always, when a fine solo was sung; when "the sound has been an echo to the sense"; when the music has been extremely simple and inartificial, the composer having attended to melody, not harmony. Then, and then only, the natural power of music to move the passions has appeared. This music was calculated for that end and effectually answered it.

Upon this ground it is that so many persons are so much affected by the Scotch or Irish airs. They are composed, not according to art, but nature; they are simple in the highest degree. There is no harmony, according to the present sense of the word, therein; but there is much melody. And this is not only heard but felt by all those who retain their native taste, whose taste is not biased (I might say, corrupted) by attending to counterpoint and complicated music. It is this, it is counterpoint, it is harmony (so called) which destroys the power of music. And if ever this should be banished from our composition, if ever we should return to the simplicity and melody of the ancients, then the effects of our music will be as surprising as any that were wrought by theirs; yea, perhaps they will be as much greater as modern instruments are more excellent than those of the ancients. (*Thoughts on the Power of Music* [June 9, 1779], in Coll. C, 338-41)

NEW BIRTH

I met Peter Böhler once more. I had now no objection to what he said of the nature of faith, namely, that it is (to use the words of our [Anglican] Church) "a sure trust and confidence which a man hath in God, that through the merits of Christ his sins are forgiven, and he reconciled to the favor of God." Neither could I deny either the happiness or holiness which he described as fruits of this living faith. "The Spirit itself beareth witness with our spirit, that we are the children of God" and "He that believeth hath the witness in himself" fully convinced me of the former, as "Whatsoever is born of God doth not commit sin" and "Whosoever believeth is born of God" did of the latter. But I could not comprehend what he spoke of an *instantaneous work*. I could not understand how this faith should be given in a moment; how a man could *at once* be thus turned from darkness to light, from sin and misery to righteousness and joy in the Holy Ghost. I searched the Scriptures again, touching this very thing, particularly the Acts of the Apostles; but to my utter astonishment found scarce any instances there of other than *instantaneous* conversions; scarce any so slow as that of St. Paul, who was three days in the pangs of the new birth. (Journal entry [April 22, 1738], quoted in Coll. B, 211-12)

They speak of the new birth as an outward thing, as if it were no more than baptism or, at most, a change from outward wickedness to outward goodness, from a vicious to (what is called) a virtuous life. I believe it to be an inward thing: a change from inward wickedness to inward goodness; an entire change of our inmost nature from the image of the devil (wherein we are born) to the image of God; a change from the love of the creature to the love of the Creator; from earthly and sensual to heavenly and holy affections. (*Conditions of Justification* [1744], in Coll. B, 181)

Justification implies only a relative, the new birth a real change. God in justifying us does something for us in begetting us again; he does the work in us . . . The one restores us to the favor, the other to the image of God. The one is the taking away of the guilt, the other the taking away the power of sin: so that, although they are joined together in point of time, yet are they of wholly distinct natures. ("The Great Privilege of Those That Are Born of God" [1748], Sermon 19, in *Works* [T], 5:180)

"Verily, verily, I say unto you, ye" also "must be born again." "Except" ye also "be born again, ye cannot see the kingdom of God." Lean no more on the staff of that broken reed, that ye *were* born again in baptism. Who denies that ye were then made children of God and heirs of the kingdom of heaven? But, notwithstanding this, ye are now children of the devil. Therefore, ye must be born again. And let not Satan put it into your heart to cavil at a word when the thing is clear. Ye have heard what are the marks of the children of God: all ye who have them not in your souls, baptized or unbaptized, must needs receive them or without doubt ye will perish everlastingly. And if ye have been baptized, your only hope is this, that those who were made the children of God by baptism but are now the children of the devil may yet again receive "power to become the sons of God," that they may receive again what they have lost, even the "Spirit of adoption, crying in their hearts, Abba, Father!" ("The Marks of the New Birth" [1748], Sermon 18, in *Works* [T], 5:179)

The new birth is not the same with sanctification. This is indeed taken for granted by many, particularly by an eminent writer in his late treatise on "The nature and grounds of Christian regeneration." To wave several other weighty objections which might be made to that tract, this is a palpable one. It all along speaks of regeneration as a progressive work, carried on in the soul by slow degrees, from the time of our first turning to God. This is undeniably true of sanctification, but of regeneration, the new birth, it is not true. This is a part of sanctification, not the whole; it is the gate to it, the entrance into it. When we are born again, then our sanctification, our inward and outward holiness, begins; and thenceforward we are gradually to "grow up in him who is our head." This expression of the apostle admirably illustrates the difference between one and the other and farther points out the exact analogy there is between natural and spiritual things. A child is born of a woman in a moment, or at least in a very short time. Afterward he gradually and slowly grows till he attains to the stature of a man. In like manner, a child is born of God in a short time, if not in a moment, but it is by slow degrees that he afterward grows up to the measure of the full stature of Christ; the same relation, therefore, which there is between our natural birth and our growth, there is also between our new birth and our sanctification. (Quoted in "Of Regeneration," chap. 11 in Coll. D, 197-98)

And as soon as his pardon or justification is witnessed to him by the Holy Ghost, he is saved. He loves God and all mankind. He has "the mind that was in Christ" and power to "walk as he also walked." From that time (unless he make shipwreck of the faith) salvation gradually increases in his soul. . . .

. . . The first sowing of this seed I cannot conceive to be other than instantaneous . . .

This beginning of that vast, inward change is usually termed the new birth. Baptism is the outward sign of this inward grace, which is supposed by our [Anglican] Church to be given with and through that sign to all infants and to those of riper years, if they repent and believe the gospel. . . . I tell a sinner, "You must be born again." "No," say you, "he was born again in baptism. Therefore, he cannot be born again now." Alas, what trifling is this? What if he was *then* a child of God? He is *now* manifestly a child of the devil, for the works of his father he doeth. Therefore, do not play upon words. He must go through an entire change of heart. In one not yet baptized, you yourself would call that change the new birth. In him, call it what you will; but remember, meantime, that if either he or you die without it your baptism will be so far from profiting you that it will greatly increase your damnation. (*Conditions of Justification* [1744], in Coll. B, 179)

I am acquainted with more than twelve or thirteen hundred persons whom I believe to be *truly pious*, and not on slight grounds, and who have severally testified to me with their own mouths that they *do know* the day when the love of God was first shed abroad in their hearts, and when his Spirit first witnessed with their spirits that they were the children of God. Now, if you are determined to think all these liars or fools, this is no evidence to you; but to me it is strong evidence, who have for some years known the men and their communication. (Letter to John Smith [probably one of the archbishops of Canterbury, Thomas Herring or Thomas Secker] [September 28, 1745], in *Works* [WL], 12:60)

From many such passages as these [from early Christian writers], which I have occasionally read, as well as from what I have myself seen and known, I am induced to believe that God's ordinary way of converting sinners to himself is by "suddenly inspiring them with an immediate testimony of his love, easily distinguishable from fancy." I am assured thus he hath wrought in all I have known (except, perhaps, three or four persons), of whom I have reasonable ground to believe that they are really turned from the power of Satan to God. (Letter to John Smith [probably one of the archbishops of Canterbury, Thomas Herring or Thomas Secker] [December 30, 1745], in *Works* [WL], 12:67)

Concerning the instantaneous and the gradual work, what I still affirm is this: that I know hundreds of persons whose hearts were one moment filled with fear and sorrow and pain, and the next with peace and joy in believing, yea, joy unspeakable, full of glory; that the same moment they experienced such a love of God and so fervent a goodwill to all mankind (attended with power over all sin) as till then they were wholly unacquainted with; that nevertheless the peace and love thus sown in their hearts received afterward a gradual increase; and that to this subsequent increase the Scriptures do manifestly refer. (*The Immediate Testimony* [December 30, 1745], in Coll. B, 198)

NEW BIRTH AND SANCTIFICATION

Concerning the instantaneous and the gradual work, what I still affirm is this: that I know hundreds of persons whose hearts were one moment filled with fear and sorrow and pain and the next with peace and joy in believing, yea, joy unspeakable, full of glory; that the same moment they experienced such a love of God and so fervent a goodwill to all mankind (attended with power over all sin), as till then they were wholly unacquainted with; that nevertheless the peace and love thus sown in their hearts received afterward a gradual increase; and that to this subsequent increase the Scriptures you mention do manifestly refer. (Letter to John Smith [probably one of the archbishops of Canterbury, Thomas Herring or Thomas Secker] [December 30, 1745], in *Works* [WL], 12:68)

It is true, a late very eminent author, in his strange "Treatise on Regeneration," proceeds entirely on the supposition that it is the whole gradual progress of sanctification. No; it is only the threshold of sanctification, the first entrance upon it. And as in the natural birth a man is born at once and then grows larger and stronger by degrees; so in the spiritual birth a man is born at once and then gradually increases in spiritual stature and strength. The new birth, therefore, is the first point of sanctification, which may increase more and more unto the perfect day. ("On God's Vineyard" [October 17, 1787], Sermon 107, in *Works* [WL], 7:205)

The Holy Ghost confers on us the graces necessary for, and our souls receive the seeds of, an immortal nature. Now surely these graces are not of so little force as that we cannot perceive whether we have them or not; if we dwell in Christ, and Christ in us, which he will not do unless we are regenerate, certainly we must be sensible of it. If we can never have any certainty of our being in a state of salvation, good reason it is that every moment should be spent, not in joy, but in fear and trembling; and then undoubtedly in this life we are of all men most miserable. God deliver us from such a fearful expectation as this! Humility is undoubtedly necessary to salvation; and if all these things are essential to humility, who can be humble, who can be saved? (Letter to his mother [June 18, 1725], in *Letters*, 41-42)

That we can never be so certain of the pardon of our sins, as to be assured they will never rise up against us, I firmly believe. We know that they will infallibly do so if ever we apostatize; and I am not satisfied what evidence there can be of our final perseverance, till we have finished our course. But I am persuaded we may know if we are now in a state of salvation, since that is expressly promised in the holy Scriptures to our sincere endeavors; and we are surely able to judge of our own sincerity. (Letter to his mother [July 29, 1725], *Letters* [JT], 1:22)

N

That "circumcision is that of the heart, in the spirit and not in the letter"; that the distinguishing mark of a true follower of Christ, of one who is in a state of acceptance with God, is not either outward circumcision or baptism or any other outward form, but a right state of soul, a mind and spirit renewed after the image of him that created it, is one of those important truths that can only be *spiritually discerned.* . . .

. . . "All things are possible to him that (thus) believeth": "the eyes of his understanding being enlightened," he *sees* what is his calling, even to *glorify God*, who hath *bought him with* so high *a price*, in his body and in his spirit, which now are God's by redemption as well as creation. He feels what is "the exceeding greatness of his power," who, as he raised up Christ from the dead, so is able to quicken us, *dead in sin*, "by his Spirit which dwelleth in us." "This is the victory which overcometh the world, even our faith": that faith which is not only an unshaken assent to all that God hath revealed in Scripture, and in particular to those important truths: "Jesus Christ came into the world to save sinners"; "He bare our sins in his own body on the tree"; "He is the propitiation for our sins; and not for ours only, but also for the sins of the whole world"; but likewise the revelation of Christ in our hearts; a divine evidence or conviction of his love, his free, unmerited love to me a sinner; a sure confidence in his pardoning mercy wrought in us by the Holy Ghost: a confidence whereby every true believer is enabled to bear witness, "I know that my Redeemer liveth"; "that I have an Advocate with the Father; that Jesus Christ the righteous is my Lord and the propitiation for my sins." I know he *hath loved* me *and given himself for* me. He *hath reconciled* me, *even* me *to God,* and I "have redemption through his blood, even the forgiveness of sins."

. . . Such a faith as this cannot fail to show evidently the power of him that inspires it, by delivering his children from the yoke of sin and "purging their consciences from dead works"; by strengthening them so that they are no longer constrained to "obey sin in the desires thereof"; but instead of "yielding their members unto it, as instruments of unrighteousness," they now *yield* themselves entirely "unto God, as those that are alive from the dead."

. . . Those who are thus by faith "born of God" have also "strong consolation through hope." This is the next thing which the *circumcision of the heart* implies: even the testimony of their own spirit, with the Spirit which witnesses in their hearts that they are the children of God. Indeed it is the same Spirit who works in them that clear and cheerful confidence that their heart is upright toward God; that good assurance that they now do, through his grace, the things which are acceptable in his sight; that they are now in the path which leadeth to life and shall, by the mercy of God, endure therein to the end. It is he who giveth them a lively expectation of receiving all good things at God's hand, a joyous prospect of that "crown of glory, which is reserved in heaven" for them. ("The Circumcision of the Heart" [January 1, 1733], Sermon 17, in *Works* [T], 5:163, 165-66)

It is now two years and almost four months since I left my native country in order to teach the Georgian Indians the nature of Christianity. But what have I learned myself in the meantime? Why (what I the least of all suspected), that I who went to America to convert others was never myself converted to God. (*Journal,* January 29, 1738. Note: in his *Second Letter to the Author of* The Enthusiasm of Methodists and Papists Compared, dated November 27, 1750, Wesley clarified a similar remark: "The first was written . . . in the anguish of my heart, to which I gave vent (between God and my own soul) by breaking out, not into 'confidence of boasting,' as you term it, but into those expressions of bitter sorrow. 'I went to America to convert the Indians. But [oh], who shall convert me?' Some of the words which follow, you have picked out, and very honestly laid before your reader, without either the beginning or end, or one word of the occasion or manner wherein they were spoken" [*Works,* 13:25].)

"Having the sentence of death" in my heart and having nothing in or of myself to plead, I have no hope but that of being justified freely "through the redemption that is in Jesus." I have no hope but that if I seek I shall find Christ and "be found in him, not having my own righteousness, [. . .] but that which is through the faith of Christ, the righteousness which is of God by faith" [Phil. 3:9].

If it be said that I have faith (for many such things have I heard, from many miserable comforters), I answer, so have the devils—a sort of faith; but still they are strangers to the covenant of promise. So the apostles had even at Cana in Galilee, when Jesus first "manifested forth his glory"; even then they, in a sort, "believed on him"; but they had not then "the faith that overcometh the world." The faith I want is (the faith of a son), "A sure trust and confidence in God, that, through the merits of Christ, my sins are forgiven, and I reconciled to the favour of God." I want that faith which St. Paul recommends to all the world, especially in his Epistle to the Romans: that faith which enables everyone that hath it to cry out, "I live not; but Christ liveth in me; and the life which I now live, I live by faith in the Son of God, who loved me, and gave himself for me." I want that faith which none can have without knowing that he hath it (though many imagine they have it, who have it not); for whosoever hath it is "freed from sin," the whole "body of sin is destroyed" in him; he is freed from fear, "having peace with God through Christ, and rejoicing in hope of the glory of God." And he is freed from doubt, "having the love of God shed abroad in his heart, through the Holy Ghost which is given unto him"; which "Spirit itself beareth witness with his spirit, that he is a child of God." (*Journal*, February 1, 1738)

I think it was about five this morning that I opened my Testament on those words, . . . "There are given unto us exceeding great and precious promises, even that ye should be partakers of the divine nature" [2 Pet. 1:4]. Just as I went out, I opened it again on those words, "Thou art not far from the kingdom of God." In the afternoon I was asked to go to St. Paul's. The anthem was, "Out of the deep have I called unto thee, O Lord: Lord, hear my voice. O let thine ears consider well the voice of my complaint. If thou, Lord, wilt be extreme to mark what is done amiss, O Lord, who may abide it? For there is mercy with thee; therefore shalt thou be feared. O Israel, trust in the Lord: for with the Lord there is mercy, and with him is plenteous redemption. And he shall redeem Israel from all his sins."

In the evening I went very unwillingly to a society in Aldersgate Street, where one was reading Luther's preface to the Epistle to the Romans. About a quarter before nine, while he was describing the change which God works in the heart through faith in Christ, I felt my heart strangely warmed. I felt I did trust in Christ, Christ alone for salvation, and an assurance was given me that he had taken away *my* sins, even *mine*, and saved *me* from the law of sin and death.

. . . I began to pray with all my might for those who had in a more especial manner despitefully used me and persecuted me. I then testified openly to all there what I now first felt in my heart. But it was not long before the enemy suggested, "This cannot be faith; for where is thy joy?" Then was I taught that peace and victory over sin are essential to faith in the Captain of our salvation; but that, as to the transports of joy that usually attend the beginning of it, especially in those who have mourned deeply, God sometimes giveth, sometimes withholdeth them, according to the counsels of his own will.

. . . After my return home I was much buffeted with temptations; but cried out, and they fled away. They returned again and again. I as often lifted up my eyes, and he "sent me help from his holy place." And herein I found the difference between this and my former state chiefly consisted. I was striving, yea, fighting with all my might, under the law as well as under grace. But then I was sometimes, if not often, conquered; now, I was always conqueror. (Journal entry [May 24, 1738], quoted in Coll. B, 219)

Now although, by the grace of God in Christ, I find a measure of some of these in myself, [namely], of peace, long-suffering, gentleness, meekness, temperance; yet others I find not. I cannot find in myself the love of God or of Christ. Hence my deadness and wanderings in public prayer; hence it is that even in the Holy Communion I have frequently no more than a cold attention.

Again, I have not that joy in the Holy Ghost—no settled, lasting joy. Nor have I such a peace as excludes the possibility either of fear or doubt. When holy men have told me I had no faith, I have often doubted whether I had or no. And those doubts have made me very uneasy, till I was relieved by prayer and the Holy Scriptures.

Yet, upon the whole, although I have not yet that joy in the Holy Ghost, nor the full assurance of faith, much less am I, in the full sense of the words, "in Christ a new creature." I nevertheless trust that I have a measure of faith and am "accepted in the Beloved." I trust "the hand-writing that was against me is blotted out" and that I am "reconciled to God" through his Son. (*Journal*, October 14, 1738)

By a Christian I mean one who so believes in Christ as that sin hath no more dominion over him; and in this obvious sense of the word I was not a Christian until May the 24th last past. For till then sin had the dominion over me, although I fought with it continually; but surely, then, from that time to this it hath not—such is the free grace of God in Christ. What sins they were which till then reigned over me and from which, by the grace of God, I am now free, I am ready to declare on the housetop, if it may be for the glory of God.

If you ask by what means I am made free (though not perfect, neither infallibly sure of my perseverance), I answer, By faith in Christ; by such a sort or degree of faith as I had not till that day. (Letter to his brother, Samuel Wesley [October 30, 1738], in *Letters*, 62)

1. I judge thus of myself, but I feel it not; therefore there is in me still the old heart of stone.

2. I judge thus of happiness, but I still hanker after creature happiness. My soul is almost continually running out after one creature or another and imagining how happy should I be in such or such a condition. I have more pleasure in eating and drinking and in the company of those I love than I have in God. I have a relish for earthly happiness. I have not a relish for heavenly. "I savour . . . the things of men, not the things of God." Therefore there is in me still the carnal heart . . .

But the eyes of my understanding are not yet fully opened.

. . . "This is the design of my life." But a thousand little designs are daily stealing into my soul. This is my ultimate design, but intermediate designs are continually creeping in upon me—designs (though often disguised) of pleasing myself, of doing my own will; designs wherein I do not eye God, at least not him singly.

Therefore my eye is not yet single, at least not always so.

. . . Are my desires new? Not all. Some are new, some old. My desires are like my designs. My great desire is to have "Christ formed in my heart by faith." But little desires are daily stealing into my soul. And so my great hopes and fears have respect to God. But a thousand little ones creep in between them.

Again, my desires, passions, and inclinations in general are mixed, having something of Christ and something of earth. I love you, for instance. But my love is only partly spiritual and partly natural. Something of my own cleaves to that which is of God. Nor can I divide the earthly part from the heavenly. (*Journal*, December 16, 1738)

My friends affirm I am mad because I said I was not a Christian a year ago. I affirm I am not a Christian now. Indeed, what I might have been I know not, had I been faithful to the grace then given, when expecting nothing less, I received such a sense of the forgiveness of my sins as till then I never knew. But that I am not a Christian at this day, I as assuredly know as that Jesus is the Christ.

For a Christian is one who has the fruits of the Spirit of Christ, which (to mention no more) are love, peace, joy. But these I have not. I have not any love of God. I do not love either the Father or the Son. Do you ask, How do I know whether I love God? I answer by another question, How do you know whether you love me? Why, as you know, whether you are hot or cold. You *feel* this moment that you do or do not love me. And I *feel* this moment I do not love God; which therefore I *know* because I *feel* it. There is no word more proper, more clear, or more strong.

And I know it also by St. John's plain rule, "If any man love the world, the love of the Father is not in him." For I love the world. I desire the things of the world, some or other of them, and have done all my life. I have always placed some part of my happiness in some or other of the things that are seen, particularly in meat and drink and in the company of those I loved. For many years I have been, yea, and still am, hankering after a happiness, in loving and being loved by one or another. And in these I have from time to time taken more pleasure than in God.

Again, joy in the Holy Ghost I have not. I have now and then some starts of joy in God; but it is not that joy, for it is not abiding. Neither is it greater than I have had on some worldly occasions. So that I can in no wise be said to "rejoice evermore"; much less to "rejoice with joy unspeakable and full of glory."

Yet again; I have not "the peace of God"—*that* peace, peculiarly so called. The peace I have may be accounted for on natural principles. I have health, strength, friends, a competent fortune, and a composed, cheerful temper. Who would not have a sort of peace in such circumstances? But I have none which can with any propriety be called a "peace which passeth all understanding."

From hence I conclude (and let all the *saints of the world* hear, that whereinsoever they boast, they may be found even as I), though I have given and do give all my goods to feed the poor, I am not a Christian. Though I have endured hardship, though I have in all things denied myself and taken up my cross, I am not a Christian. My works are nothing, my sufferings are nothing; I have not the fruits of the Spirit of Christ. Though I have constantly used all the means of grace for twenty years, I am not a Christian. (*Journal,* January 4, 1739. Note: Wesley explained the context of "despairing" remarks such as these in his *Second Letter to the Author of* The Enthusiasm of Methodists and Papists Compared, from November 27, 1750, citing his own *Journal:* "That some time after, I 'was strongly assaulted again, and after recovering peace and joy, was thrown into perplexity afresh by a letter, asserting, that no doubt or fear could consist with true faith: that my weak mind could not then bear to be thus *sawn asunder';* will not appear strange to any who are not utter novices in experimental religion. No more than that one night the next year, 'I had no life or spirit in me and was much in doubt whether God would not lay me aside and send other laborers into his harvest'" [*Works,* 13:32].)

You say you cannot reconcile some parts of my behavior with the character I have long supported. No, nor ever will. Therefore I have disclaimed that character on every possible occasion. I told all in our ship, all at Savannah, all at Frederica, and that over and over, in express terms, "I am not a Christian; I only follow after, if haply I may attain it." When they urged my works and self-denial, I answered short, "Though I give all my goods to feed the poor, and my body to be burned, I am nothing: for I have not charity; I do not love God with all my heart." If they added, "Nay, but you could not preach as you do, if you [were] not a Christian," I again confronted them with St. Paul: "Though I speak with the tongue of men and angels, and have not charity, I am nothing." (Letter to James Hervey, in *Journal*, June 11, 1739)

I am one who for twenty years used outward works not only as "acts of goodness" but as commutations (though I did not indeed profess this), instead of inward holiness. I knew I was not holy. But I quieted my conscience by doing such and such outward works; and therefore I hoped I should go to heaven, even without inward holiness. . . .

. . . It would doubtless be wrong to insist thus on these things if they were "not necessary to final salvation." But we believe they are; unless in the case of invincible ignorance. In this case, undoubtedly many thousands are saved who never heard of these doctrines; and I am inclined to think this was our own case, both at Oxford and for some time after. (Letter to John Smith [probably one of the archbishops of Canterbury, Thomas Herring or Thomas Secker] [December 30, 1745], in *Works* [WL], 12:65, 70)

"I know everyone *under the Law* is even as I was," namely, from the time I was twelve years old till considerably above thirty. (*A Second Letter to the Author of* The Enthusiasm of Methodists and Papists Compared [November 27, 1750], in *Works*, 13:32)

The second passage (written January 24, 1737-8) is this, "In a storm I think, What if the gospel be not true? Then thou art of all men most foolish. For what hast thou given thy goods, thy ease, thy friends, thy reputation, thy country, thy life? For what art thou wandering over the face of the earth? A dream? A cunningly devised fable?"

I am here describing the thoughts which passed through my mind when I was confessedly an unbeliever. . . .

. . . You recite more at large one passage more. The whole paragraph stands thus.

"St. Paul tells us, 'The fruit of the Spirit is love, joy, peace, long-suffering, gentleness, meekness, temperance.' . . . Now, although, by the grace of God in Christ, I find a measure of some of these in myself, [namely], of peace, long-suffering, gentleness, meekness, temperance; yet others I find not. I cannot find in myself the love of God or of Christ. Hence my deadness and wanderings in public prayer. Hence it is that even in the Holy Communion I have rarely any more than a cold attention. Hence, when I hear of the highest instance of God's love, my heart is still senseless and unaffected. Yea, at this moment (October 14, 1738), I feel no more love to him than one I had never heard of."

To any who knew something of inward religion I should have observed that this is what serious divines mean by *desertion*. But all expressions of this kind are jargon to you. So, allowing it to be whatever you please, I ask only, Do you know how long I continued in this state? How many years, months, weeks, or days? If not, how can you infer what my state of mind is now, from what it was above eleven years ago?

Sir, I do not tell you or any man else, that "I cannot *now* find the love of God in myself" or that *now*, in the year 1751, I rarely feel more than a cold attention in the Holy Communion. So that your whole argument, built on this supposition, falls to the ground at once. (*A Second Letter to the Author of* The Enthusiasm of Methodists and Papists Compared [November 27, 1750], in *Works*, 13:39-41)

But how came this opinion [perfection] into my mind? I will tell you with all simplicity. In 1725 I met with Bishop Taylor's *Rules of Holy Living and Dying*. I was struck particularly with the chapter upon Intention and felt a fixed intention to give myself up to God. In this I was much confirmed soon after by the Christian Pattern and longed to give God all my heart. This is just what I mean by Perfection now: I sought after it from that hour.

In 1727 I read Mr. Law's *Christian Perfection* and *Serious Call* and more explicitly resolved to be all devoted to God in body, soul, and spirit. In 1730 I began to be *homo unius libri* ["A man of one book"]; to study (comparatively) no book but the Bible. I then saw in a stronger light than ever before that only one thing is needful, even faith that worketh by the love of God and man, all inward and outward holiness; and I groaned to love God with all my heart and to serve him with all my strength.

January 1, 1733, I preached the sermon on the Circumcision of the Heart, which contains all that I now teach concerning salvation from all sin and loving God with an undivided heart. In the same year I printed (the first time I ventured to print anything) for the use of my pupils *A Collection of Forms of Prayer*; and in this I spoke explicitly of giving "the whole heart and the whole life to God." This was then, as it is now, my idea of Perfection, though I should have started at the word.

In 1735 I preached my farewell sermon at Epworth, in Lincolnshire. In this likewise I spoke with the utmost clearness of having one design, one desire, one love, and of pursuing the one end of our life in all our words and actions. (Letter to John Newton, in *Journal*, May 14, 1765)

In the year 1726, I met with Kempis's *Christian's Pattern*. The nature and extent of inward religion, the religion of the heart, now appeared to me in a stronger light than ever it had done before. I saw that giving even *all my life* to God (supposing it possible to do this, and go no farther) would profit me nothing, unless I gave my heart, yea, *all my heart*, to him.

I saw, that "simplicity of intention, and purity of affection," *one design* in all we speak or do, and *one desire* ruling all our tempers, are indeed "the wings of the soul" without which she can never ascend to the mount of God.

. . . A year or two after, Mr. Law's *Christian Perfection* and *Serious Call* were put into my hands. These convinced me, more than ever, of the absolute impossibility of being *half a Christian*; and I determined, through his grace (the absolute necessity of which I was deeply sensible of), to be *all-devoted* to God, to give him *all* my soul, my body, and my substance.

Will any considerate man say that this is carrying matters too far? or that anything less is due to him who has given himself for us than to give him ourselves—all we have and all we are? (*A Plain Account of Christian Perfection* [1767; rev. 1777], in *Works* [WL], 11:366-67)

The truth is, from the year 1725, I saw more and more of the nature of inward religion, chiefly by reading the writings of Mr. Law and a few other *mystic* writers. Yet I never was "in the way of *mysticism*" at all; this is another mistake. Although I did not clearly see that we *are saved by faith* till the year 1738, I then published the sermon on "Salvation by Faith," every sentence of which I subscribe to now. (*Some Remarks on Mr. Hill's Review of All the Doctrines Taught by Mr. John Wesley* [September 9, 1772], in *Works* [T], 9:498)

Let me be again an Oxford Methodist! I am often in doubt whether it would not be best for me to resume all my Oxford rules, great and small. I did then walk closely with God and redeem the time. But what have I been doing these thirty years? (Letter to Charles Wesley [December 15, 1772], in Coll. C, 353)

NUDITY (IN ART)

Of pictures I do not pretend to be a judge, but there is one by Paul Rubens which particularly struck me, both with the design and the execution of it. It is Zacharias and Elisabeth with John the Baptist, two or three years old, coming to visit Mary, and our Lord sitting upon her knee. The passions are surprisingly expressed, even in the children, but I could not see either the decency or common sense of painting them stark naked. Nothing can defend or excuse this; it is shockingly absurd. . . . I allow, a man who paints thus may have a good hand but certainly *cerebrum non habet* [no brains]. (*Journal*, February 7, 1772)

ORDINATION (HOLY ORDERS); PRIESTHOOD

When asked . . . by what authority I did these things, I replied, "By the authority of Jesus Christ, conveyed to me by the archbishop of Canterbury when he laid his hands upon me." (Quoted in "Of Holy Orders," chap. 8 in Coll. A, 54)

But does not the Scripture say, "No man taketh this honour to himself, but he that is called of God, as was Aaron"? Nor do these. The *honor* here mentioned is the priesthood. But they no more take upon them to be priests than to be kings [anticipating the plea sometimes urged from Rev. 1:6]. They take not upon them to administer the sacraments, an honor *peculiar* to the *priests of God.* Only according to their power they exhort their brethren to continue in the grace of God. (*A Farther Appeal to Men of Reason and Religion* [1745], pt. 3, in *Works,* 12:253)

Before those words which you suppose limit the exercise of the *sacerdotal* powers to that congregation whereunto each *priest* shall be appointed—were those spoken without any restraint or limitation at all, which I apprehend to convey an *indelible* character, "Receive the Holy Ghost, for the office and work of a priest in the Church of God, now committed unto thee, by the imposition of our hands." (Quoted in "Of Holy Orders," chap. 8 in Coll. A, 53)

We believe there is, and always was, in every Christian church (whether dependent on the bishop of Rome or not) an *outward priesthood* ordained by Jesus Christ. (Quoted in "Of the Holy Communion," chap. 5 in Coll. A, 17)

Ministers . . . [should be] authorized to exercise that office by those who are empowered to convey that authority. (I believe bishops are empowered to do this and have been so from the apostolic age.) (*A Letter to a Clergyman* [May 4, 1748], in Coll. C, 250-51)

The bishop said, when you were ordained, "Receive thou the Holy Ghost." But that was the least of your care. Let who will receive this, so you receive the money, the revenue of a good benefice. While you minister the Word and sacraments before God, he gives the Holy Ghost to those who duly receive them: so that *through your hands* likewise *the Holy Ghost is* in this sense *given.* (Quoted in "Of Holy Orders," chap. 8 in Coll. A, 53-54)

Whoever [lay preacher or non-ordained Methodist] among us undertakes to baptize a child is *ipso facto* excluded from our connection. (Letter to Joseph Thompson [July 18, 1772], in *Letters,* 229)

It is not worth disputing whether ordination should be called a sacrament or not. Let the word then pass. (*Popery Calmly Considered* [1779], in *Works,* 15:192)

ORIGINAL SIN

Man did disobey God. He "ate of the tree, of which God commanded him, saying, Thou shalt not eat of it." And in that day he was condemned by the righteous judgment of God. Then also the sentence, whereof he was warned before, began to take place upon him. For the moment he tasted that fruit he died. His soul died, was separated from God; separate from whom the soul has no more life than the body has when separate from the soul. His body, likewise, became corruptible and mortal, so that death then took hold on this also. And being already dead in spirit, dead to God, dead in sin, he hastened on to death everlasting—to the destruction both of body and soul in the fire never to be quenched.

Thus "by one man sin entered into the world, and death by sin. And so death passed upon all men," as being contained in him who was the common father and representative of us all. Thus, "through the offence of one" all are dead—dead to God, dead in sin, dwelling in a corruptible, mortal body—shortly to be dissolved and under the sentence of death eternal. For as "by one man's disobedience" all "were made sinners," so by that offense of one "judgment came upon all men to condemnation" [Rom. 5:12, etc.].
(Quoted in "Of Man," chap. 7 in Coll. D, 119)

Perhaps you will say, "They are not condemned for actual, but for original sin." What do you mean by this term? The inward corruption of our nature? If so, it has been spoken of before. Or do you mean the sin which Adam committed in paradise? That this is imputed to all men, I allow; yea, that by reason hereof "the whole creation groaneth and travaileth in pain together until now." But that any will be damned for this alone, I allow not, till you show me where it is written. Bring me plain proof from the Scripture, and I submit. But till then I utterly deny it. (*Predestination Calmly Considered* [1752], in *Works* [T], 9:391)

That we are all born under the guilt of Adam's sin, and that all sin deserves eternal misery, was the unanimous sense of the ancient church, as it is expressed in the ninth article of our own. And the Scripture plainly asserts that we were "shapen in iniquity, and in sin did our mother conceive us," that "we were all by nature children of wrath, and dead in trespasses and sins," that "in Adam all die," that "by one man's disobedience all were made sinners," that "by one man sin entered into the world, and death by sin; which came upon all men, because all had sinned." This plainly includes infants, for they too die; therefore they have sinned, but not by actual sin; therefore by original, else what need have they of the death of Christ? Yea, "death reigned from Adam to Moses, even over those who had not sinned" actually "according to the similitude of Adam's transgression." This, which can relate to infants only, is a clear proof that the whole race of mankind are obnoxious both to the guilt and punishment of Adam's transgression. (*A Treatise on Baptism* [November 11, 1756], in Coll. B, 225-26)

The true and rational way of accounting for the general wickedness of mankind, in all ages and nations, is pointed out in these words. In Adam *all die*. In and through their first parent, all his posterity died in a spiritual sense: and they remain wholly "dead in trespasses and sins" till the Second Adam makes them alive. By this "one man's sin entered into the world and passed upon all men." And through the infection which they derive from him, all men are and ever were *by nature entirely* "alienated from the life of God, without hope, without God in the world." (*The Doctrine of Original Sin: According to Scripture, Reason, and Experience* [1757], in *Works* [T], 9:216)

ORTHODOXY (CORRECT BELIEFS)

For neither does religion consist in *orthodoxy* or *right opinions* which, although they are properly outward things, are not in the heart but the understanding. A man may be orthodox in every point; he may not only espouse right opinions but zealously defend them against all opposers; he may think justly concerning the incarnation of our Lord, concerning the ever blessed Trinity, and every other doctrine contained in the oracles of God; he may assent to all the three creeds—that called the Apostles', the *Nicene,* and the *Athanasian*—and yet it is possible he may have no religion at all . . . He may be almost as orthodox as the devil (though, indeed, not altogether—for every man errs in something, whereas we cannot well conceive him to hold any erroneous opinion) and may, all the while, be as great a stranger as he to the religion of the heart. ("The Way to the Kingdom" [June 6, 1742], Sermon 7, in *Works* [T], 5:65-66)

But we do not lay the main stress of our religion on any opinions, right or wrong; neither do we ever begin or willingly join in any dispute concerning them. The weight of all religion, we apprehend, rests on holiness of heart and life. And consequently, wherever we come, we press this with all our might. . . .

. . . I will not quarrel with you about any opinion. Only see that your heart be right toward God, that you know and love the Lord Jesus Christ, that you love your neighbor and walk as your Master walked, and I desire no more. I am sick of opinions; I am weary to bear them. My soul loathes this frothy food. Give me solid and substantial religion. Give me a humble, gentle lover of God and man—a man full of mercy and good fruits, without partiality, and without hypocrisy; a man laying himself out in the work of faith, the patience of hope, the labor of love. Let my soul be with these Christians, wheresoever they are, and whatsoever opinion they are of. "Whosoever" thus "doth the will of my Father which is in heaven, the same is my brother, and sister, and mother." . . .

It is a poor excuse to say, "[Oh], but the people are brought into several erroneous opinions." It matters not a straw whether they are or not (I speak of such opinions as do not touch the foundation); it is scarcely worthwhile to spend ten words about it. Whether they embrace this religious opinion or that is no more concern to me than whether they embrace this or that system of astronomy. Are they brought to holy tempers and holy lives? This is mine and should be your inquiry, since on this both social and personal happiness depend—happiness, temporal and eternal. Are they brought to the love of God and the love of their neighbor? Pure religion and undefiled is this, how long then will you darken counsel by words without knowledge? (*A Farther Appeal to Men of Reason and Religion* [1745], pt. 3, in *Works,* 12:275-76, 278)

One who lives and dies in error or in dissent from our [Anglican] Church may yet be saved, but one who lives and dies in sin must perish. . . . I would to God we could all agree both in opinions and outward worship. But if this cannot be, may we not agree in holiness? (Letter to the Rev. Mr. Clarke [July 3, 1756], in *Works,* 16:27)

I have written severally and printed against deists, Papists, mystics, Quakers, Anabaptists, Presbyterians, Calvinists, and antinomians. An odd way of ingratiating myself with them, to strike at the apple of their eye! Nevertheless, in all things indifferent (but not at the expense of truth) I rejoice to "please all men for their good to edification"; if haply I may "gain more proselytes" to genuine, scriptural Christianity, if I may prevail upon the more to love God and their neighbor and to walk as Christ walked.

So far as I find them obstructive of this, I oppose wrong opinions with my might; though even then, rather by guarding those who are yet free than by disputing with those who are deeply infected. I need not dispute with many of these to know there is no probability of convincing them. (Second letter to the Rev. Mr. Clarke [September 10, 1756], in *Works* [S], 7:286-87)

My design in publishing the following tracts is not to reclaim but to preserve, not to convince those who are already perverted but to prevent the perversion of others. I do not therefore enter deep into the controversy even with deists, Socinians, Arians, or Papists, much less with those who are not so dangerously mistaken—mystics, Quakers, Anabaptists, Presbyterians, predestinarians, or antinomians. I only recite, under each head, a few plain arguments which, by the grace of God, may farther confirm those who already know "the truth as it is in Jesus." (Preface to *A Preservative against Unsettled Notions in Religion* [1758], in *Works* [S], 7:537)

You have admirably well expressed what I mean by an opinion, contradistinguished from an essential doctrine. Whatever is "compatible with love to Christ, and a work of grace," I term an *opinion*. And certainly the holding particular election and final perseverance is compatible with these. (Letter to John Newton, in *Journal*, May 14, 1765)

Though *right tempers* cannot subsist without *right opinion*, yet *right opinion* may subsist without *right tempers*. There may be a right opinion of God, without either love or one right temper toward him. Satan is a proof of it. (*Some Remarks on a Defence of the Preface to the Edinburgh Edition of* Aspasio Vindicated [May 1766], in *Works*, 13:114)

There are ten thousand mistakes which may consist with real religion with regard to which every candid, considerate man will think and let think. But there are some truths more important than others. It seems there are some which are of deep importance. I do not term them *fundamental* truths, because that is an ambiguous word and hence there have been so many warm disputes about the number of *fundamentals*. But surely there are some, which it nearly concerns us to know, as having a close connection with vital religion. ("On the Trinity" [May 8, 1775], Sermon 59, in *Works* [T], 6:209)

One circumstance more is quite peculiar to the people called Methodists; that is, the terms upon which any person may be admitted into their society. They do not impose, in order to their admission, any opinions whatever. Let them hold particular or general redemption, absolute or conditional decrees; let them be churchmen or dissenters, Presbyterians or Independents, it is no obstacle. Let them choose one mode of baptism or another, it is no bar to their admission. The Presbyterian may be a Presbyterian still; the Independent or Anabaptist use his own mode of worship. So may the Quaker; and none will contend with him about it. They think and let think. One condition and one only is required—a real desire to save their soul. Where this is, it is enough. They desire no more; they lay stress upon nothing else. They ask only, "Is thy heart herein as my heart? If it be, give me thy hand."

Is there any other society in Great Britain or Ireland that is so remote from bigotry? that is so truly of a catholic spirit? so ready to admit all serious persons without distinction? ("Thoughts upon a Late Phenomenon" [July 13, 1788], in *Works* [S], 7:321)

O

PEACE OF GOD

What peace? *The peace of* God which God only can give and the world cannot take away; the peace which "passeth all understanding," all (barely) rational conception; being a supernatural sensation, a divine taste of "the powers of the world to come" such as the natural man knoweth not, how wise soever in the things of this world; nor, indeed, can he know it in his present state "because it is spiritually discerned." It is a peace that banishes all doubt, all painful uncertainty; the Spirit of God bearing witness with the spirit of a Christian that he is *a child of God.* And it banishes fear, all such fear as hath torment—the fear of the wrath of God, the fear of hell, the fear of the devil, and in particular, the fear of death—he that hath the peace of God, desiring, if it were the will of God, "to depart, and to be with God." ("The Way to the Kingdom" [June 6, 1742], Sermon 7, in *Works* [T], 5:67)

PEER PRESSURE

I received your letter and rejoiced to find that you are still determined to save yourself, by the grace of God, from this perverse generation. But this cannot possibly be done at Cambridge (I speak from long experience) unless you can make and keep one resolution—to have no acquaintance but such as fear God. I know it may be some time before you will find any that truly bear this character. If so, it is best to be alone till you do and to converse only with your absent friends by letter. But if you are carried away with the stream into frequent conversation with harmless, good-natured, honest triflers, they will soon steal away all your strength and stifle all the grace of God in your soul. (Letter to the Rev. Samuel Furley [March 30, 1754], in *Letters*, 422-23)

You are now, as it were, in the crisis of your fate—just launching into life and ready to fix your choice, whether you will have God or the world for your happiness. Scripture and reason tell you now what experience will confirm, if it pleases God to prolong your life, that he "made your heart for himself; and it cannot rest till it rests in him." You will be in danger of being diverted from this thought by the fashion of the world. The example of those that are round about us is apt to get within our guard. And indeed their spirit steals upon us in an unaccountable manner and inclines us to think as they think. (Letter to Charles Wesley Jr. [September 8, 1781], in *Letters*, 442)

PELAGIANISM; WORKS SALVATION (FALSITY OF)

Abundance of people I have likewise known, and many I do know at this day, who "are so grossly superstitious as to think devotion may be put upon God instead of honesty"; as to fancy, going to church and sacrament will bring them to heaven, though they practice neither justice nor mercy. (Letter to John Smith [probably one of the archbishops of Canterbury, Thomas Herring or Thomas Secker] [December 30, 1745], in *Works* [WL], 12:65)

I believe firmly, and that in the most literal sense, that "without God we can do nothing," that we cannot think or speak or move a hand or an eye without the concurrence of the divine energy, and that all our natural faculties are God's gift, nor can the meanest be exerted without the assistance of his Spirit. What then do I mean by saying that faith, hope, and love are not the effect of any, or all, our natural faculties? I mean this: that supposing a man to be now void of faith and hope and love, he cannot effect any degree of them in himself by any possible exertion of his understanding and of any or all his other natural faculties, though he should enjoy them in the utmost perfection. A distinct power from God, not implied in any of these, is indispensably necessary before it is possible he should arrive at the very lowest degree of Christian faith or hope or love. In order to his having any of these (which, on this very consideration, I suppose St. Paul terms the "fruits of the Spirit") he must be created anew, thoroughly and inwardly changed by the operation of the Spirit of God, by a power equivalent to that which raises the dead and which calls the things which are not as though they were. (Letter to John Smith [probably one of the archbishops of Canterbury, Thomas Herring or Thomas Secker] [June 25, 1746], in *Works* [WL], 12:73-74)

Whereas the doctrinal points in the minutes of a conference held in London, August 7, 1770, have been understood to favor "justification by works," now the Rev. John Wesley and others, assembled in conference, do declare that we had no such meaning and that we abhor the doctrine of "justification by works" as a most perilous and abominable doctrine. And as the said minutes are not sufficiently guarded in the way they are expressed, we hereby solemnly declare in the sight of God that we have no trust or confidence but in the alone merits of our Lord and Savior Jesus Christ for justification or salvation, either in life, death, or the day of judgment. . . . our works have no part in meriting or purchasing our justification, from first to last, either in whole or in part. (Minutes, August 9, 1771, in *Works* [WL], 1:xxxi-xxxii)

PENANCE

You say, "The matter of a sacrament is something sensible," perceivable by our senses. But if so, penance is not a sacrament. For surely contrition is not something perceivable by the outward senses! (*Popery Calmly Considered* [1779], in *Works,* 15:191)

P

Exhort all our brethren steadily to wait upon God in the appointed means of fasting and prayer, the former of which has been almost universally neglected by the Methodists both in England and Ireland. But it is a true remark of Kempis: "The more thou deniest thyself, the more thou wilt grow in grace." (Letter to James McDonald [October 23, 1790], in *Works* [S], 7:215)

PERFECTION (ENTIRE SANCTIFICATION)

We . . . believe that there is *no such perfection* in this life as implies an entire deliverance—either from ignorance or mistake in things not essential to salvation or from manifold temptations or from numberless infirmities wherewith the corruptible body more or less presses down the soul. We cannot find any ground in Scripture to suppose that any inhabitant of a house of clay is wholly exempt either from bodily infirmities or from ignorance of many things or to imagine any is incapable of mistake or falling into divers temptations.

. . . But whom then do you mean by *one that is perfect*? We mean one in whom is "the mind which was in Christ" and who so "walketh as Christ also walked," a man "that hath clean hands and a pure heart" or that is "cleansed from all filthiness of flesh and spirit," one in whom is "no occasion of stumbling" and who, accordingly, "does not commit sin." To declare this a little more particularly: We understand by that scriptural expression, "a perfect man," one in whom God hath fulfilled his faithful word, "From all your filthiness and from all your idols I will cleanse you: I will also save you from all your uncleannesses." We understand hereby one whom God hath "sanctified throughout in body, soul, and spirit," one who "walketh in the light as he is in the light, in whom is no darkness at all; the blood of Jesus Christ his Son having cleansed him from all sin." (*A Plain Account of Christian Perfection* [1767; rev. 1777], in *Works* [WL], 11:383-84)

Have you not another objection nearly allied to this, namely, that we preach perfection? True; but what perfection? The term you cannot object to, because it is scriptural. All the difficulty is to fix the meaning of it according to the Word of God. And this we have done again and again, declaring to all the world that Christian perfection does not imply an exemption from ignorance or mistake or infirmities or temptations, but that it does imply the being so crucified with Christ as to be able to testify, "I live not, but Christ liveth in me" [Gal. 2:20], and hath "purified my heart by faith" [Acts 15:9]. It does imply "the casting down every high thing that exalteth itself against the knowledge of God, and bringing into captivity every thought to the obedience of Christ." It does imply "the being holy, as he that hath called us is holy, in all manner of conversation" [2 Cor. 10:5; 1 Pet. 1:15]; and, in a word, "the loving the Lord our God with all our heart, and serving him with all our strength."

... Come with boldness to the throne of grace and be assured that when you ask this of God, you shall have the petition you ask of him. We know indeed that to man, to the natural man, this is impossible. But we know also that as no word is impossible with God, so "all things are possible to him that believeth." (*An Earnest Appeal to Men of Reason and Religion* [1743], in Coll. C, 223-24)

Q. ... What will become of a heathen, a Papist, a Church of England man, if he dies without being thus sanctified?

A. He cannot see the Lord. But none who seeks it sincerely shall or can die without it; though possibly he may not attain it, till the very article of death.

Q. ... Is it ordinarily given till a little before death?

A. It is not, to those that expect it no sooner, nor consequently ask for it, at least, not in faith.

Q. ... But ought we to expect it sooner?

A. Why not? For although we grant, (1) that the generality of believers whom we have hitherto known were not so sanctified till near death; (2) that few of those to whom St. Paul wrote his Epistles were so at the time he wrote; (3) nor he himself at the time of writing his former Epistles: yet this does not prove that we may not today. (*Minutes of Some Late Conversations* [August 2, 1745], in *Works* [S], 5:201-2)

We grant . . . that many of those who have died in the faith, yea, the greater part of them we have known, were not sanctified throughout—not made perfect in love—till a little before death. (*Minutes of Some Late Conversations* [June 17, 1747], in *Works* [S], 5:208)

Q. Is there any clear Scripture *promise* of this, that God will save us from *all* sin?

A. There is: "He shall redeem Israel from *all his sins*" [Ps. 130:8].

This is more largely expressed in the prophecy of Ezekiel: "Then will I sprinkle clean water upon you, and ye shall be clean: from *all* your filthiness and from *all* your idols will I cleanse you. [. . .] I will also save you from all your uncleannesses" [36:25, 29]. No promise can be more clear. And to this the apostle plainly refers in that exhortation: "Having these promises, let us cleanse ourselves from all filthiness of flesh and spirit, perfecting holiness in the fear of God" [2 Cor. 7:1]. Equally clear and express is that ancient promise: "The Lord thy God will circumcise thy heart, and the heart of thy seed, to love the Lord thy God with all thy heart and with all thy soul" [Deut. 30:6]. (*A Plain Account of Christian Perfection* [1767; rev. 1777], in *Works* [WL], 11:388-89)

P

Q. Does the New Testament afford any farther ground for expecting to be saved from all sin?

A. Undoubtedly it does, both in those prayers and commands, which are equivalent to the strongest assertions.

Q. What prayers do you mean?

A. Prayers for entire sanctification which, were there no such thing, would be mere mockery of God. Such in particular are, (1) "Deliver us from evil." Now, when this is done, when we are delivered from all evil, there can be no sin remaining. (2) "Neither pray I for these alone, but for them also who shall believe on me through their word; that they all may be one; as thou, Father, art in me, and I in thee, that they also may be one in us; I in them, and thou in me, that they may be made perfect in one" [John 17:20-23]. (3) "I bow my knees unto the God and Father of our Lord Jesus Christ, [. . .] that he would grant you, [. . .] that ye, being rooted and grounded in love, may be able to comprehend with all saints what is the breadth, and length, and depth, and height; and to know the love of Christ, which passeth knowledge, that ye may be filled with all the fulness of God" [Eph. 3:14, 16-19]. (4) "The very God of peace sanctify you wholly: and I pray God your whole spirit, soul, and body may be preserved blameless unto the coming of our Lord Jesus Christ" [1 Thess. 5:23].

Q. What command is there to the same effect?

A. (1) "Be ye perfect, as your Father who is in heaven is perfect" [Matt. 5:48]. (2) "Thou shalt love the Lord thy God with all thy heart, and with all thy soul, and with all thy mind" [Matt. 22:37]. But if the love of God fill all the heart, there can be no sin therein. (*A Plain Account of Christian Perfection* [1767; rev. 1777], in *Works* [WL], 11:389-90)

What follows you did not design for argument, but wit. "I cannot help thinking that Paul, with all his infirmities, might more reasonably be looked upon as an inspired prophet than Mr. Wesley, though arrived, in his own imagination, to a sinless perfection." I never told you so, nor anyone else. I no more imagine that I have already attained, that I already love God with all my heart, soul, and strength, than that I am in the third heavens. (Letter to John Smith [probably one of the archbishops of Canterbury, Thomas Herring or Thomas Secker] [March 22, 1748], in *Works* [WL], 12:103)

Q. How are we to wait for this change?

A. Not in careless indifference or indolent inactivity, but in vigorous, universal obedience, in a zealous keeping of all the commandments, in watchfulness and painfulness, in denying ourselves, and taking up our cross daily; as well as in earnest prayer and fasting and a close attendance on all the ordinances of God. And if any man dream of attaining it any other way (yea, or of keeping it when it is attained, when he has received it even in the largest measure), he deceiveth his own soul. It is true, we receive it by simple faith. But God does not, will not, give that faith unless we seek it with all diligence in the way which he has ordained. (*A Plain Account of Christian Perfection* [1767; rev. 1777], in *Works* [WL], 11:402-3)

Q. What is Christian perfection?

A. The loving God with all our heart, mind, soul, and strength. This implies that no wrong temper, none contrary to love, remains in the soul and that all the thoughts, words, and actions are governed by pure love.

Q. Do you affirm that this perfection excludes all infirmities, ignorance, and mistake?

A. I continually affirm quite the contrary, and always have done so.

Q. But how can every thought, word, and work be governed by pure love, and the man be subject at the same time to ignorance and mistake?

A. I see no contradiction here: "A man may be filled with pure love and still be liable to mistake." Indeed I do not expect to be freed from actual mistakes till this mortal puts on immortality. I believe this to be a natural consequence of the soul's dwelling in flesh and blood. For we cannot now *think* at all but by the mediation of those bodily organs which have suffered equally with the rest of our frame. And hence we cannot avoid sometimes *thinking wrong* till this corruptible shall have put on incorruption. (*A Plain Account of Christian Perfection* [1767; rev. 1777], in *Works* [WL], 11:394)

Certainly sanctification (in the proper sense) is "an instantaneous deliverance from all sin" and includes "an instantaneous power then given, always to cleave to God." Yet this sanctification (at least, in the lower degrees) does not include a power never to think a useless thought nor ever speak a useless word. I myself believe that such a perfection is inconsistent with living in a corruptible body, for this makes it impossible "always to think right." While we breathe, we shall, more or less, mistake. If, therefore, Christian perfection implies this, we must not expect it till after death.

I want you to be all love. This is the perfection I believe and teach. . . . to set perfection too high (so high as no man that we ever heard or read of attained) is the most effectual (because unsuspected) way of driving it out of the world. (Letter to Miss Furly [September 15, 1762], in *Works* [WL], 12:192)

As to the word *perfection*, it is scriptural. Therefore neither you nor I can in conscience object to it unless we would send the Holy Ghost to school and teach him to speak who made the tongue.

P

By Christian perfection, I mean (as I have said again and again) the so loving God and our neighbor as to "rejoice evermore, pray without ceasing, and in everything give thanks." He that experiences this is scripturally perfect. And if you do not, yet you may experience it. You surely will if you follow hard after it, for the Scripture cannot be broken.

What then does their arguing reprove, who object against Christian perfection? Absolute or infallible perfection I never contended for. Sinless perfection I do not contend for, seeing it is not scriptural. A perfection such as enables a person to fulfill the whole law and so needs not the merits of Christ—I acknowledge no such perfection; I do now and always did protest against it.

"But is there no sin in those who are perfect in love?" I believe not, but be that as it may, they feel none; no temper contrary to pure love, while they rejoice, pray, and give thanks continually. And whether sin is suspended or extinguished I will not dispute, it is enough that they feel nothing but love. This you allow we should daily press after. And this is all I contend for. (Letter to Mrs. Maitland [May 12, 1763], in *Works* [WL], 12:241)

Absolute perfection belongs not to man, nor to angels, but to God alone. (*A Plain Account of Christian Perfection* [1767; rev. 1777], in *Works* [WL], 11:442)

Where Christian perfection is not strongly and explicitly preached, there is seldom any remarkable blessing from God and, consequently, little addition to the society and little life in the members of it. (Letter to Mr. Merryweather [February 8, 1766], in *Works* [WL], 12:254)

Concerning setting perfection too high. That perfection which I believe I can boldly preach because I think I see five hundred witnesses of it. Of that perfection which you preach you think you do not see any witness at all. Why, then, you must have far more courage than me or you could not persist in preaching it. I wonder you do not, in this article, fall in plumb with Mr. Whitefield. For do not you, as well as he, ask, "Where are the perfect ones?" I verily believe there are none upon earth, none dwelling in the body. I cordially assent to his opinion that there is no such perfection here as you describe, at least I never met with an instance of it and I doubt I never shall. Therefore I still think to set perfection so high is effectually to renounce it. (Letter to Charles Wesley [July 9, 1766], in *Works* [WL], 12:121-22)

Some thoughts occurred to my mind this morning concerning Christian perfection and the manner and time of receiving it, which I believe may be useful to set down.

    1. By perfection I mean the humble, gentle, patient love of God and our neighbor ruling our tempers, words, and actions.

    I do not include an impossibility of falling from it, either in part or in whole. Therefore, I retract several expressions in our Hymns which partly express, partly imply, such an impossibility.

    And I do not contend for the term *sinless*, though I do not object against it. (*A Plain Account of Christian Perfection* [1767; rev. 1777], in *Works* [WL], 11:446)

Five or six and thirty years ago, I much admired the character of a perfect Christian drawn by Clemens Alexandrinus. Five or six and twenty years ago, a thought came into my mind of drawing such a character myself, only in a more scriptural manner and mostly in the very words of Scripture. This I entitled *The Character of a Methodist*, believing that curiosity would incite more persons to read it and also that some prejudice might thereby be removed from candid men. But that none might imagine I intended a panegyric either on myself or my friends, I guarded against this in the very title page, saying, both in the name of myself and them, "Not as though I had already attained, either were already perfect." To the same effect I speak in the conclusion, "These are the principles and practices of our sect; these are the marks of a true Methodist," [that is], a true Christian, as I immediately after explain myself: "By these alone do those who are in derision so called *desire* to be distinguished from other men" . . . "By these marks do we *labor* to distinguish ourselves from those whose minds or lives are not according to the Gospel of Christ" . . .

Upon this Rusticulus, or Dr. Dodd, says, "A Methodist, according to Mr. Wesley, is one who is perfect and sinneth not in thought, word, or deed."

Sir, have me excused. This is not "according to Mr. Wesley." I have told all the world I am not perfect, and yet you allow me to be a Methodist. *I tell you flat, I have not attained the character I draw.* Will you pin it upon me in spite of my teeth?

"But Mr. Wesley says, the other Methodists have." I say no such thing. What I say, after having given a scriptural account of a perfect Christian, is this: "By these marks the Methodists *desire* to be distinguished from other men; by these we *labor* to distinguish ourselves." And do you not yourself *desire* and *labor* after the very same thing?

But you insist, "Mr. Wesley affirms the Methodists" ([that is], all Methodists) "to be perfectly holy and righteous." Where do I affirm this? Not in the tract before us. In the front of this I affirm just the contrary, and that I affirm it anywhere else is more than I know. Be pleased, sir, to point out the place. . . . the Methodists (so called) may still declare (without any impeachment of their sincerity) that they do not come to the holy table "trusting in their own righteousness, but in God's manifold and great mercies." (Letter to the editor of *Lloyd's Evening Post* [March 5, 1767], in *Letters*, 121-23)

P

Entire sanctification, or Christian perfection, is neither more nor less than pure love; love expelling sin and governing both the heart and life of a child of God. The refiner's fire purges out all that is contrary to love and that many times by a pleasing smart. Leave all this to him that does all things well and that loves you better than you do yourself. (Letter to Walter Churchey [February 21, 1771], in *Works* [S], 7:82)

The perfection I hold is so far from being contrary to the doctrine of our Church that it is exactly the same which every clergyman prays for every Sunday: "Cleanse the thoughts of our hearts by the inspiration of thy Holy Spirit, that we may perfectly love thee and worthily magnify thy holy name." I mean neither more nor less than this. In doctrine, therefore, I do not dissent from the Church of England. (*An Answer to Mr. Rowland Hill's Tract, Entitled, "Imposture Detected"* [June 28, 1777], in *Works* [WL], 10:450)

I advise you frequently to read and meditate upon the thirteenth chapter of the First Epistle to the Corinthians. There is the true picture of Christian perfection! Let us copy after it with all our might. (Letter to Miss Ann Loxdale [April 12, 1782], in *Letters*, 372)

I have no particular fondness for the term [*perfection*]. It seldom occurs either in my preaching or writings. It is my opponents who thrust it upon me continually and ask me what I mean by it. So did Bishop Gibson till by his advice I publicly declared what I did not mean by it and what I did. (*An Answer to the Rev. Mr. Dodd* [1782], in *Works* [WL], 11:450)

You proceed: "You allow in another sermon, in evident contradiction to yourself, that the true children of God could, and did, commit sin." This is no contradiction to anything I ever advanced. I everywhere allow that a child of God can and will commit sin, if he does not keep himself. . . . If they keep themselves, they do not; otherwise, they can and do commit sin. . . . But "hence," you say, "we conclude that he who is born of God may possibly commit sin." An idle conclusion as ever was formed, for who ever denied it? . . . The only conclusion which I deny is that "all Christians do and will commit sin as long as they live." (*An Answer to the Rev. Mr. Dodd* [1782], in *Works* [WL], 11:452-53)

I am glad brother D_____ has more light with regard to full sanctification. This doctrine is the grand depositum which God has lodged with the people called Methodists, and for the sake of propagating this chiefly he appeared to have raised us up. (Letter to Robert C. Brackenbury, Esq. [September 15, 1790], in Coll. C, 397)

PERSEVERANCE: UNCONDITIONAL (FALSITY OF)

With regard to . . . final perseverance, I believe,

That there is a state attainable in this life from which a man cannot finally fall.

That he has attained this who is, according to St. Paul's account, "a new creature," that is, who can say, "Old things are passed away; all things" in me "are become new."

And I do not deny, that all those eminently styled, "the elect," will infallibly persevere to the end. (Journal entry [August 24, 1743], in *Works* [S], 7:481)

You see the blessed effects of unconditional perseverance! It leads the way, by easy steps, first to presumption and then to black despair! There will be no way to recover your poor friend to a scriptural faith but by taking away that broken reed from her and by convincing her that if she dies in her present state she will perish eternally. It will indeed be a medicine that will put her to pain, but it will be the only one that will save her soul alive. What a blessing it is, my dear Harriet, that you have been saved from this poisonous doctrine! and that you are enabled to follow after that holiness without which we cannot see the Lord! So run, that you may obtain. The prize is before you. Never be weary or faint in your mind. In due time you will reap, if you faint not. (Letter to Miss Rebecca Ingram [August 3, 1789], in *Works* [S], 7:214)

POLEMICS; CONTROVERSY

In writing practically, I seldom argue concerning the meaning of texts; in writing controversially, I do. (Letter to John Smith [probably one of the archbishops of Canterbury, Thomas Herring or Thomas Secker] [December 30, 1745], in *Works* [WL], 12:64)

It is at least as much with a view to learn myself, as to show others (what I think) the truth, that I intend to set down a few reflections on some parts of the tract you have lately published. I say, *some* parts, for it is not my design to answer every sentence in this any more than in the former. Many things I pass over because I think them true, many more because I think them not material, and some because I am determined not to engage in a useless if not hurtful controversy.

. . . Fear indeed is one cause of my declining this: fear (as I said elsewhere) not of my *adversary* but of *myself.* I fear my own spirit, lest "I fall where many mightier have been slain." I never knew one (or but one) man write controversy with what I thought a right spirit. Every disputant seems to think (as every soldier) that he may hurt his opponent as much as he can; nay, that he *ought* to do his worst to him or he cannot make the best of his own cause; that so he do not belie or willfully misrepresent him, he must expose him as much as he is able. It is enough, we suppose, if we do not show heat or passion against our adversary. But not to despise him, or endeavor to make others do so, is quite a work of supererogation.

. . . But ought these things to be so? (I speak on the Christian scheme.) Ought we not to love our neighbor as ourselves? And does a man cease to be our neighbor because he is of a different opinion? Nay, and declares himself to be? Ought we not, for all this, to do to him as we would he should do to us? But do we ourselves love to be *exposed* or set in the worst light? Would we willingly be treated with contempt? If not, why do we treat others thus? And yet, who scruples it? Who does not hit every blot he can, however foreign to the merits of the cause? Who, in controversy, casts the mantle of love over the nakedness of his brother? Who keeps steadily and uniformly to the question without ever striking at the person? Who shows in every sentence that he loves his brother only less than the truth?

. . . I fear neither you nor I have attained to this. (*The Principles of a Methodist Farther Explained* [1746], in *Works*, 12:329)

I apprehend you are the person that "wriggle on this head" because the argument pinches. You appear to me to twist and wind to and fro, because

I "distinguish away" not my doctrines but your objections, unraveling the fallacies, showing what part is false and what part true, but nothing to the purpose. Since you move it again, I will resume the point once more. You will pardon me if I speak home, that it may be seen which of us two it is that has hitherto given the "evasive answers." (Letter to John Smith [probably one of the archbishops of Canterbury, Thomas Herring or Thomas Secker] [March 22, 1748], in *Works* [WL], 12:100)

I have preached twenty years in some of Mr. Whitefield's societies, yet to this day I never contradicted him among his own people. I did not think it honest, neither necessary at all. I could preach salvation by faith and leave all controversy untouched. (Letter to Alexander Coats [July 7, 1761], in *Works*, 16:66)

I have entirely lost my taste for controversy. I have lost my readiness in disputing, and I take this to be a providential discharge from it. All I can now do with a clear conscience is not to enter into a formal controversy about the new birth or justification by faith, any more than Christian perfection, but simply to declare my judgment and to explain myself as clearly as I can upon any difficulty that may arise concerning it. (Letter to the Rev. Mr. F. [September 15, 1762], in *Works* [S], 7:36)

He is too warm and impatient of contradiction, otherwise he must be lost to all common sense, to preach against final perseverance in Scotland. From the first hour that I entered the kingdom, it was a sacred rule with me never to preach on any controverted point, at least *not in a controversial way.* Anyone may see that this is only to put a sword into our enemies' hands. It is the direct way to increase all their prejudices and to make all our labors fruitless. (Letter to Lady Maxwell [January 24, 1771], in *Letters*, 409)

I commend you for meddling with points of controversy as little as possible. It is abundantly easier to lose our love in that rough field than to find truth. This consideration has made me exceedingly thankful to God for giving me a respite from polemical labors. I am glad he has given to others both the power and the will to answer them that trouble me, so that I may not always be forced to hold my weapons in one hand while I am building with the other. (Letter to Lady Maxwell [February 8, 1772], in Coll. C, 357-58)

POPES; PAPACY

They [the apostles] were to prove their assertions by the written Word. You and I are to do the same. Without such proof I ought no more to have believed St. Peter himself, than St. Peter's pretended successor. (Letter to

John Smith [probably one of the archbishops of Canterbury, Thomas Herring or Thomas Secker] [September 28, 1745], in *Works* [WL], 12:57)

Q. . . . Was there any thought of uniformity in the government of all churches, until the time of Constantine?

A. It is certain there was not; nor would there have been then, had men consulted the Word of God only. (Minutes of the Methodist Conference, June 15, 1747, in *Minutes*, 36)

The primitive church knew of no such thing as a universal head. (*The Advantages of the Members of the Church of England over Those of the Church of Rome* [1753], in *Works*, 15:206)

I believe the Romish Antichrist is already so fallen that he will not again lift up his head in any considerable degree. The bishop of Rome has little more power now than any other of the Italian princes. I therefore concur with you in believing his tyranny is past never to return. (Letter to Joseph Benson [December 8, 1777], in *Works* [S], 7:79)

We read in Scripture that Christ is the Head of the church, "from whom the whole body is fitly joined together" [Eph. 4:16]. The Scripture does not mention any visible head of the church, much less does it mention the pope as such . . .

. . . The Papists say the pope is Christ's vicar, St. Peter's successor, and has the supreme power on earth over the whole church.

We answer, Christ gave no such power to St. Peter himself. He gave no apostle preeminence over the rest. Yea, St. Paul was so far from acknowledging St. Peter's supremacy that he withstood him to the face [Gal. 2:11] and asserted himself, "not to be behind the chief of the apostles."

Neither is it certain that St. Peter was bishop of Rome; no, nor that he ever was there. (*Popery Calmly Considered* [1779], in *Works*, 15:177-78)

I care not who is the head of the church, provided *you* be a *Christian*! (Letter to Samuel Wesley Jr. [at that time a Catholic] [March 18, 1788], *Letters* [JT], 8:47)

POPULARITY (IN OLD AGE)

I preached at St. Thomas's Church in the afternoon and at St. Swithin's in the evening. The tide is now turned, so that I have more invitations to preach in churches than I can accept of. (*Journal*, January 19, 1783)

In the afternoon, as we could not pass by the common road, we procured leave to drive round by some fields and got to Falmouth in good time. The last time I was here, about forty years ago, I was taken prisoner by an immense mob, gaping and roaring like lions. But how is the tide turned! High and low now lined the street from one end of the town to the other, out of stark love and kindness, gaping and staring as if the king were going by. In the evening I preached on the smooth top of the hill, at a small distance from the sea, to the largest congregation I have ever seen in Cornwall, except in or near Redruth. And such a time I have not known before, since I returned from Ireland. God moved wonderfully on the hearts of the people, who all seemed to know the day of their visitation. (*Journal*, August 18, 1789)

PRAYER

And first, prayer: For thus saith the Lord, "Ask and it shall be given you; if any man lack wisdom, let him ask of God." Here God plainly ordains prayer as the means of receiving whatsoever grace we want, particularly that wisdom from above, which is the chief fruit of the grace of God.

Here likewise God commands all to pray who desire to receive any grace from him. Here is no restriction as to believers or unbelievers but, least of all, as to unbelievers, for such doubtless were most of those to whom he said, "Ask and it shall be given you."

We know, indeed, that the prayer of an unbeliever is full of sin. Yet let him remember that which is written of one who could not then believe, for he had not so much as heard the gospel: "Cornelius, thy prayers and thine alms are come up for a memorial before God." (*Journal*, April 25, 1740)

He that prays in faith, at whatsoever time, is heard. In every time and place, God accepts him who "lifts up holy hands, without wrath or doubting." (*A Letter to a Person Lately Joined to the People Called Quakers* [February 2, 1748], in *Works* [T], 9:114)

Nature and the devil will always oppose private prayer, but it is worthwhile to break through. That it is a cross will not hinder its being a blessing; nay, often the more reluctance, the greater blessing. (Letter to Miss Furly [September 25, 1757], in *Works* [WL], 12:186)

If you have resolution to break through a thousand hindrances and allow some time every day for private prayer, I doubt not but you will receive every gospel blessing in this world and in the world to come. (Letter to Ebenezer Blackwell [August 15, 1761], in *Works* [WL], 12:175)

Indeed nothing will avail without prayer. Pray, whether you can or not: when you are cheerful, when you are heavy, pray; with many or few words or none at all. You will surely find an answer of peace. (Letter to John Valton [June 30, 1764], in *Works* [S], 7:121)

Whatever other ends are answered by prayer, this is one, and it seems a primary one, that we may have the petitions which we ask of him. Asking is the appointed means of receiving and that for others as well as for ourselves; as we may learn partly from reason itself but more fully from our own experience and more clearly still from revelation. Reason teaches us to argue from analogy. If you (because you have a regard for me) would do more for a third person at my request than otherwise you would have done, how much more will God, at the request of his beloved children, give blessings to those they pray for which otherwise he would not have given! And how does all experience confirm this! How many times have the petitions of others been answered to our advantage, and ours on the behalf of others!

But the most decisive of all proofs is the Scripture: "Go to my servant Job, and he shall pray for you; for him will I accept." It was not a temporal blessing which was here in question, but a spiritual—the forgiveness of their sin. . . . In proof of the general truth that God gives us both temporal and spiritual blessings, in answer to each other's prayers, I need only remind you of one scripture more: "Let them pray over him; and the prayer of faith shall save the sick; and if he have committed sins, they shall be forgiven him." The promise in the following verse is still more comprehensive: "Pray one for another, and ye shall be healed" of whatsoever you have confessed to each other. (Letter to Miss Bishop [December 26, 1776], in *Works* [S], 7:169-70)

PRAYERS: EXTEMPORARY

I do not *slight or contemn the offices* of the church. I esteem them very highly. And yet I do not, at all times, worship God, even in public, in the very terms of those offices. Nor yet do I knowingly *slight or contemn her rules.* For it is not clear to my apprehension that she has any rule which forbids using extemporary prayer, suppose between the morning and evening service. And if I am *not worthy to be called her minister* (which I dare by no means affirm myself to be), yet *her minister I am* and must always be, unless I should be judicially deposed from my ministry.

Your second argument is this: "If you suppose the Scripture enjoins you to use extemporary prayer, then you must suppose our liturgy to be inconsistent with Scripture, and, consequently, unlawful to be used." That does not follow: unless I supposed the Scripture to enjoin, to use extemporary prayer, *and no other.* Then it would follow that a form of prayer was inconsistent with Scripture. But this I never did suppose. (*The Principles of a Methodist Farther Explained* [1746], in *Works*, 12:355)

I use the Service of the Church every Lord's Day, and it has never yet appeared to me that any rule of the Church forbids my using extemporary prayer on other occasions. (Letter to John Smith [probably one of the archbishops of Canterbury, Thomas Herring or Thomas Secker] [June 25, 1746], in *Works* [WL], 12:79)

PRAYERS: FORMAL

But to speak freely, I myself find more life in the Church prayers, than in any formal extemporary prayers of Dissenters. (Letter to Miss Bishop [1778], quoted in Coll. C, 260n†)

By our reading prayers we prevent our people's contracting a hatred for forms of prayer, which would naturally be the case if we always prayed extempore. (Letter to William Percival [February 17, 1787], *Letters* [JT], 7:370)

PRAYERS FOR THE DEAD

[Oh,] grant that we, with those who are already dead in thy faith and fear, may together partake of a joyful resurrection. (Quoted in "Of Prayers for the Dead," chap. 13 in Coll. A, 84)

Bring us, with all those who have pleased thee from the beginning of the world, into the glories of thy Son's kingdom. (Quoted in "Of Prayers for the Dead," chap. 13 in Coll. A, 84)

By thy infinite mercies, vouchsafe to bring us, with those that are dead in thee, to rejoice together before thee. (Quoted in "Of Prayers for the Dead," chap. 13 in Coll. A, 84)

In these words, "Thy kingdom come," we pray for the coming of his everlasting kingdom, the kingdom of glory in heaven, which is the continuation and perfection of the kingdom of grace on earth; consequently this (as well as the preceding petition) is *offered up for the whole intelligent creation*, who are all interested in this grand event, the final restoration of all things, by God's putting an end to misery and sin, to infirmity and death, taking all things into his own hands and "setting up the kingdom which endureth throughout all ages." Exactly answerable to all this are those awful words in the prayer at the burial of the dead—"Beseeching thee that it may please thee of thy gracious goodness shortly to accomplish the number of thine elect and to hasten thy kingdom, that we, with all those that are departed in the true faith of thy holy name, may have our perfect consummation and bliss, both in body and soul, in thy everlasting glory." (Quoted in "Of Prayers for the Dead," chap. 13 in Coll. A, 86-87)

"It is certain praying for the dead was common in the second century," you might have said, and in the first also; seeing that petition, "Thy kingdom come," manifestly concerns the saints in paradise as well as those on earth. . . . Praying thus far for the dead, "That God would shortly accomplish the number of his elect and hasten his kingdom," you will not easily prove to be any corruption at all. (Quoted in "Of Prayers for the Dead," chap. 13 in Coll. A, 85-86)

Your fourth argument is that in a collection of prayers, I cite the words of an ancient liturgy—"For the Faithful Departed." Sir, whenever I use those words in the burial service, I pray to the same effect: "That we, with all those who are departed in thy faith and fear, may have our perfect consummation of bliss, both in body and soul." Yea, and whenever I say, "Thy kingdom come," for I mean both the kingdom of grace and glory. In this kind of general prayer, therefore, for the faithful departed, I conceive myself to be clearly justified, both by the earliest antiquity, by the Church of England, and by the Lord's Prayer. (Quoted in "Of Prayers for the Dead," chap. 13 in Coll. A, 85)

PREACHING

For what can be more undeniable than this, that our preaching also is vain, unless it be attended with the power of that Spirit who alone pierceth the heart? And that your hearing is vain, unless the same power be present to heal your soul and to give you a faith which standeth not in the wisdom of man but in the power of God? (*A Farther Appeal to Men of Reason and Religion* [1745], pt. 1, in *Works*, 12:97)

The following sermons contain the substance of what I have been preaching for between eight and nine years last past. During that time I have frequently spoken in public on every subject in the ensuing collection, and I am not conscious that there is any one point of doctrine on which I am accustomed to speak in public which is not here incidentally, if not professedly, laid before every Christian reader. Every serious man who peruses these will therefore see, in the clearest manner, what these doctrines are which I embrace and teach as the essentials of true religion.

. . . But I am thoroughly sensible, these are not proposed in such a manner as some may expect. Nothing here appears in an elaborate, elegant, or oratorical dress. If it had been my desire or design to write thus, my leisure would not permit. But, in truth, I at present designed nothing less, for I now write as I generally speak, *ad populum*—to the bulk of mankind, to those who neither relish nor understand the art of speaking but who, notwithstanding, are competent judges of those truths which are necessary to present and future happiness. I mention this that curious readers may spare themselves the labor of seeking for what they will not find.

. . . I design plain truth for plain people. Therefore, of set purpose, I abstain from all nice and philosophical speculations, from all perplexed and intricate reasonings, and, as far as possible, from even the show of learning, unless in sometimes citing the original Scripture. I labor to avoid all words which are not easy to be understood, all which are not used in common life, and, in particular, those kinds of technical terms that so frequently occur in bodies of divinity—those modes of speaking which men of reading are intimately acquainted with but which to common people are an unknown tongue. Yet I am not assured that I do not sometimes slide into them unawares. It is so extremely natural to imagine that a word which is familiar to ourselves is so to all the world. (Preface to *Sermons on Several Occasions* [1746], in *Works* [T], 5:3)

It is not my own will to preach at all. It is quite contrary to my will. Many a time have I cried out, "Lord, send by whom thou wilt send. Only send not me!" But I am moved by the Spirit of God to preach. He clearly shows me it is his will I should and that I should do it *when* and *where* the greatest number of poor sinners may be gathered together. Moved by him, I give up my will and appoint a time and place when by his power I trust to speak in his name. (*A Letter to a Person Lately Joined to the People Called Quakers* [February 2, 1748], in *Works* [T], 9:113)

Be their talents ever so great, they will ere long grow dead themselves, and so will most of those that hear them. I know, were I myself to preach one whole year in one place, I should preach both myself and most of my congregation asleep. Nor can I believe it was ever the will of our Lord that any congregation should have one teacher only. We have found by long and constant experience that a frequent change of teachers is best. This preacher has one talent; that another. No one whom I ever yet knew has all the talents which are needful for beginning, continuing, and perfecting the work of grace in a whole congregation. (Letter to the Rev. Mr. Walker [September 3, 1756], in *Works* [S], 7:277)

I preach about eight hundred sermons in a year. (Letter to John Newton, in *Journal,* May 14, 1765)

You and I are called to this—to save souls from death, to watch over them as those that must give account! If our office implied no more than preaching a few times in a week, I could play with it. So might you. But how small a part of our duty (yours, as well as mine) is this! God says to you, as well as me, "Do all thou canst, be it more or less, to save the souls for whom my Son has died." Let this voice be ever sounding in our ears, then shall we give up our account with joy. . . . I am ashamed of my indolence and inactivity. The good Lord help us both! (Letter to Charles Wesley [March 25, 1772], in *Works* [WL], 12:128)

It is a shame for any Methodist preacher to confine himself to one place. We are debtors to all the world. We are called to warn everyone, to exhort everyone, if by any means we may save some. (Letter to Joseph Benson [December 11, 1772], in *Works* [S], 7:72)

PREACHING AND OPPOSITION (RIOTS, ETC.)

"But it is plain, peace is broke and disturbances do arise, in consequence of your preaching." I grant it. But what would you infer? Have you never read the Bible? Have you not read that the Prince of Peace himself was, in this sense, a disturber of the public peace? When he came into Jerusalem [Matt. 21:10], all the city was moved . . . shaken as with an earthquake. And the disturbance arose higher and higher till the whole multitude cried out together, "Away with him; crucify him, crucify him, and Pilate gave sentence it should be done." Such another disturber of the public peace was that Stephen, even from the time he began "disputing with the Libertines and Cyrenians, till the people stopped their ears, and ran upon him with one accord, and cast him out of the city and stoned him." Such disturbers of the peace were all those ringleaders of the sect of the Nazarenes (commonly called apostles) who wherever they came "turned the world upside down." And above all the rest, that Paul of Tarsus, who occasioned so much disturbance at Damascus [Acts 9], at Antioch of Pisidia [chap. 13], at Iconium [chap. 14], Lystra [v. 19], at Philippi [chap. 16], at Thessalonica [chap. 17], and, particularly, at Ephesus. The consequence of his preaching there was that "the whole city was filled with confusion." And "they all ran together with one accord, some crying one thing, some another: inasmuch that the greater part of them knew not wherefore they were come together."

. . . And can we expect it to be any otherwise now? . . . But of all this, our Lord hath told us before. "Think not that I am come to send peace upon earth," that this will be the immediate effect wherever my gospel is preached with power. "I am not come to send peace, but a sword," this . . . will be the first consequence of my coming, whenever my word turns sinners from darkness to light, from the power of Satan unto God. (*A Farther Appeal to Men of Reason and Religion* [1745], pt. 1, in *Works*, 12:131-32)

I never saw before, no, not at Walsal itself, the hand of God so plainly shown as here. There I had many companions who were willing to die with me; here, not a friend but one simple girl, who likewise was hurried away from me in an instant as soon as ever she came out of Mrs. B.'s door. There I received some blows, lost part of my clothes, and was covered over with dirt. Here, although the hands of perhaps some hundreds of people were lifted up to strike or throw, yet they were one and all stopped in the midway, so that not a man touched me with one of his fingers, neither was anything thrown from first to last; so that I had not even a speck of dirt on my clothes. Who can deny that God heareth prayer or that he hath all power in heaven and earth? (*Journal,* August 4, 1745)

At one I went to the Cross in Bolton. There was a vast number of people, but many of them utterly wild. As soon as I began speaking, they began thrusting to and fro, endeavoring to throw me down from the steps on which I stood. They did so once or twice, but I went up again and continued my discourse. They then began to throw stones. At the same time some got upon the Cross behind me to push me down; on which I could not but observe how God overrules even the minutest circumstances. One man was bawling just at my ear, when a stone struck him on the cheek and he was still. A second was forcing his way down to me till another stone hit him on the forehead; it bounded back, the blood ran down, and he came no farther. The third, being close to me stretched out his hand and in the instant a sharp stone came upon the joints of his fingers. He shook his hand and was very quiet till I concluded my discourse and went away. (*Journal,* August 28, 1748)

One evening, when Mr. [Edward] Perronet preached in my absence, a crew of sailors procured a fiddle and made an attempt to interrupt, but they met with small encouragement. A company of colliers turned upon them, broke their fiddle in pieces, and used those of them they could overtake so roughly that they have not made their appearance since. (Letter to Ebenezer Blackwell [October 2, 1749], in *Letters,* 307)

That any of the Methodist preachers are alive is a clear proof of an overruling providence. (Letter to Ebenezer Blackwell [July 21, 1750], in *Letters,* 309)

Even the Methodists are now at peace throughout the kingdom. It is well if they bear this so well as they did war. I have seen more make shipwreck of the faith in a calm than in a storm. We are apt in sunshiny weather to lie down and sleep, and who can tell what may be done before we awake. (Letter to Ebenezer Blackwell [April 16, 1752], in *Letters,* 316)

I was obliged to preach abroad. One buffoon labored much to interrupt, but as he was bawling, with his mouth wide open, some arch boys gave him such a mouthful of dirt as quite satisfied him. (*Journal,* March 17, 1775)

PREACHING IN THE FIELDS

God in Scripture commands me, according to my power, to instruct the ignorant, reform the wicked, confirm the virtuous. Man forbids me to do this in another's parish; that is, in effect, to do it at all; seeing I have now no parish of my own, nor probably ever shall. Whom then shall I hear, God or man? "If it be just to obey man rather than God, judge you." "A dispensation of the gospel is committed to me; and woe is me if I preach not the gospel." But where shall I preach it upon the principles you mention? Why, not in Europe, Asia, Africa, or America; not in any of the Christian parts, at least, of the habitable earth: for all these are, after a sort, divided into parishes. . . .

Suffer me now to tell you my principles in this matter. I look upon all the world as my parish; thus far I mean that in whatever part of it I am, I judge it meet, right, and my bounden duty to declare unto all that are willing to hear, the glad tidings of salvation. This is the work which I know God has called me to, and sure I am that his blessing attends it. Great encouragement have I, therefore, to be faithful in fulfilling the work he hath given me to do. His servant I am and, as such, am employed according to the plain direction of his Word, "As I have opportunity, doing good unto all men." And his providence clearly concurs with his Word, which has disengaged me from all things else that I might singly attend on this very thing, "and go about doing good." (Letter to James Hervey, in *Journal*, June 11, 1739)

In the evening I reached Bristol and met Mr. Whitefield there. I could scarcely reconcile myself at first to this strange way of preaching in the fields, of which he set me an example on Sunday; having been all my life (till very lately) so tenacious of every point relating to decency and order that I should have thought the saving of souls almost a sin if it had not been done in a church. (*Journal*, March 29, 1739)

In the evening (Mr. Whitefield being gone) I began expounding our Lord's Sermon on the Mount (one pretty remarkable precedent of field preaching, though I suppose there were churches at that time also). (*Journal*, April 1, 1739)

At four in the afternoon, I submitted to be more vile and proclaimed in the highways the glad tidings of salvation, speaking from a little eminence in a ground adjoining to the city to about three thousand people. The scripture on which I spoke was this (is it possible anyone should be ignorant that it is fulfilled in every true minister of Christ?): "The Spirit of the Lord is upon me, because he hath anointed me to preach the gospel to the poor; he hath sent me to heal the brokenhearted, to preach deliverance to the captives, and recovering of sight to the blind, to set at liberty them that are bruised, to proclaim the acceptable year of the Lord." (*Journal*, April 2, 1739)

Permit me to speak plainly. If by catholic principles you mean any other than scriptural, they weigh nothing with me; I allow no other rule, whether of faith or practice, than the Holy Scriptures. But on scriptural principles, I do not think it hard to justify whatever I do. God in Scripture commands me, according to my power, to instruct the ignorant, reform the wicked, confirm the virtuous. Man forbids me to do this in another's parish; that is, in effect, to do it at all, seeing I have now no parish of my own, nor probably ever shall. Whom then shall I hear, God or man?

. . . I look upon all the world as my parish; thus far I mean that in whatever part of it I am, I judge it meet, right, and my bounden duty to declare unto all that are willing to hear, the glad tidings of salvation. This is the work which I know God has called me to, and sure I am that his blessing attends it. Great encouragement have I, therefore, to be faithful in fulfilling the work he hath given me to do. His servant I am and, as such, am employed according to the plain direction of his Word, "As I have opportunity, doing good unto all men." And his providence clearly concurs with his Word, which has disengaged me from all things else that I might singly attend on this very thing, "and go about doing good." (*Journal,* June 11, 1739)

Be pleased to observe, (1) That I was forbidden, as by a general consent, to preach in any church, though not by any judicial sentence, "for preaching such doctrine." This was the open, avowed cause: there was at that time no other, either real or pretended. (2) That I had no desire or design to preach in the open air till long after this prohibition. (3) That when I did, as it was no matter of choice, so neither of premeditation. There was no scheme at all previously formed, which was to be supported thereby; nor had I any other end in view than this, to save as many souls as I could. (4) *Field preaching* was therefore a sudden expedient, a thing submitted to rather than chosen; and therefore submitted to because I thought preaching even thus better than not preaching at all. First, in regard to my own soul, because a dispensation of the gospel being committed to me, I did not dare, not to preach the gospel. Secondly, in regard to the souls of others, whom I everywhere saw, *seeking death in the error of their life.* (*A Farther Appeal to Men of Reason and Religion* [1745], pt. 1, in *Works,* 12:123)

But suppose field preaching to be, in a case of this kind, ever so expedient, or even necessary, yet who will contest with us for this province? May we not enjoy this quiet and unmolested? Unmolested, I mean by any competitors. For who is there among you, brethren, that is willing (examine your own hearts) even to save souls from death at this price? Would not you let a thousand souls perish, rather than you would be the instrument of rescuing them thus? I do not speak now with regard to conscience, but to the inconveniences that must accompany it. Can you sustain them, if you would? Can you bear the summer sun to beat upon your naked head? Can you suffer the wintry rain or wind, from whatever quarter it blows? Are you able to stand in the open air, without any covering or defense, when God casteth abroad his snow like wool or scattereth his hoarfrost like ashes? And yet these are some of the smallest inconveniences which accompany field preaching. For beyond all these are the contradiction of sinners, the scoffs both of the great vulgar and the small; contempt and reproach of every kind; often more than verbal affronts, stupid, brutal violence, sometimes to the hazard of health or limbs or life. Brethren, do you envy us this honor? What, I pray, would buy you to be a field preacher? Or what, think you, could induce any man of common sense to continue therein one year, unless he had a full conviction in himself that it was the will of God concerning him? Upon this conviction it is (were we to submit to these things on any other motive whatsoever, it would furnish you with a better proof of our distraction than any that has yet been found) that we now do, for the good of souls, what you cannot, will not, dare not do. And we desire not that you should; but this one thing we may reasonably desire of you: do not increase the difficulties which are already so great, that without the mighty power of God we must sink under them. Do not assist in trampling down a little handful of men who for the present stand in the gap between ten thousand poor wretches and destruction, till you find some others to take their places. (*A Farther Appeal to Men of Reason and Religion* [1745], pt. 3, in *Works,* 12:260-61)

P

It were better for me to die than not to preach the gospel of Christ; yea, and in the fields, either where I may not preach in the church or where the church will not contain the congregation. (Letter to John Smith [probably one of the archbishops of Canterbury, Thomas Herring or Thomas Secker] [June 25, 1746], in *Works* [WL], 12:79)

Among my parishioners in Lincolnshire I tried for some years, but I am well assured I did far more good to them by preaching three days on my father's tomb than I did by preaching three years in his pulpit.

But you "know no call I have to preach up and down; to play the part of an itinerant evangelist." Perhaps you do not. But I do; I know God hath required this at my hands. To me, his blessing my work is an abundant proof, although such a proof as often makes me tremble. But "is there not pride or vanity in my heart"? There is; yet this is not my motive to preaching. I know and feel that the spring of this is a deep conviction that it is the will of God and that, were I to refrain, I should never hear that word, "Well done, good and faithful servant" but "Cast ye the unprofitable servant into outer darkness, where is weeping, and wailing, and gnashing of teeth." (Letter to John Smith [probably one of the archbishops of Canterbury, Thomas Herring or Thomas Secker] [March 25, 1747], in *Works* [WL], 12:88-89)

I no otherwise assume the apostolate of England (if you choose to use the phrase) than I assume the apostolate of all Europe or, rather, of all the world; that is, in plain terms, wherever I see one or a thousand men running into hell—be it in England, Ireland, or France, yea, in Europe, Asia, Africa, or America—I will stop them if I can: as a minister of Christ I will beseech them, in his name, to turn back and be reconciled to God. Were I to do otherwise, were I to let any soul drop into the pit whom I might have saved from everlasting burnings, I am not satisfied God would accept my plea, "Lord, he was not of my parish." (Letter to John Smith [probably one of the archbishops of Canterbury, Thomas Herring or Thomas Secker] [March 22, 1748], in *Works* [WL], 12:100)

I wonder at those who still talk so loud of the indecency of field preaching. The highest indecency is in St. Paul's Church, when a considerable part of the congregation are asleep or talking or looking about, not minding a word the preacher says. On the other hand, there is the highest decency in a churchyard or field, when the whole congregation behave and look as if they saw the Judge of all and heard him speaking from heaven. (*Journal*, August 28, 1748)

A vast majority of the immense congregation in Moorfields were deeply serious. One such hour might convince any impartial man of the expediency of field preaching. What building, except St. Paul's Church, would contain such a congregation? And if it would, what human voice could have reached them there? By repeated observations I find I can command thrice the number in the open air that I can under a roof. And who can say the time for field preaching is over while (1) greater numbers than ever attend; (2) the converting, as well as convincing power of God is eminently present with them? (*Journal*, September 23, 1759)

As to *irregularity*, I hope none of those who cause it do then complain of it. Will they throw a man into the dirt and beat him because he is dirty? Of all men living, those clergymen ought not to complain who believe I preach the gospel (as to the substance of it). If they do not ask me to preach in their churches, *they* are accountable for my preaching in the fields. (Letter to the Rev. Mr. Venn [June 22, 1765], in *Works*, 16:60)

Let us consider this matter from the very beginning. Two young clergymen, not very remarkable any way, of middle age, having a tolerable measure of health though rather weak than strong, began, about fifty years ago, to call sinners to repentance. This they did, for a time, in many of the churches in and about London. But two difficulties arose: First, the churches were so crowded that many of the parishioners could not get in. Secondly, they preached new doctrines—that we are saved by faith and that "without holiness no man could see the Lord." For one or other of these reasons, they were not long suffered to preach in the churches. They then preached in Moorfields, Kennington Common, and in many other public places. The fruit of their preaching quickly appeared. Many sinners were changed both in heart and life. ("On God's Vineyard" [October 17, 1787], Sermon 107, in *Works* [WL], 7:206)

PREDESTINATION: CONDITIONAL

The Scripture tells us plainly what predestination is: it is God's fore-appointing obedient believers to salvation, not without, but "according to his foreknowledge" of all their works "from the foundation of the world." And so likewise he predestinates or fore-appoints all disobedient unbelievers to damnation, not without, but "according to his foreknowledge" of all their works "from the foundation of the world."

We may consider this a little further. "God, from the foundation of the world, foreknew all men's believing or not believing. And according to this his foreknowledge, he chose or *elected* all obedient believers, as such, to salvation and refused or *reprobated* all disobedient unbelievers, as such, to damnation. Thus the Scriptures teach us to consider *election* and *reprobation* "according to the foreknowledge of God from the foundation of the world." (Quoted in "Of God," chap. 3 in Coll. D, 67)

As to your main objection, convince me that it is my duty to preach on controverted subjects, predestination in particular, and I will do it. At present, I think it would be a sin. I think it would create still more divisions. And are there not enough already? (*Some Remarks on a Defence of the Preface to the Edinburgh Edition of* Aspasio Vindicated [May 1766], in *Works*, 13:124)

My chief objection to Milton's doctrine of election is that I cannot reconcile it to the words of St. Peter, which manifestly refer to the eternal state of men: "God is no respecter of persons." Now, how can we allow this if we believe he places one man, as it were, suspended between heaven and hell while he fixes another, ere ever he is born, under an absolute impossibility of missing heaven? (Letter to Mrs. Elizabeth Bennis [July 20, 1771], in *Works* [S], 7:54)

PRIESTS

But before those words . . . were those spoken [in the Anglican rite of ordination] without any restraint or limitation at all, which I apprehend to convey an indelible character, "Receive the Holy Ghost, for the office and work of a priest in the church of God, now committed unto thee by the imposition of our hands. Whose sins thou dost forgive, they are forgiven, and whose sins thou dost retain, they are retained. And be thou a faithful dispenser of the

Word of God and of his holy sacraments, in the name of the Father and of the Son and of the Holy Ghost." (*A Farther Appeal to Men of Reason and Religion* [1745], pt. 1, in *Works*, 12:129)

PRIVATE JUDGMENT

Q. . . . It was then inquired, "How far does each of us agree to submit to the unanimous judgment of the rest?" [A.] And it was answered, "In speculative things each can only submit as far as his judgment shall be convinced; in every practical point, as far as we can without wounding our several consciences."

Q. . . . Can a Christian submit any farther than this to any man or number of men upon earth?

A. It is undeniably plain he cannot: either to pope, council, bishop, or convocation. And this is that grand principle of every man's right to private judgment, in opposition to implicit faith in man, on which Calvin, Luther, Melanchthon, and all the ancient reformers, both at home and abroad, proceeded, "Every man must think for himself, since every man must give an account for himself to God." (Minutes of the Methodist Conference, June 15, 1747 in *Minutes*, 34-35)

I know it is commonly supposed that the place of our birth fixes the church to which we ought to belong; that one, for instance, who is born in England ought to be a member of that which is styled the Church of England, and consequently, to worship God in the particular manner which is prescribed by that Church. I was once a zealous maintainer of this, but I find many reasons to abate of this zeal. I fear it is attended with such difficulties that no reasonable man can get over. Not the least of which is that if this rule had taken place there could have been no Reformation from popery; seeing it entirely destroys the right of private judgment on which that whole Reformation stands. ("Catholic Spirit" [1750], Sermon 41, in *Works* [T], 5:413-14)

PURGATORY; PREPARATION FOR HEAVEN IN THE AFTERLIFE (AND THIS LIFE)

"You make sinless perfection necessary after justification in order to make us meet for glory." And who does not? Indeed men do not agree in the time. Some believe it is attained before death, some in the article of death, some in an after state, in the *mystic* or the *popish* purgatory. But all writers whom I have ever seen till now (the Romish themselves not excepted) agree, that we must be *fully cleansed from all sin* before we can enter into glory. (*The Principles of a Methodist Farther Explained* [1746], in *Works*, 12:346)

But it is far from certain that "the purpose of this [praying for the dead] was to procure relief and refreshment to the departed souls in some intermediate state of expiatory pains" or that this was the general "opinion of those times." (*A Letter to the Rev. Dr. Conyers Middleton Occasioned by His Late "Free Inquiry"* [January 4, 1749], *Works* [S], 5:711)

As to the manner, I believe this perfection is always wrought in the soul by a simple act of faith; consequently, in an instant.

But I believe a gradual work, both preceding and following that instant.

As to the time, I believe this instant generally is the instant of death, the moment before the soul leaves the body. But I believe it may be ten, twenty, or forty years before.

I believe it is usually many years after justification but that it may be within five years or five months after it. I know no conclusive argument to the contrary. (*A Plain Account of Christian Perfection* [1767; rev. 1777], in *Works* [WL], 11:446)

Conflicts and various exercises of soul are permitted; these also are for good. If Satan has desired to have you to sift you as wheat, this likewise is for your profit. You will be purified in the fire, not consumed, and strengthened unto all longsuffering with joyfulness. (Letter to Mrs. Mary Savage [May 6, 1771], in *Works* [WL], 12:481)

That those who die in a state of grace go into a place of torment, in order to be purged in the other world, is utterly contrary to Scripture. Our Lord said to the penitent thief upon the cross, "To day shalt thou be with me in paradise." Now, if a purgation in another world were necessary for any, he that did not repent and believe till the last hour of his life might well be supposed to need it and consequently ought to have been sent to purgatory, not to paradise. (*Popery Calmly Considered* [1779], in *Works*, 15:182)

Gold is tried in the fire, and acceptable men in the furnace of adversity.

You say, "I know not whither I am going." I will tell you whither. You are going the straight way to be swallowed up in God. "I know not what I am doing." You are suffering the will of God and glorifying him in the fire. "But I am not increasing in the divine life." That is your mistake. Perhaps you are now increasing therein faster than ever you did since you were justified. It is true that the usual method of our Lord is to purify us by joy in the Holy Ghost and a full consciousness of his love. But I have known several exempt cases, and I am clearly satisfied yours is one. (Letter to Miss Loxdale [March 9, 1782], in *Works*, 16:164)

PURITANS

I am sensible, even these excellent writers are not without their blemishes. . . . One of these is that they drag in controversy on every occasion, nay, without any occasion or pretense at all. Another is that they generally give a low and imperfect view of sanctification or holiness. . . .

. . . But abundant recompense is made for all their blemishes by the excellencies which may be observed in them. . . .

. . . Particularly, they do indeed exalt Christ. They set him forth in all his offices. They speak of him as those that have seen his glory, full of grace and truth. They sum up all things in Christ, deduce all things from him, and refer all things to him.

. . . And, next to God himself, they honor his word. They are men mighty in the Scriptures, equal to any of those who went before them and far superior to most that have followed them. They prove all things hereby. (Preface to *Extracts from the Works of the Puritans,* in *Works* [S], 7:530-31)

P

QUAKERS

Friend, you have an honest heart but a weak head; you have a zeal but not according to knowledge. You were zealous once for the love of God and man, for holiness of heart and holiness of life. You are now zealous for particular forms of speaking, for a set of phrases and opinions. Once your zeal was against ungodliness and unrighteousness, against evil tempers and evil works. Now it is against forms of prayer, against singing psalms or hymns, against appointing times of praying or preaching, against saying *you* to a single person, uncovering your head, or having too many buttons on your coat. [Oh,] what a fall is here! What poor trifles are these that now well nigh engross your thoughts! Come back, come back to the weightier matters of the law, spiritual, rational, scriptural religion. No longer waste your time and strength in beating the air, in vain controversies and strife of words, but bend your whole soul to the growing in grace and in the knowledge of our Lord Jesus Christ, to the continually advancing in that holiness, without which you cannot see the Lord. (*A Letter to a Person Lately Joined to the People Called Quakers* [February 2, 1748], in *Works* [T], 9:117-18)

When you enter into your closet, and shut the door, and pray to your Father who seeth in secret; then is the time to groan, to him who reads the heart, the unutterable prayer. But to be silent in the congregation of his people is wholly new and therefore wholly wrong. A silent meeting was never heard of in the church of Christ for sixteen hundred years. (Letter to James Bogie [August 10, 1772], in *Works* [S], 7:143)

Q

READING

History, poetry, and philosophy I commonly read on horseback. (*Journal,* March 21, 1770)

REFORMATION: PROTESTANT

Yet there is not found among them [those in the Methodist revival] that *bitter zeal* in points either of small or of great importance, that spirit of *persecution*, which has so often accompanied the spirit of Reformation. . . . all the children of disobedience will, on a thousand different pretenses and in a thousand different ways, so far as God permits, persecute the children of God. But what is still more to be lamented is that the children of God themselves have so often used the same weapons and persecuted others, when the power was in their own hands.

Can we wholly excuse those venerable men, our great Reformers themselves, from this charge? I fear not, if we impartially read over any history of the Reformation. (*A Farther Appeal to Men of Reason and Religion* [1745], pt. 3, in *Works*, 12:230)

When the Reformation began, what mountainous offenses lay in the way, of even the sincere members of the Church of Rome! They saw such failings in those great men, Luther and Calvin! Their vehement tenaciousness of their own opinion, their bitterness towards all who differed from them, their impatience of contradiction and utter want of forbearance, even with their own brethren.

But the grand stumbling block of all was their open, avowed separation from the Church, their rejecting so many of the doctrines and practices which the others accounted the most sacred, and their continual invectives against the Church they separated from, so much sharper than Michael's reproof of Satan.

Were there fewer stumbling blocks attending the Reformation in England? Surely not; for what was Henry the Eighth? Consider either his character, his motives to the work, or his manner of pursuing it! And even King Edward's ministry we cannot clear of persecuting in their turns, yea, and burning heretics. The main stumbling block also still remained, [namely], open separation from the Church. (*A Farther Appeal to Men of Reason and Religion* [1745], pt. 3, in *Works*, 12:273-74)

REGENERATION

According to the whole tenor of Scripture, the being born again does really signify the being inwardly changed by the almighty operation of the Spirit of God: changed from sin to holiness; renewed in the image of him that created us. And why must we be so changed? Because "without holiness no man shall see the Lord" and because without this change, all our endeavors after holiness are ineffectual. God hath, indeed, "endowed us with understanding, and given us abundant means," but our understanding is as insufficient for that end as are the outward means, if not attended with inward power. (*Regeneration* [January 25, 1757], in Coll. B, 182)

Of the new birth, you say, "The terms of being *regenerated*, of being *born again*, of being *born of God* are often used to express *the works* of gospel righteousness." I cannot allow this. I know not that they are ever used in Scripture to express any outward work at all. They always express an inward work of the Spirit, whereof baptism is the outward sign. . . .

. . . You proceed: "Our holy [Anglican] Church doth teach us that by the laver of regeneration in baptism we are received into the number of the children of God; this is the first part of the new birth." What is the first part of the new birth? baptism? It is the outward sign of that inward and spiritual grace, but no part of it at all. It is impossible that it should be. The outward sign is no more a part of the inward grace than the body is a part of the soul. Or do you mean that regeneration is a part of the new birth? Nay, this is the whole of it. (Letter to the Rev. Mr. Potter [November 4, 1758], in Coll. B, 186)

We do believe regeneration, or in plain English, the new birth, to be as miraculous or supernatural a work now as it was seventeen hundred years ago. We likewise believe that the spiritual life, which commences when we are born again, must in the nature of the thing, have a *first moment* as well as the natural. But we say again and again, we are concerned for the *substance* of the work, not the *circumstance*. Let it be wrought at all, and we will not contend whether it be wrought gradually or instantaneously. "But what are the signs that it is wrought?" We never said or thought that they were either "frightful tremors of body" or "convulsive agonies of mind." I presume you mean, agonies of mind attended with bodily convulsions. Although we know many persons who *before* this change was wrought felt much fear and sorrow of mind which in some of these had such an effect on the body as to make all their bones to shake. (Letter to the Rev. Mr. Downes [November 17, 1759], in *Works*, 13:97)

REPENTANCE

If to this lively conviction of thy inward and outward sins, of thy utter guiltiness and helplessness, there be added suitable affections, sorrow of heart for having despised thy own mercies, remorse, and self-condemnation, having thy mouth stopped, shame to lift up thine eyes to heaven, fear of the wrath of God abiding on thee, of his curse hanging over thy head, and of the fiery indignation ready to devour those who forget God and obey not our Lord Jesus Christ, earnest desire to escape from that indignation, to cease from evil, and learn to do well: then I say unto thee in the name of the Lord, "Thou art not far from the kingdom of God." One step more and thou shalt enter in. Thou dost *repent*. Now, "Believe the gospel." ("The Way to the Kingdom" [1746], Sermon 7, in *Works* [T], 5:70)

REPROBATION: UNCONDITIONAL (FALSITY OF)

Impartially consider how it is possible to reconcile reprobation with the following scriptures:

[Gen. 3:17, 19], "Because thou hast eaten of the tree of which I commanded thee, saying, Thou shalt not eat of it; [. . .] in the sweat of thy face shalt thou eat bread." The curse shall come on thee and thine offspring, not because of any absolute decree of mine, but because of thy sin.

[Gen. 4:7], "If thou doest well, shalt thou not be accepted? And if thou doest not well, sin lieth at the door." Sin only, not the decree of reprobation, hinders thy being accepted.

[Deut. 7:9-10], "Know that the Lord thy God, he is the faithful God, which keepeth covenant and mercy with them that love him and keep his commandments to a thousand generations: and repayeth them that hate him to their face, to destroy them." [V. 12], "Wherefore if ye hearken to these judgments, and keep and do them, the Lord thy God shall keep unto thee the covenant which he sware unto thy fathers."

[Deut. 11:26-28], "Behold, I set before you this day a blessing and a curse; a blessing, if you obey the commandments of the Lord your God; and a curse, if you will not obey."

[Deut. 30:15-19], "See, I have set before thee this day life and good, and death and evil: in that I command thee this day to love the Lord thy God, to walk in his ways and keep his commandments, and the Lord thy God shall bless thee. But if thou wilt not hear, I denounce unto you this day, that ye shall surely perish. [. . .] I call heaven and earth to record this day, that I have set before you life and death, blessing and cursing. Therefore choose life, that both thou and thy seed may live."

[2 Chron. 15:1-2], "And the Spirit of God came upon Azariah, and he said, The Lord is with you while ye be with him: and if ye seek him, he will be found of you: but if ye forsake him, he will forsake you."

[Ezra 9:13-14], "After all that is come upon us for our evil deeds, and for our great trespass, [. . .] Should we again break thy commandments, [. . .] wouldst thou not be angry with us, till thou hadst consumed us?"

[Job 36:5], "Behold, God is mighty, and despiseth not any." Could he then reprobate any?

[Ps. 145:9], "The Lord is good to all, and his tender mercies are over all his works."

[Prov. 1:23-24, 26, 28, 29], "Turn you at my reproof; behold I will pour out my Spirit upon you. Because I have called and ye refused, I have stretched out my hand, and no man regarded." "I also will laugh at your calamity; I will mock when your fear cometh." "Then shall they call upon me, but I will not answer; they shall seek me early, but they shall not find me." Why? Because of my decree? No. "But because they hated knowledge, and did not choose the fear of the Lord."

[Isa. 65:2-3, 7, 12, 15], "I have spread out my hands all the day unto a rebellious people; a people that provoked me to anger continually to my face; [. . .] therefore will I measure their former work into their bosom. [. . .] Ye shall all bow down to the slaughter, because when I called ye did not answer. [. . .] Therefore ye shall leave your name for a curse unto my chosen: for the Lord God shall slay thee, and call his servants by another name."

[Ezek. 18:20, 23], "The soul that sinneth, it shall die. The son shall not bear (*eternally*) the iniquity of the father, neither shall the father bear the iniquity of the son. [. . .] Have I any pleasure at all that the wicked should die, saith the Lord: and not that he should return from his ways and live?"

[Matt. 7:26], "Every one that heareth these sayings of mine, and doeth them not, shall be likened unto a foolish man, which built his house upon the sand." Nay, he could not help it, if he were ordained thereto.

[Matt. 11:20-24], "Then began he to upbraid the cities wherein most of his mighty works were done, because they repented not. Woe unto thee, Chorazin! woe unto thee, Bethsaida! for if the mighty works which were done in you, had been done in Tyre and Sidon, they would have repented long ago in sackcloth and ashes." (What if they were not *elected*? And if they of Bethsaida had been *elected*, would they not have repented too?) "Therefore I say unto you, it shall be more tolerable for Tyre and Sidon in the day of judgment, than for you. And thou, Capernaum, which art exalted unto heaven, shalt be brought down to hell. For if the mighty works which have been done in thee, had been done in Sodom, it would have remained until this day. But I say unto you, it shall be more tolerable for the land of Sodom in the day of judgment, than for thee."

[Matt. 12:41], "The men of Nineveh shall rise in judgment with this generation, and shall condemn it; because they repented at the preaching of Jonas; and behold a greater than Jonas is here." But what was this to the purpose, if *the men of Nineveh* were elected and *this generation* of men were not?

[Matt. 13:11-12], "It is given unto you to know the mysteries of the kingdom of heaven, but unto them it is not given. For whosoever hath ([that is], uses what he hath), to him shall be given, and he shall have more abundance. But whosoever hath not, from him shall be taken away even that he hath." [22:8], "They which were called were not worthy," were shut out from the marriage of the Lamb: Why so? Because "they would not come" [v. 3]. The whole twenty-fifth chapter requires and will reward your most serious consideration. If you can reconcile unconditional reprobation with this, you may reconcile it with the 18th of Ezekiel.

[John 3:19], "This is the condemnation, that light is come into the world, and men love (or choose) darkness rather than light." [5:44], "How can ye believe, who receive honour one of another, and seek not the honour that cometh of God only?" Observe the reason why they *could* not believe: it was not in God but in themselves.

[Acts 8:20-22], "Thy money perish with thee (and so doubtless it did). [. . .] Thou hast neither part nor lot in this matter; for thy heart is not right in the sight of God. Repent therefore of this thy wickedness, and pray God, if perhaps the thought of thy heart may be forgiven thee." So that St. Peter had no thought of any absolute reprobation, even in the case of Simon Magus.

[Rom. 1:20-21, 24-28], "They are without excuse; because when they knew God, they glorified him not as God: [. . .] wherefore God also gave them up to uncleanness, [. . .] who changed the truth of God into a lie, [. . .]

For this cause God gave them up to vile affections, [. . .] As they did not like to retain God in their knowledge, God gave them over to a reprobate mind, to do those things which are not convenient."

[2 Thess. 2:10-12], "Them that perish, because they received not the love of the truth, that they might be saved. And for this cause God shall send them strong delusions, to believe a lie: that they all might be damned who believed not the truth, but had pleasure in unrighteousness." (*Predestination Calmly Considered* [1752], in *Works* [T], 9:382-84)

But as the apostle was aware, how deeply the Jews were offended at the whole tenor of his doctrine, and more especially at his asserting, (1) that the Jews themselves could not be saved without believing in Jesus; and, (2) that the heathens, by believing in him, might partake of the same salvation; he spends the whole ninth chapter [of Romans] upon them: wherein, (1) he declares the tender love he had for them [vv. 1, 3]; (2) allows the great national privileges they enjoyed above any people under heaven [vv. 4-5]; (3) answers their grand objection to his doctrine, taken from the justice of God, to their fathers [vv. 6-13]; (4) removes another objection, taken from the justice of God, interweaving all along strong reproofs to the Jews, for priding themselves on those privileges which were owing merely to the good pleasure of God, not to their fathers' goodness, any more than their own [vv. 14, 23]; (5) resumes and proves by Scripture his former assertion, that many Jews would be lost and many heathens saved [vv. 24-29]. And, lastly, sums up the general drift of this chapter, and indeed of the whole epistle. *What shall we say then?* What is the conclusion from the whole? The sum of all which has been spoken? Why, that many Gentiles already partake of the great salvation, and many Jews fall short of it. *Wherefore?* Because they would not receive it by faith. And whosoever believeth not cannot be saved; whereas, *whosoever believeth* in Christ, whether Jew or Gentile, *shall not be ashamed* [vv. 30, 33].

. . . Those words, "Hath not the potter power over his own clay? are part of St. Paul's answer to that objection, that it was unjust for God to show that mercy to the Gentiles which he withheld from his own people. This he first simply denies, saying, *God forbid!* And then observes that according to his own words to Moses, God has a right to fix the terms on which he will show mercy, which neither the will nor the power of man can alter [vv. 15-16]; and to withdraw his mercy from them who, like Pharaoh, will not comply with those terms [v. 17]. And that accordingly, "he hath mercy on whom he will have mercy," namely, those that truly believe; *and whom he will*, namely, obstinate unbelievers he suffers to be *hardened*. (*Predestination Calmly Considered*

[1752], in *Works* [T], 9:388-89)

Should you not rather say that unbelief is the damning sin? and that those who are condemned in that day will be therefore condemned, "because they believed not on the name of the only-begotten Son of God?" But could they believe? Was not this faith both the gift and the work of God in the soul? And was it not a gift which he had eternally decreed never to give them? Was it not a work which he was of old unchangeably determined never to work in their souls? Shall these men then be condemned because God would not work, because they did not receive what God would not give? Could they "ungrasp the hold of his right hand, or force omnipotence"? (*Predestination Calmly Considered* [1752], in *Works* [T], 9:391-92)

Suppose now the Judge of all the earth, having just pronounced the awful sentence, *Depart, ye cursed, into everlasting fire, prepared for the devil and his angels*, should say to one on the left hand, "What canst thou offer in thy own behalf?" Might he not on this [Calvinist] scheme, answer, "Lord, why am I doomed to dwell with everlasting burnings? For not doing good? Was it ever in my power to do any good action? Could I ever do any, but by that grace which thou hadst determined not to give me? For doing evil? Lord, did I ever do any which I was not bound to do by thy own decree? Was there ever a moment when it was in my power either to do good or to cease from evil? Didst not thou fix whatever I should do or not do or ever I came into the world? And was there ever one hour, from my cradle to my grave, wherein I could act otherwise than I did?" (*Thoughts upon Necessity* [May 14, 1774], in *Works* [T], 9:465)

REPROOF; REBUKE

I am exceedingly obliged by the pains you have taken to point out to me what you think to be mistakes. It is a truly Christian attempt, an act of brotherly love, which I pray God to repay sevenfold into your bosom. Methinks I can scarce look upon such a person, on one who is "a contender for truth and not for victory," whatever opinion he may entertain of me, as any adversary at all. For what is friendship, if I am to account him my enemy who endeavors to open my eyes or to amend my heart? (Letter to John Smith [probably one of the archbishops of Canterbury, Thomas Herring or Thomas Secker] [September 28, 1745], in *Works* [WL], 12:57)

Always take advice or reproof as a favor; it is the surest mark of love.

I advised you once, and you took it as an affront; nevertheless I will do it once more. . . .

. . . If you cannot take advice from others, surely you might take it from your affectionate brother. (Letter to John King [July 28, 1775], in *Letters*, 253)

REVIVAL

Just at this time, when we wanted little of "filling up the measure of our iniquities," two or three clergymen of the Church of England began vehemently to *call sinners to repentance*. In two or three years they had sounded the alarm to the utmost borders of the land. Many thousands gathered together to hear them; and in every place where they came, many began to show such a concern for religion, as they never had done before. A stronger *impression* was made on their minds of the importance of things eternal, and they had more earnest *desires* of serving God than they had ever had from their earliest childhood. Thus did God begin to draw them toward himself with the cords of love, with the bands of a man.

Many of these were in a short time deeply *convinced* of the *number* and *heinousness* of their *sins*. They were also made thoroughly sensible of those *tempers* which are justly hateful to God and man and of their utter *ignorance* of God and entire *inability* either to know, love, or serve him. At the same time, they saw in the strongest light the *insignificancy* of their *outside religion*, nay, and often confessed it before God as the most abominable *hypocrisy*. Thus did they sink deeper and deeper into that *repentance* which must ever precede *faith* in the Son of God. And from hence sprung "fruits meet for repentance." The drunkard commenced sober and temperate; the whoremonger abstained from adultery and fornication; the unjust from oppression and wrong. He that had been accustomed to curse and to swear for many years now swore no more. The sluggard began to work with his hands that he might eat his own bread. The miser learned to deal his bread to the hungry and to cover the naked with a garment. Indeed the whole form of their life was changed. They had *left off doing evil, and learned to do well*.

. . . But this was not all. Over and above this *outward change*, they began to experience *inward* religion: "The love of God was shed abroad in their hearts," which they continue to enjoy to this day. They love him "because he first loved us" and withheld not from us his Son, his only Son. And this love constrains them to love all mankind, all the children of the Father of heaven and earth, and inspires them with every holy and heavenly temper, the whole mind that was in Christ. . . .

. . . In what age has such a work been wrought, considering the *swiftness* as well as the *extent* of it? When have such *numbers* of sinners, in so *short* a time, been recovered from the error of their ways? When hath religion, I will not say since the Reformation but since the time of Constantine the Great, made so large a progress in any nation within so small a space? I believe, hardly can either ancient or modern history supply us with a parallel instance. (*A Farther Appeal to Men of Reason and Religion* [1745], pt. 3, in *Works*, 12:225-27)

The clear and undeniable fact stands thus: A few years ago Great Britain and Ireland were covered with vice from sea to sea. Very little of even the form of religion was left and still less of the power of it. Out of this darkness God commanded light to shine. In a short space, he called thousands of sinners to repentance. They were not only reformed from their outward vices but likewise changed in their dispositions and tempers; filled with a serious, sober sense of true religion, with love to God and all mankind, with a holy faith producing good works of every kind, works both of piety and mercy. (*A Letter to the Author of* The Enthusiasm of Methodists and Papists Compared [1750], in *Works,* 13:15)

Where Christian perfection is not strongly and explicitly preached there is seldom any remarkable blessing from God and, consequently, little addition to the society and little life in the members of it. . . . Speak and spare not. Let not regard for any man induce you to betray the truth of God. Till you press the believers to expect full salvation *now,* you must not look for any revival. (Letter to Mr. Merriweather [February 8, 1766], in Coll. B, 527)

The fields in every part of England are indeed white for the harvest. There is everywhere an amazing willingness in the people to receive either instruction or exhortation. We find this temper now even in many of the higher rank, several of whom cared for none of these things. But surely the time is coming for these also; for the Scripture must be fulfilled: "They shall all know me, from the least even to the greatest." (Letter to Ebenezer Blackwell [May 6, 1766], in *Letters,* 351)

I seldom find it profitable to converse with any who are not athirst for full salvation and who are not big with earnest expectation of receiving it every moment. (Letter to the Rev. John Fletcher [March 20, 1768], in Coll. B, 529)

The remark of Luther, "that a revival of religion seldom continues above thirty years," has been verified many times in several countries. But it will not always hold. The present revival of religion in England has already continued fifty years. And, blessed be God, it is at least as likely to continue, as it was twenty or thirty years ago. Indeed, it is far more likely, as it not only spreads wider but sinks deeper than ever, more and more persons being able to testify that the blood of Christ cleanses from all sin. (Letter to Miss Elizabeth Ritchie [February 12, 1779], in *Letters,* 379)

It is certain there has been, for these forty years, such an outpouring of the Spirit and such an increase of vital religion as has not been in England for many centuries, and it does not appear that the work of God at all decays. In many places there is a considerable increase of it, so that we have reason to hope that the time is at hand when the kingdom of God shall come with power and all the people of this poor heathen land shall know him, from the least to the greatest. (Letter to Miss H. A. Roe [June 25, 1782], in *Works* [S], 7:195)

I do not wonder at all that after that great and extraordinary work of God there should be a remarkable decay. So we have found it in almost all places. A swift increase is generally followed by a decrease equally swift. All we can do to prevent it is continually to exhort all who have tasted that the Lord is gracious to remember our Lord's words, "Watch and pray that ye enter not into temptation." (Letter to William Black [July 13, 1783], in *Letters*, 260)

It is indeed a matter of joy that our Lord is still carrying on his work throughout Great Britain and Ireland. In the time of Dr. Jonathan Edwards, there were several gracious showers in New England, but there were large intermissions between one and another; whereas, with us there has been no intermission at all for seven-and-forty years, but the work of God has been continually increasing. (Letter to William Black [November 26, 1786], in *Letters*, 270)

REVOLUTION: AMERICAN

I do not intend to enter upon the question, whether the Americans are in the right or in the wrong? Here all my prejudices are against the Americans, for I am a High Churchman, the son of a High Churchman, bred up from my childhood in the highest notions of passive obedience and nonresistance; and yet, in spite of all my long-rooted prejudices, I cannot avoid thinking, if I think at all, these, an oppressed people, asked for nothing more than their legal rights, and that in the most modest and inoffensive manner that the nature of the thing would allow.

But waiving this, waiving all considerations of right and wrong, I ask, Is it common sense to use force toward the Americans? A letter now before me, which I received yesterday, says, "Four hundred of the regulars and forty of the militia were killed in the late skirmish." What a disproportion is this! And this is the first essay of raw men against regular troops. You see, my Lord, whatever has been affirmed, these men will not be frightened; and it seems they will not be conquered so easily as was at first imagined. They will probably dispute every inch of ground, and if they die, die sword in hand. Indeed, some of our valiant officers say, "Two thousand men will clear America of these rebels." No, nor twenty thousand, be they rebels or not, nor perhaps treble that number. They are as strong men as you; they are as valiant as you, if not abundantly more valiant, for they are one and all enthusiasts— enthusiasts for liberty. They are calm, deliberate enthusiasts, and we know how this principle breathes into softer souls stern love of war and thirst of vengeance and contempt of death. We know men, animated with this spirit, will leap into a fire or rush into a cannon's mouth.

"But they have no experience in war." And how much more have our troops?—Very few of them ever saw a battle. "But they have no discipline." That is an entire mistake. Already they have near as much as our army, and they will learn more of it every day; so that in a short time, if the fatal occasion continue, they will understand it as well as their assailants. "But they are divided amongst themselves." So you are informed by various letters and memorials. So, doubt not, was poor Rehoboam informed concerning the ten tribes! . . .

These men think, one and all, be it right or wrong, that they are contending . . . for their wives, children, and liberty. What an advantage have they herein over many that fight only for pay! None of whom care a straw for the cause wherein they are engaged; most of whom strongly disapprove of it. Have they not another considerable advantage? Is there occasion to recruit the troops? Their supplies are at hand and all round about them. Ours are three thousand miles off! Are we then able to conquer the Americans, suppose they are left to themselves, suppose all our neighbors should stand stock still and leave us and them to fight it out? (Letter to the Right Honourable Lord North [June 15, 1775], in *Letters,* 474-75)

R

"But a few years ago he himself thought the Americans were in the right." I did; for then I thought that they sought nothing but legal liberty. But as soon as I was convinced they sought independency, I knew they were in the wrong. (*An Answer to Mr. Rowland Hill's Tract, Entitled, "Imposture Detected"* [June 28, 1777], in *Works* [WL], 10:452)

REWARDS IN HEAVEN

When the Son of Man shall come in his glory and assign every man his own reward, that reward will undoubtedly be proportioned, (1) to our inward holiness, our likeness to God; (2) to our works; and, (3) to our sufferings. Therefore, whatever you suffer in time, you will be an unspeakable gainer in eternity. (Letter to Miss Bolton [December 15, 1790], in *Works* [S], 7:120)

RICHES; LOVE OF MONEY

Indeed if I lay up riches at all, it must be *to leave them behind me,* seeing my fellowship is a provision for life. But I cannot understand this. What comfort would it be to my soul, now launched into eternity, that I had *left behind me* gold as the dust and silver as the sand of the sea? Will it follow me over the great gulf? Or can I go back to it? Thou that liftest up thy eyes in hell, what do thy riches profit thee now? Will all thou once hadst under the sun gain thee a drop of water to cool thy tongue? O the comfort of *riches* left *behind* to one who is tormented in that flame! . . .

. . . As to gold and silver, I count it dung and dross; I trample it under my feet. I (yet not I, but by the grace of God that is in me) esteem it just as mire in the streets. I desire it not; I seek it not. I only fear lest any of it should cleave to me, and I should not be able to shake it off before my spirit returns to God. It must indeed pass through my hands, but I will take care (God being my helper) that the mammon of unrighteousness shall only pass through; it shall not rest there. (*An Earnest Appeal to Men of Reason and Religion* [1743], in Coll. C, 231-32)

I love the poor; in many of them I find pure, genuine grace, unmixed with paint, folly, and affection. (Letter to Miss Furly [September 25, 1757], in *Works* [WL], 12:185)

I am almost ashamed (having done it twenty times before) to answer this stale calumny again. But the bold, frontless manner wherein you advance it obliges me so to do. . . . I love money no more than I love the mire in the streets: that I seek it not. And I have it not, any more than suffices for food and raiment, for the plain conveniences of life. I pay no court to it at all or to those that have it, either with cunning or without. For myself, for my own use, I raise no contributions either great or small. The weekly contributions of our community (which are freely given, not *squeezed* out of any), as well as the gifts and offerings of the Lord's Table, never come into my hands. I have no concern with them, not so much as "the beholding them with my eyes." They are received every week by the stewards of the society, men of well-known character in the world, and by them constantly distributed within the week to those whom they know to be in real necessity. (Letter to the Rev. Mr. Downes [November 17, 1759], in *Works*, 13:101-2)

Money never stays with *me*; it would burn me if it did. I throw it out of my hands as soon as possible, lest it should find a way into my heart. (Letter to his sister, Mrs. Martha Hall [October 6, 1768], in *Letters*, 66)

There is one way, and there is no other under heaven. If those who "gain all they can" and "save all they can" will likewise "give all they can," then the more they gain, the more they will grow in grace and the more treasure they will lay up in heaven. (*Thoughts upon Methodism* [August 4, 1786], in *Works* [S], 7:317)

Most of those in England who have riches love money, even the Methodists—at least those who are called so. The poor are the Christians. I am quite out of conceit with almost all those who have this world's goods. (Letter to the Rev. Freeborn Garrettson [September 30, 1786], in *Letters*, 270)

It is no more sinful to be rich than to be poor. But it is dangerous beyond expression. Therefore, I remind all of you that are of this number, that have the conveniences of life and something over, that ye walk upon slippery ground. Ye continually tread on snares and deaths. Ye are, every moment, on the verge of hell. ("The Rich Man and Lazarus" [March 25, 1788], Sermon 48, in *Works* [T], 6:55)

I left no money to anyone in my will, because I had none. (*Journal*, January 9, 1789)

RIGHTEOUSNESS OF FAITH

"By the righteousness which is of faith" is meant that condition of justification (and in consequence, of present and final salvation if we endure therein unto the end) which was given by God, to *fallen man*, through the merits and mediation of his only begotten Son. ("The Righteousness of Faith" [1746], Sermon 6, in *Works* [T], 5:58)

RULE OF FAITH

Permit me to speak plainly. If by catholic principles you mean any other than scriptural, they weigh nothing with me. I allow no other rule, whether of faith or practice, than the Holy Scriptures; but on scriptural principles I do not think it hard to justify whatever I do. (Letter to James Hervey, in *Journal*, June 11, 1739)

R

This whole demand, common as it is, of proving our doctrine by miracles, proceeds from a double mistake: (1) A supposition, that what we preach is not provable from Scripture; for if it be, what need we farther witnesses? "To the law and to the testimony!" (2) An imagination, that a doctrine not provable by Scripture might nevertheless be proved by miracles. I believe not. I receive the written word as the whole and sole rule of my faith. . . .
. . . What is scriptural in any church, I hold fast. For the rest, I let it go. (Letter to John Smith [probably one of the archbishops of Canterbury, Thomas Herring or Thomas Secker] [September 28, 1745], in *Works* [WL], 12:57, 59)

When I say, "The apostles themselves were to prove their assertions by the written word," I mean the word written before their time, the Law and the Prophets; and so they did. . . . I desire none to receive my words unless they are confirmed by Scripture and reason. (Letter to John Smith [probably one of the archbishops of Canterbury, Thomas Herring or Thomas Secker] [December 30, 1745], in *Works* [WL], 12:64)

But then remember, "That Scripture" (to use the words which you cite from *our learned and judicious* Hooker) "is *not* the only rule of all things which in this life may be done by men." (*The Principles of a Methodist Farther Explained* [1746], in *Works*, 12:369)

The Scriptures are the touchstone whereby Christians examine all (real or supposed) revelations. In all cases they appeal *to the law and* to *the testimony*, and *try* every *spirit* thereby. . . .

. . . Though the Spirit is our *principal leader*, yet he is not our rule at all; the Scriptures are the rule whereby he leads us into all truth. Therefore, only talk good English; call the Spirit our guide (which signifies an intelligent Being) and the Scriptures our rule (which signifies something used by an intelligent being), and all is plain and clear. (*A Letter to a Person Lately Joined to the People Called Quakers* [February 2, 1748], in *Works* [T], 9:110-11)

I lay this down as an undoubted truth, "The more the doctrine of any church agrees with the Scripture, the more readily ought it to be received." And on the other hand, "The more the doctrine of any church differs from the Scripture, the greater cause we have to doubt of it." . . .

. . . Every Christian has a right to know and read the Scripture, that he may be sure what he hears from his teachers agrees with the revealed Word of God. (*The Advantages of the Members of the Church of England over Those of the Church of Rome* [1753], in *Works*, 15:199)

On Scripture and common sense I build all my principles. Just so far as it agrees with these, I regard human authority. (Letter to Samuel Sparrow, Esq. [October 9, 1773], in *Works* [S], 7:112)

Upon the head of authority we are quite agreed. Our guides are Scripture and reason. (Letter to Samuel Sparrow, Esq. [December 28, 1773], in *Works* [S], 7:113)

St. Paul says, "All Scripture is given by inspiration of God, and is profitable for doctrine, for reproof, for correction, for instruction in righteousness, that the man of God may be perfect, thoroughly furnished unto all good works."

The Scripture therefore being delivered by men divinely inspired is a rule sufficient of itself, so it neither needs nor is capable of any farther addition. (*Popery Calmly Considered* [1779], in *Works* 15:178)

In all cases the Church is to be judged by the Scripture, not the Scripture by the Church. (*Popery Calmly Considered* [1779], in *Works*, 15:180)

From the very beginning, from the time that four young men united together, each of them was *homo unius libri*—"a man of one book." God taught them all to make his "word a lantern unto their feet, and a light in all their paths." They had one, and only one, rule of judgment with regard to all their tempers, words, and actions, namely, the oracles of God. They were one and all determined to be Bible Christians. They were continually reproached for this very thing; some terming them, in derision, Bible bigots; others, Bible moths—feeding, they said, upon the Bible, as moths do upon cloth. And indeed, unto this day, it is their constant endeavor to think and speak as the oracles of God. ("On God's Vineyard" [October 17, 1787], Sermon 107, in *Works* [WL], 7:203)

The Bible is the whole and sole rule both of Christian faith and practice. (*Thoughts upon Methodism* [August 4, 1786], in *Works* [S], 7:315)

R

SABBATH

How many are they, in every city as well as in this, who profane the Sabbath with a high hand! How many in this that openly defy both God and the king, that break the laws both divine and human by working at their trade, delivering their goods, receiving their pay, or following their ordinary business, in one branch or another, and "wiping their mouth and saying, *I do no evil!*" How many buy and sell on the Day of the Lord, even in the open streets of this city! How many open or (with some modesty) half open their shops! And when they have not the pretense of perishable goods; without any pretense at all, money is their god, and gain their godliness. (*A Farther Appeal to Men of Reason and Religion* [1745], pt. 2, in *Works,* 12:176)

About thirty years ago a motion was made in Parliament for raising and embodying the militia and for exercising them, to save time, on Sunday. When the motion was like to pass, an old gentleman stood up and said, "Mr. Speaker, I have one objection to this: I believe an old book called the Bible." The members looked at one another and the motion was dropped.

Must not all others who believe the Bible have the same objection? And, from what I have seen, I cannot but think these are still three-fourths of the nation. Now, setting religion out of the question, is it expedient to give such a shock to so many millions of people at once? And certainly it would shock them extremely: it would wound them in a very tender part. For would not they, would not all England, would not all Europe, consider this as a virtual repeal of the Bible? And would not all serious persons say, "We have little religion in the land now, but by this step we shall have less still." (Letter to the Lord Shelburne [December 7, 1782], in *Letters*, 481-82)

We cannot allow a baker to remain in our society if he sells bread on the Lord's Day. But if he only bakes pies, as they call it, we do not exclude him: although we are convinced that to abstain even from this is the more excellent way. (Letter to Thomas Carlill [May 6, 1785], in *Letters*, 227)

SACRAMENTS

By *means of grace* I understand outward signs, words, or actions ordained of God and appointed for this end to be the ordinary channels whereby he might convey to men preventing, justifying, or sanctifying grace. . . .

Our own Church . . . teaches us that a Sacrament is "an outward sign of inward *grace* and a *means* whereby we receive the same." (Quoted in "Of the Sacraments," chap. 2 in Coll. A, 4)

The validity of the ordinance doth not depend on the goodness of him who administers but on the faithfulness of him that ordained it, who will and doth meet us in his appointed ways. ("On Our Lord's Sermon on the Mount: Discourse 12" [1750], Sermon 34, in *Works* [T], 5:352)

If you say, "Believe, and thou shalt be saved." True; but how shall I believe? You reply, "Wait upon God." Well? But how am I to wait? In the means of grace, or out of them? (Quoted in "Of the Sacraments," chap. 2 in Coll. A, 4)

SAINTS: COMMUNION OF

It has, in all ages, been allowed that the communion of saints extends to those in paradise as well as those upon earth; as they are all one body united under one head. . . . But it is difficult to say either what kind or what degree of union may be between them. It is not improbable their fellowship with us is far more sensible than ours with them. Suppose any of them are present, they are hid from our eyes, but we are not hid from their sight. They, no doubt, clearly discern all our words and actions, if not all our thoughts too. For it is hard to think these walls of flesh and blood can intercept the view of an angelic being. But we have, in general, only a faint and indistinct perception of their presence, unless in some peculiar instances, where it may answer some gracious ends of divine providence. Then it may please God to permit that they should be perceptible, either by some of our outward senses or by an internal sense for which human language has not any name. But I suppose this is not a common blessing. I have known but few instances of it. To keep up constant and close communion with God is the most likely means to obtain this also. (Letter to Miss Bishop [June 12, 1773], in Coll. B, 540-41)

All Saints' Day, a day that I peculiarly love. (*Journal,* November 1, 1789)

May we not probably suppose that the spirits of the just, though generally lodged in paradise, may yet sometimes, in conjunction with the holy angels, minister to the heirs of salvation? May they not "Sometimes on errands of love / Revisit their brethren below?" It is a pleasing thought that some of these human spirits, attending us with or in the room of angels, are of the number of those that were dear to us while they were in the body. So that there is no absurdity in the question—"Have ye your own flesh forgot; / By a common ransom bought? / Can death's interposing tide / Spirits one in Christ divide?" But be this as it may, it is certain human spirits (after death) swiftly increase in knowledge, in holiness and in happiness. . . . All those holy souls who have been discharged from the body, from the beginning of the world unto this day, will be continually ripening for heaven, will be perpetually holier and happier, till they are received into "the Kingdom prepared for them from the foundation of the world." (Quoted in "Of the Communion of Saints," chap. 12 in Coll. A, 83)

SAINTS: HONORING OF

November 1 was a day of triumphant joy, as All Saints' Day generally is. How superstitious are they who scruple giving God solemn thanks for the lives and deaths of his saints! (*Journal,* November 1, 1756)

SAINTS: INTERCESSION OF

And suppose the angels or saints intercede for us in heaven, yet may we no more worship them than because *there are gods many on earth,* we may worship them as we do the true God. (*Popery Calmly Considered* [1779], in *Works,* 15:184)

SALVATION

By salvation I mean not barely, according to the vulgar notion, deliverance from hell or going to heaven but a present deliverance from sin, a restoration of the soul to its primitive health, its original purity; a recovery of the divine nature; the renewal of our souls after the image of God, in righteousness and true holiness, in justice, mercy, and truth. (*Conditions of Justification* [1744], in Coll. B, 178)

I cannot call those uncommon words which are the constant language of holy writ. These I purposely use; desiring always to express Scripture sense in Scripture phrase. And this I apprehend myself to do, when I speak of salvation as a present thing. How often does our Lord himself do thus! how often his apostles, St. Paul particularly! Insomuch that I doubt whether we can find six texts in the New Testament, perhaps not three, where it is otherwise taken. (Letter to John Smith [probably one of the archbishops of Canterbury, Thomas Herring or Thomas Secker] [September 28, 1745], in *Works* [WL], 12:58)

With regard to the condition of salvation, it may be remembered that I allow, not only faith, but likewise holiness or universal obedience to be the ordinary condition of final salvation. (*A Farther Appeal to Men of Reason and Religion* [1745], pt. 1, in *Works*, 12:73)

In order to converse profitably, may you not select a few persons who . . . are vigorously working out their salvation, who are athirst for full redemption, and every moment expecting it if not already enjoying it? (Letter to the Rev. John Fletcher [March 20, 1768], in Coll. B, 530)

Salvation is carried on by *convincing grace*, usually in Scripture termed *repentance*, which brings a larger measure of self-knowledge and a farther deliverance from the heart of stone. Afterward we experience the proper Christian salvation whereby "through grace" we "are saved by faith," consisting of those two grand branches, justification and sanctification. By justification we are saved from the guilt of sin and restored to the favor of God; by sanctification we are saved from the power and root of sin and restored to the image of God. All experience, as well as Scripture, show this salvation to be both instantaneous and gradual. It begins the moment we are justified, in the holy, humble, gentle, patient love of God and man. It gradually increases from that moment, as "a grain of mustard seed which, at first, is the least of all seeds," but afterward puts forth large branches and becomes a great tree: till, in another instant, the heart is cleansed from all sin and filled with pure love to God and man. But even that love increases more and more till we "grow up in all things into him that is our head," till we "attain the measure of the fulness of the stature of Christ." (Quoted in "Of Salvation," chap. 13 in Coll. D, 209-10)

SALVATION AND INVINCIBLE IGNORANCE

We know not how far invincible ignorance may excuse. "Love hopeth all things." . . . we allow there may be very many degrees of seeing God; even as many as are between seeing the sun with the eyelids closed and with the eyes open. (Letter to Mr. Richard Tompson [February 5, 1756], in Coll. B, 208)

Touching the charity due to those who are in error, I suppose, we both like-wise agree, that really invincible ignorance never did, nor ever shall, exclude any man from heaven. And hence, I doubt not but God will receive thousands of those who differ from me, even where I hold the truth. (Letter to John Smith [probably one of the archbishops of Canterbury, Thomas Herring or Thomas Secker] [June 25, 1746], in *Works* [WL], 12:72)

SALVATION: ASSURANCE OF FINAL (FALSITY OF)

Exhort them all in the name of the Lord Jesus that they love and study the oracles of God more and more; that they work out their salvation with fear and trembling, never imagining they have already attained or are already perfect; never deceiving themselves, as if they had now less need than before to be serious, watchful, lowly-minded. (Letter to Charles Wesley [August 4, 1738], in *Letters*, 69)

The gospel promises to you and me and our children and all that are afar off, even as many of those whom the Lord God shall call, as are not disobedient unto the heavenly vision, "the witness of God's Spirit with their spirit, that they are the children of God"; that they are now, at this hour, all accepted in the Beloved; but it witnesses not that they shall be. It is an assurance of present salvation only; therefore, not necessarily perpetual, neither irreversible. (Letter to his brother, Samuel Wesley [May 10, 1739], in Coll. C, 346)

On this authority I believe a saint may fall away, that one who is holy or righteous in the judgment of God himself may nevertheless so fall from God as to perish everlastingly.

. . . For thus saith the Lord: "When the righteous turneth away from his righteousness, and committeth iniquity; [. . .] in his trespass that he hath trespassed, and in his sin that he hath sinned, in them shall he die" [Ezek. 18:24].

That this is to be understood of eternal death appears from the twenty-sixth verse: "When a righteous man turneth away from his righteousness and committeth iniquity, and dieth in them" (here is temporal death); "for his iniquity that he hath done he shall die" (here is death eternal).

It appears farther from the whole scope of the chapter, which is to prove, "The soul that sinneth, it shall die" [v. 4].

If you say, "The soul here means the body," I answer, that will die whether you sin or no. . . .

If you say, "But it was particularly revealed to me that God had loved me with an everlasting love," I answer: Suppose it was (which might bear a dispute); it proves no more, at the most, than that you in particular shall persevere, but does not affect the general question, whether others shall or shall not.

. . . One who is endued with the faith that purifies the heart, that produces a good conscience, may nevertheless so fall from God as to perish everlastingly.

For thus saith the inspired apostle: "War a good warfare; holding faith, and a good conscience; which some having put away concerning faith have made shipwreck" [1 Tim. 1:18-19].

Observe, (1) These men (such as Hymeneus and Alexander) had once the faith that purifies the heart, that produces a good conscience, which they once had, or they could not have "put it away."

Observe, (2) They made "shipwreck" of the faith, which necessarily implies the total and final loss of it. For a vessel once wrecked can never be recovered. It is totally and finally lost.

And the apostle himself, in his Second Epistle to Timothy, mentions one of these two as irrecoverably lost. "Alexander," says he, "did me much evil: the Lord reward him according to his works" [2 Tim. 4:14]. Therefore, one who is endued with the faith that purifies the heart, that produces a good conscience, may nevertheless so fall from God as to perish everlastingly.

"But how can this be reconciled with the words of our Lord, 'He that believeth shall be saved'?"

Do you think these words mean, "he that believes" at this moment "shall" certainly and inevitably "be saved"?

If this interpretation be good, then, by all the rules of speech, the other part of the sentence must mean, "He" that does "not believe" at this moment "shall" certainly and inevitably "be damned."

Therefore, that interpretation cannot be good. The plain meaning then of the whole sentence is, "He that believeth," if he continue in faith, "shall be saved; he that believeth not," if he continue in unbelief, "shall be damned." (*The Perseverance of the Saints* [1746], in Coll. B, 237, 239)

What will this [Rom. 8:38-39] prove? Just thus much—that the apostle was at that time fully persuaded of his own perseverance. And I doubt not but many believers at this day have the very same persuasion, termed in Scripture "the full assurance of hope." But this does not prove that every believer shall persevere, any more than that every believer is thus fully persuaded of his perseverance. (*The Perseverance of the Saints* [1746], in Coll. B, 242)

(1) A child of God, that is, a true believer (for he that believeth is born of God), while he continues a true believer, cannot go to hell. But (2) if a believer make shipwreck of the faith, he is no longer a child of God. And then he may go to hell; yea, and certainly will if he continues in unbelief. (3) If a believer may make shipwreck of a faith, then a man that believes now may be an unbeliever some time hence; yea, very possibly, tomorrow; but, if

so, he who is a child of God today may be a child of the devil tomorrow. For (4) God is the Father of them that believe, so long as they believe. But the devil is the father of them that believe not, whether they did once believe or no. (*The Perseverance of the Saints* [1746], in Coll. B, 248)

I am not one jot more concerned in instantaneous justification as your lordship explains it, [namely], "A sudden instantaneous justification, by which the person receives from God, a certain seal of his salvation or absolute *assurance* of being saved at last. . . . Such an instantaneous working of the Holy Spirit as finishes the business of salvation once for all." . . . I neither teach nor believe and am therefore clear of all the consequences that may arise therefrom. I believe "a gradual improvement in grace and goodness," I mean in the knowledge and love of God, is a good "testimony of our present sincerity toward God," although I dare not say, it is "the only true ground of humble assurance" or the only foundation on which a Christian builds his "hopes of acceptance and salvation." (Letter to the bishop of London [June 11, 1747], in *Works*, 12:409)

"After these sudden conversions," say you, "they receive their assurances of salvation." . . . you had before you, while you wrote, the very tract wherein I . . . explicitly declared, "The assurance whereof I speak is not an assurance of salvation." And the very passages you cite from me prove the same: everyone of which (as you yourself know in your own conscience) relates wholly and solely to present pardon, not to future salvation. (*A Letter to the Author of* The Enthusiasm of Methodists and Papists Compared [1750], in *Works*, 13:10)

You add, . . . "But it is a considerable offense to charge another wrongfully and contradict himself about the doctrine of assurance." To prove this upon me, you bring my own words. "The assurance we preach is of quite another kind from that Mr. Bedford writes against. We speak of an assurance of our present pardon; not, as he does, of our final perseverance" [*Journal*, October 6, 1738]. "Mr. Wesley might have considered (you say) that when they talk of *assurance of pardon and salvation*, the world will extend the meaning of the words to our eternal state." I do consider it, Sir. And therefore I never use that phrase either in preaching or writing. "Assurance of pardon and salvation" is an expression that never comes out of my lips. . . .

. . . (1) That *faith* is one thing; the *full assurance of faith* another. (2) That even the full assurance of faith does not imply the full assurance of perseverance. This bears another name; being styled by St. Paul, *The full assurance of hope*. (3) Some Christians have only the first of these. They have faith, but mixed with doubts and fears. Some have also the full assurance of faith, a full conviction of *present* pardon and yet not the full assurance of hope; not a full conviction of their future perseverance. (4) The faith which we preach, as necessary to all Christians, is the first of these, and no other. Therefore, (5) It is no evasion at all to say, "This (the faith which we preach as necessary to all Christians) is not *properly* an assurance of what is future." (*A Second Letter to the Author of* The Enthusiasm of Methodists and Papists Compared [November 27, 1750], in *Works,* 13:36-37)

"The doctrine of assurance of pardon and salvation, present and future, causes a false security, to the neglect of future endeavors." Blunder upon blunder again. That all Christians have an assurance of *future salvation* is no Methodist doctrine: and an assurance of present pardon is so far from causing negligence that it is of all others the strongest motive to vigorous endeavors after universal holiness. (*A Second Letter to the Author of* The Enthusiasm of Methodists and Papists Compared [November 27, 1750], in *Works,* 13:53)

I begin with the subject of your third charge, *Assurances*: because what I have to say upon this head will be comprised in few words. Some are fond of the expression, I am not; I hardly ever use it. But I will simply declare (having neither leisure nor inclination to draw the sword of controversy concerning it) what are my present sentiments with regard to the *thing* which is usually meant thereby.

I believe a few, but very few Christians have an assurance from God of everlasting salvation: and that is the thing which the apostle terms, *the plerophory* or *full assurance of hope.*

I believe more have such an assurance of being *now* in the favor of God, as excludes all doubt and fear. And this, if I do not mistake, the apostle means by *the plerophory* or *full assurance of faith.*

I believe a consciousness of being in the favor of God (which I do not term *plerophory* or *full assurance,* since it is frequently weakened, nay, perhaps interrupted, by returns of doubt or fear) is the common privilege of Christians, fearing God and working righteousness. (Letter to the Rev. Dr. Rutherforth [March 28, 1768], in *Works,* 13:127-28)

It is true, the full assurance of hope excludes all doubt of our final salvation, but it does not, and cannot, continue any longer than we walk closely with God. And it does not include any assurance of our future behavior; neither do I know any word in all the Bible which gives us any authority to look for a testimony of this kind. (Letter to a young disciple [May 20, 1771], in *Works* [S], 7:89)

SANCTIFICATION

They speak of sanctification (or holiness) as if it were an outward thing, as if it consisted chiefly, if not wholly, in those two points: (1) the doing no harm;

(2) the doing good (as it is called), that is, the using the means of grace and helping our neighbor.

I believe it to be an inward thing, namely, the life of God in the soul of man; a participation of the divine nature; the mind that was in Christ; or, the renewal of our heart after the image of him that created us. (*Conditions of Justification* [1744], in Coll. B, 181)

On Monday, June 25, 1744, our First Conference began, six clergymen and all our preachers being present. The next morning we seriously considered the doctrine of sanctification, or perfection. The questions asked concerning it, and the substance of the answers given, were as follows:

Q. What is it to be sanctified?

A. To be renewed in the image of God, "in righteousness and true holiness."

Q. What is implied in being a perfect Christian?

A. The loving God with all our heart and mind and soul [Deut. 6:5].

Q. Does this imply that all inward sin is taken away?

A. Undoubtedly; or how can we be said to be "saved from all our uncleannesses"? [Ezek. 36:29].

Our Second Conference began August 1, 1745. The next morning we spoke of sanctification as follows:

Q. When does inward sanctification begin?

A. In the moment a man is justified. (Yet sin remains in him; yea, the seed of all sin, till he is sanctified throughout.) From that time a believer gradually dies to sin and grows in grace. (*A Plain Account of Christian Perfection* [1767; rev. 1777], in *Works* [WL], 11:387)

Q. . . . But how do you know that you are sanctified, saved from your inbred corruption?

A. I can know it no otherwise than I know that I am justified. "Hereby know we that we are of God," in either sense, "by the Spirit that he hath given us."

We know it by the witness and by the fruit of the Spirit. And first, by the witness. As, when we were justified, the Spirit bore witness with our spirit, that our sins were forgiven; so, when we were sanctified, he bore witness that they were taken away. Indeed, the witness of sanctification is not always clear at first (as neither is that of justification); neither is it afterward always the same, but, like that of justification, sometimes stronger and sometimes fainter. Yea, and sometimes it is withdrawn. Yet, in general, the latter testimony of the Spirit is both as clear and as steady as the former. (*A Plain Account of Christian Perfection* [1767; rev. 1777], in *Works* [WL], 11:420)

I do not suppose any man who is justified is a slave to sin. Yet, I do suppose, sin remains (at least for a time) in all that are justified. . . .

. . . He is not proud or self-willed in the same sense that unbelievers are, that is, *governed* by pride or self-will. Herein he differs from unregenerate men. They *obey* sin, he does not. Flesh is in them both. But they *walk after the flesh*: he *walks after the Spirit*. . . .

. . . Although we are renewed, cleansed, purified, sanctified, the moment we truly believe in Christ, yet we are not then renewed, cleansed, purified altogether: but the flesh, the evil nature still *remains* (though subdued) and wars *against* the Spirit. So much the more, let us use all diligence in "fighting the good fight of faith." So much the more earnestly let us "watch and pray" against the enemy within. The more carefully let us *take* to ourselves and "put on the whole armour of God," that, although "we wrestle" both "with flesh and blood, and with principalities, and powers, and wicked spirits in high places," we "may be able to withstand in the evil day, and having done all, to stand." ("On Sin in Believers," March 28, 1763, Sermon 13, in *Works* [T], 5:126-27)

"I will sprinkle clean water upon you, and ye shall be clean; from all your filthiness and from all your idols will I cleanse you." "I will circumcise thy heart" (from all sin) "to love the Lord thy God with all thy heart, and with all thy soul." This I term sanctification (which is both an instantaneous and a gradual work), or perfection, the being perfected in love, filled with love, which still admits of a thousand degrees. But I have no time to throw away in contending for words, especially where the thing is allowed. And you allow the whole thing which I contend for; an entire deliverance from sin, a recovery of the whole image of God, the loving God "with all our heart, soul, and strength." And you believe God is able to give you this; yea, to give it you in an instant. You trust he will. [Oh], hold fast this also; this blessed hope, which he has wrought in your heart! And with all zeal and diligence confirm the brethren, (1) In holding fast that whereto they have attained; namely, the remission of all their sins by faith in a bleeding Lord. (2) In expecting a second change, whereby they shall be saved from all sin and perfected in love. (Letter to Joseph Benson [December 28, 1770], in *Works* [S], 7:71)

A will steadily and uniformly devoted to God is essential to a state of sanctification, but not a uniformity of joy or peace or happy communion with God. These may rise and fall in various degrees; nay, and may be affected either by the body or by diabolical agency, in a manner which all our wisdom can neither understand nor prevent. (Letter to Mrs. Elizabeth Bennis [January 18, 1774], in *Works*, 16:182)

SANCTIFICATION AND SALVATION

Far other qualifications are required, in order to our standing before God in glory, than were required in order to his giving us faith and pardon. In order to this, nothing is *indispensably* required but repentance, or conviction of sin. But in order to the other it is indispensably required that we be fully *cleansed from all sin*, that the very God *of peace* sanctify us wholly, even . . . our entire body, soul, and spirit. It is not necessary therefore (nor indeed possible), that we should *before* justification, *patiently wait upon God, by lowliness, meekness, and resignation, in all the ways of his holy law*. And yet it is necessary in the highest degree that we should thus wait upon him *after* justification. Otherwise, how shall we be "meet to be partakers of the inheritance of the saints in light"? (*Answer to the Rev. Mr. Church's "Remarks on the Rev. Mr. Wesley's Last Journal"* [February 2, 1745], in *Works,* 12:299)

"Without holiness no man shall see the LORD," shall see the face of God in glory. Nothing under heaven can be more sure than this: "For the mouth of the Lord hath spoken it." And though heaven and earth pass away, yet his "word shall not pass away." As well therefore might God fall from heaven, as this word fall to the ground. No, it cannot be: None shall live with God, but he that now *lives to God*. None shall enjoy the glory of God in heaven, but he that bears the image of God on earth. None that is not saved from sin here can be saved from hell hereafter. None can see the kingdom of God above unless the kingdom of God be in him below. Whosoever will reign with Christ in heaven must have Christ reigning in him on earth. He must have "that mind in him which was in Christ," enabling him "to walk as Christ also walked."

. . . And yet as sure as this is, and as clearly as it is taught in every part of the Holy Scripture, there is scarcely one among all the truths of God which is less received with men. . . .

. . . How shall they hope to see God without holiness? Why, by doing no harm, doing good, going to the church and sacrament. And many thousands sit down content with this, believing they are in the high road to heaven. (*A Blow at the Root* [1762], in *Works* [T], 9:453-54)

SATAN AND HIS DEMONS (FALLEN ANGELS)

I am more and more convinced that the devil himself desires nothing more than that the people should be half-awakened and then left to themselves to fall asleep again. (*Journal,* March 13, 1743)

I grant, . . . that extraordinary circumstances have attended this conviction [i.e., sense of personal sinfulness] in some instances. A particular account of these I have frequently given. While the Word of God was preached, some persons have dropped down as dead; some have been, as it were, in strong convulsions; some have roared aloud, though not with an articulate voice; and others spoke the anguish of their souls. This, I suppose, you believe to be perfect madness. But it is easily accounted for, either on principles of reason or Scripture. . . .

. . . We are to add to the consideration of natural causes the agency of those spirits who still excel in strength and, as far as they have leave from God, will not fail to torment whom they cannot destroy; to tear those that are coming to Christ. It is also remarkable that there is plain Scripture precedent of every symptom which has lately appeared. So that we cannot allow even the conviction attended with these to be madness, without giving up both reason and Scripture. (*A Farther Appeal to Men of Reason and Religion* [1745], pt. 1, in *Works,* 12:143-44)

I presume, you do not deny that a believer, one who has the witness in himself, may make "shipwreck of the faith" and, consequently, lose the witness (however it be explained) which he once had of his being a child of God. The darkness which then covers his soul again, I ascribe (in part) to the energy of Satan, who . . . *worketh,* according to the apostle, in the children of unbelief, whether they did once believe or no. And has he not much power even on the children of God? to disturb, though not to destroy? to throw fiery darts without number; especially against those who, as yet, are but weak in the faith? to inject doubts and fears? sometimes unbelieving, sometimes even blasphemous thoughts? And how frequently will they be wounded thereby, if they have not put on the whole armor of God! (Letter to John Smith [probably one of the archbishops of Canterbury, Thomas Herring or Thomas Secker] [July 10, 1747], in *Works* [WL], 12:94)

Of the power of the evil spirits to afflict the minds of men, none can doubt who believe there are any such beings. And of their power to afflict the body we have abundant proof both in the history of Job and that of the gospel demoniacs.

I do not mean, Sir, to accuse *you* of believing these things . . . But, alas! the fathers were not so far enlightened. And because they were bigoted to that old book, they, of consequence, held for truth what you assure us was mere delusion and imposture. (*A Letter to the Rev. Dr. Conyers Middleton Occasioned by His Late "Free Inquiry"* [January 4, 1749], *Works* [S], 5:730-31)

As to *conflicts* with Satan, "Nor can Mr. Wesley," you say, "escape the attacks of this infernal spirit, namely, suggesting distrustful thoughts and buffeting him with inward temptations." Sir, did you never hear of anyone so attacked, unless among the Papists or Methodists? How deeply then are you experienced both in the ways of God and the devices of Satan? (*A Second Letter to the Author of* The Enthusiasm of Methodists and Papists Compared [November 27, 1750], in *Works,* 13:30)

It cannot be doubted but your heaviness was owing in part to diabolical agency. Nay, and Satan sometimes, by God's permission, weakens the body. Nevertheless, we are, even in that weakness, to use natural means, just as if it was owing to natural causes. I believe it would be of use, if you took a cup-full of the decoction of burdock (sweetened or unsweetened) both morning and evening. (Letter to Miss Ball [May 23, 1773], in *Works* [S], 7:100)

Undoubtedly Satan, who well understands the manner how the mind is influenced by the body, can, by means of those parts in the animal machine which are more immediately subservient to thinking, raise a thousand perceptions and emotions in the mind, so far as God is pleased to permit. I doubt not but he was the chief agent in your late painful exercises. And you gave him advantage by reasoning with him, that is, fighting him with his own weapons; instead of simply looking up and saying, "Thou shalt answer for me, O Lord my God." (Letter to Miss Bolton [September 27, 1777], in *Works* [S], 7:117)

One circumstance more we may learn from the Scripture concerning the evil angels; they do not wander at large but are all united under one common head. It is he that is styled by our blessed Lord, "The prince of this world"; yea, the apostle does not scruple to call him, "The god of this world." He is frequently styled Satan the adversary, being the great adversary both of God and man. He is termed "the devil" by way of eminence; "Apollyon," or the destroyer; "the old serpent," from his beguiling Eve under that form; and "the angel of the bottomless pit." We have reason to believe that the other evil angels are under his command, that they are ranged by him according to their several orders, that they are appointed to their several stations and have from time to time their several works and offices assigned them. And undoubtedly they are connected (though we know not how; certainly not by love) both to him and to each other. (Quoted in "Of Angels," chap. 18 in Coll. D, 351)

They are (remember! so far as God permits) . . . "Governors of the world!" So that there may be more ground than we are apt to imagine, for that strange expression of Satan [Matt. 6:8-9], when he showed our Lord "all the kingdoms of the world, and the glory of them," "All these things will I give thee, if thou wilt fall down and worship me." It is a little more particularly expressed in the fourth chapter of St. Luke, "The devil showed unto him all the kingdoms of the world in a moment of time." (Such an astonishing measure of power is still left in the prince of darkness!) "And the devil said, All this power will I give thee, and the glory of them: for that is delivered unto me; and to whomsoever I will I give it" [vv. 5, 6]. They are "the rulers of the darkness of this age" (so the words are literally translated), of the present state of things, during which "the whole world lieth in the wicked one." He is the element of the children of men, only those who fear God being excepted. He and his angels, in connection with, and in subordination to him, dispose all the ignorance, all the error, all the folly, and particularly all the wickedness of men, in such a manner as may most hinder the kingdom of God and most advance the kingdom of darkness. ("Of Evil Angels," January 7, 1783, Sermon 77, in *Works* [T], 6:359)

Next to the love of God, there is nothing which Satan so cordially abhors as the love of our neighbor. He uses, therefore, every possible means to prevent or destroy this; to excite either private or public suspicions, animosities, resentment, quarrels; to destroy the peace of families or of nations and to banish unity and concord from the earth. And this, indeed, is the triumph of his art; to embitter the poor, miserable children of men against each other and, at length, urge them to do his own work; to plunge one another into the pit of destruction.

. . . This enemy of all righteousness is equally diligent to hinder every good word and work. If he cannot prevail upon us to do evil, he will, if possible, prevent our doing good. He is peculiarly diligent to hinder the work of God from spreading in the hearts of men. What pains does he take to prevent or obstruct the general work of God! And how many are his devices to stop its progress in particular souls! To hinder their continuing or growing in grace, in the knowledge of our Lord Jesus Christ! To lessen, if not destroy that love, joy, peace; that long-suffering, gentleness, goodness; that fidelity, meekness, and temperance which our Lord works, by his loving Spirit, in them that believe and wherein the very essence of religion consists.

. . . To effect these ends, he is continually laboring with all his skill and power to infuse evil thoughts of every kind into the hearts of men. And certainly it is as easy for a spirit to speak to our heart as for a man to speak to our ears. But sometimes it is exceedingly difficult to distinguish these from our own thoughts, those which he injects so exactly resembling those which naturally arise in our own minds. Sometimes, indeed, we may distinguish one from the other by this circumstance. The thoughts which naturally arise in our minds are generally, if not always, occasioned by or at least connected with some inward or outward circumstance that went before. But those that are preternaturally suggested, have, frequently, no relation to or connection (at least, none that we are able to discern) with anything which preceded. On the contrary, they shoot in, as it were, across and thereby show that they are of a different growth.

. . . He likewise labors to awaken evil passions or tempers in our souls. He endeavors to inspire those passions and tempers which are directly opposite to the "fruit of the Spirit." He strives to instill unbelief, atheism, ill-will, bitterness, hatred, malice, envy; opposite to faith and love: fear, sorrow, anxiety, worldly care; opposite to peace and joy: impatience, ill-nature, anger, resentment; opposite to long-suffering, gentleness, meekness: fraud, guile, dissimulation; contrary to fidelity: love of the world, inordinate affection, foolish desires; opposite to the love of God. One sort of evil desires he may probably raise or inflame, by touching the springs of this animal machine. Endeavoring thus, by means of the body, to disturb or sully the soul. ("Of Evil Angels," January 7, 1783, Sermon 77, in *Works* [T], 6:361-62)

It is no wonder that Satan should fight for his own kingdom, when such inroads are made upon it. . . . After we have observed a day of fasting and prayer, I have known the most violent commotions quelled at once. (Letter to Robert C. Brackenbury [September 24, 1785], in *Works* [S], 7:151)

SCHISM; SEPARATION

There is yet another circumstance which is quite peculiar to yourselves: whereas every other religious set of people, as soon as they were joined to each other, separated themselves from their former societies or congregations, you, on the contrary, do not; nay, you absolutely disavow all desire of separating from them. You openly and continually declare you have not, nor ever had, such a design. And whereas the congregations to which those separatists belonged have generally spared no pains to prevent that separation, those to which you belong spare no pains (not to prevent, but) to occasion this separation, to drive you from them, to force you on that division to which you declare you have the strongest aversion. (*Advice to the People Called Methodists* [October 10, 1745], in Coll. B, 50)

I cannot take schism for a separation from a church, true or false; because I cannot find it is ever so taken in Scripture. The first time I read the term there, is [1 Cor. 1]: I meet with it again [in 11:18]. But it is plain, by schisms in both places is meant not any separation from the church but uncharitable divisions in it. For the Corinthians continued to be one church, and, notwithstanding all their strife and contention, there was no separation of any one party from the rest, with regard to external communion. It is in the same sense the word is used [in 12:25]. And these are the only places in the New Testament where it occurs. Therefore, the indulging any unkind temper toward our fellow Christians is the true scriptural schism. (Second letter to the Rev. Mr. Clarke [September 10, 1756], *Works* [S], 7:286)

Beware of schism, of making a rent in the church of Christ. That inward disunion, the members ceasing to have a reciprocal love "one for another" [1 Cor. 12:25], is the very root of all contention and every outward separation. Beware of everything tending thereto. Beware of a dividing spirit; shun whatever has the least aspect that way. Therefore, say not, "I am of Paul or of Apollos"; the very thing which occasioned the schism at Corinth. Say not, "This is my preacher; the best preacher in England. Give me him, and take all the rest." All this tends to breed or foment division, to disunite those whom God hath joined. . . .

. . . Suffer not one thought of separating from your brethren, whether their opinions agree with yours or not. (*A Plain Account of Christian Perfection* [1767; rev. 1777], in *Works* [WL], 11:433)

SCRIPTURE AND LEARNING

Is not a knowledge of profane history, likewise, of ancient customs, of chronology and geography, though not absolutely necessary yet highly expedient, for him that would thoroughly understand the Scriptures; since the want even of this knowledge is but poorly supplied by reading the comments of other men?

. . . Some knowledge of the sciences also, is, to say the least, equally expedient. Nay, may we not say that the knowledge of one (whether art or science), although now quite unfashionable, is even necessary next, and in order to, the knowledge of the Scripture itself? I mean logic. For what is this, if rightly understood, but the art of good sense? of apprehending things clearly, judging truly, and reasoning conclusively? . . .

Is not some acquaintance with what has been termed the second part of logic (metaphysics), if not so necessary as this, yet highly expedient: (1) In order to clear our apprehension (without which it is impossible either to judge correctly or to reason closely or conclusively), by ranging our ideas under general heads? And (2) In order to understand many useful writers who can very hardly be understood without it?

Should not a minister be acquainted too with at least the general grounds of natural philosophy? Is not this a great help to the accurate understanding several passages of Scripture? (*An Address to the Clergy* [February 6, 1756], in Coll. C, 265-66)

SCRIPTURE AND PATRISTIC INTERPRETATION

From five to seven (each morning) we read the Bible together, carefully comparing it—that we might not lean to our own understandings—with the writings of the earliest ages. (Quoted in "Of the Catholic Faith," chap. 1 in Coll. A, 3)

You receive not the ancient but the modern mystics as the best interpreters of Scripture, and, in conformity to these, you mix much of man's wisdom with the wisdom of God; you greatly refine the plain religion taught by the letter of Holy Writ and philosophize on almost every part of it, to accommodate it to the mystic theory. (Letter to the Church of God at Herrnhut [Moravians], in *Journal*, August 8, 1741)

It is their [Methodists'] one desire and design to be downright Bible Christians—taking the Bible *as interpreted* by the primitive church and our own for *their whole and sole rule.* (Quoted in "Of the Catholic Faith," chap. 1 in Coll. A, 3)

SCRIPTURE: CHAPTER DIVISIONS

The division of the New Testament into chapters . . . [was] made in the dark ages, and very incorrectly; often separating things that are closely joined and joining those that are entirely distinct from each other. (Preface to *Explanatory Notes upon the New Testament* [January 4, 1754], in *Works* [S], 7:536)

SCRIPTURE: "DIFFICULTIES" IN

I believe just what is revealed, and no more; but I do not pretend to account for it or to solve the difficulties that may attend it. Let angels do this, if they can. (Letter to Joseph Benson [September 17, 1788], in *Works* [S], 7:81-82)

SCRIPTURE: FORMAL SUFFICIENCY

I reject the word *sufficient*, because it is ambiguous. . . . The Scriptures are a complete rule of faith and practice, and they are clear in all necessary points. And yet their clearness does not prove that they need not be explained, nor their completeness that they need not be enforced. (*A Letter to the Rev. Dr. Conyers Middleton Occasioned by His Late "Free Inquiry"* [January 4, 1749], *Works* [S], 5:715)

SCRIPTURE: HERMENEUTICS (INTERPRETATION)

No less necessary is a knowledge of the Scriptures, which teach us how to teach others; yea, a knowledge of all the Scriptures; seeing scripture interprets scripture; one part fixing the sense of another. So that, whether it be true or not, that every good textuary is a good divine, it is certain none can be a good divine who is not a good textuary. None else can be mighty in the Scriptures, able both to instruct and to stop the mouths of gainsayers.

In order to do this accurately, ought he not to know the literal meaning of every word, verse, and chapter; without which there can be no firm foundation on which the spiritual meaning can be built? Should he not likewise be able to deduce the proper corollaries, speculative and practical, from each text; to solve the difficulties which arise and answer the objections which are or may be raised against it; and to make a suitable application of all to the consciences of his hearers?

. . . But can he do this, in the most effectual manner, without a knowledge of the original tongues? Without this, will he not frequently be at a stand, even as to texts which regard practice only? But he will be under still greater difficulties with respect to controverted scriptures. He will be ill able to rescue these out of the hands of any man of learning that would pervert them: for whenever an appeal is made to the original, his mouth is stopped at once. (*An Address to the Clergy* [February 6, 1756], in Coll. C, 264-65)

Have I . . . such a knowledge of Scripture, as becomes him who undertakes so to explain it to others, that it may be a light in all their paths? Have I a full and clear view of the analogy of faith, which is the clue to guide me through the whole? Am I acquainted with the several parts of Scripture, with all parts of the Old Testament and the New? Upon the mention of any text, do I know the context and the parallel places? Have I that point at least of a good divine, the being a good textuary? Do I know the grammatical construction of the four Gospels, of the Acts, of the Epistles, and am I a master of the spiritual sense (as well as the literal) of what I read? Do I understand the scope of each book and how every part of it tends thereto? Have I skill to draw the natural inferences deducible from each text? Do I know the objections raised to them or from them by Jews, deists, Papists, Arians, Socinians, and all other sectaries who more or less corrupt or cauponize the Word of God? Am I ready to give a satisfactory answer to each of these objections? And have I learned to apply every part of the sacred writings, as the various states of my hearers require? . . .

. . . Do I understand so much of profane history as tends to confirm and illustrate the sacred? Am I acquainted with the ancient customs of the Jews and other nations mentioned in Scripture? Have I a competent knowledge of chronology, that at least which refers to the sacred writings? And am I so far (if no farther) skilled in geography as to know the situation and give some account of all the considerable places mentioned therein? (*An Address to the Clergy* [February 6, 1756], in Coll. C, 274-76)

Scripture is the best expounder of Scripture. The best way, therefore, to understand it is carefully to compare scripture with scripture and thereby learn the true meaning of it. (*Popery Calmly Considered* [1779], in *Works*, 15:180)

SCRIPTURE: INSPIRATION AND INFALLIBILITY OF

I am as fully assured today, as I am of the shining of the sun, that the Scriptures are of God. I cannot possibly deny or doubt of it now. (Letter to John

Smith [probably one of the archbishops of Canterbury, Thomas Herring or Thomas Secker] [March 25, 1747], in *Works* [WL], 12:85)

The Scripture, therefore, of the Old and New Testament is a most solid and precious system of divine truth. Every part thereof is worthy of God, and all together are one entire body wherein is no defect, no excess. It is the fountain of heavenly wisdom, which they who are able to taste prefer to all writings of men, however wise or learned or holy. (Preface to *Explanatory Notes upon the New Testament* [January 4, 1754], in *Works* [S], 7:536)

For if there be one falsehood in the Bible, there may be a thousand; neither can it proceed from the God of truth. (A*n Extract of a Letter to the Rev. Mr. Law* [January 6, 1756], in *Works,* 13:357)

SCRIPTURE: MATERIAL SUFFICIENCY

This is a lantern unto a Christian's feet and a light in all his paths. This alone he receives as his rule of right or wrong, of whatever is really good or evil. He esteems nothing good but what is here enjoined, either directly or by plain consequence; he accounts nothing evil but what is here forbidden, either in terms or by undeniable inference. Whatever the Scripture neither forbids nor enjoins, either directly or by plain consequence, he believes to be of an indifferent nature; to be in itself neither good nor evil; this being the whole and sole outward rule whereby his conscience is to be directed in all things. (Quoted in "Of the Scriptures," chap. 1 in Coll. D, 2-3)

You easily observe I therein build on no authority, ancient or modern, but the Scripture. If this supports any doctrine, it will stand; if not, the sooner it falls, the better. Neither the doctrine in question, nor any other, is anything to me, unless it be the doctrine of Christ and his apostles. If, therefore, you will please to point out to me any passages in that sermon which are either contrary to Scripture or not supported by it, and to show that they are not, I shall be full as willing to oppose as ever I was to defend them. I search for truth— plain, Bible truth—without any regard to the praise or dispraise of men. (*On Christian Perfection: To the Rev. Mr. Dodd* [February 5, 1756], in *Works* [WL], 11:449)

SCRIPTURE: OLD TESTAMENT

It should be observed that this [2 Tim 3:15-17] is spoken primarily and directly of the Scriptures which Timothy had *known from a child*, which must have been those of the Old Testament, for the New was not then written. How far then was St. Paul (though he was "not a whit behind the very chief of the apostles," nor, therefore, I presume, behind any man now upon earth) for making light of the Old Testament! Behold this, lest ye one day "wonder and perish," ye who make so small account of one half of the oracles of God! Yea, and that half, of which the Holy Ghost expressly declares, that it is *profitable*, as a mean ordained of God for this very thing, "for doctrine, for reproof, for correction, for instruction in righteousness: to the end the man of God may be perfect, thoroughly furnished unto all good works." ("The Means of Grace," November 15, 1739, Sermon 16, in *Works* [T], 5:156-57)

SCRIPTURE: UNREASONABLE DEMAND FOR EXPLICIT PROOF TEXTS

Another objection was, "There is no scripture for this, for classes and I know not what." I answer . . . There is no scripture against it. You cannot show one text that forbids them. . . . You seem not to have observed that the Scripture, in most points, gives only general rules and leaves the particular circumstances to be adjusted by the common sense of mankind. The Scripture, for instance, gives that general rule, "Let all things be done decently and in order." But common sense is to determine, on particular occasions, what order and decency require. So, in another instance, the Scripture lays it down as a general, standing direction: "Whether ye eat or drink, or whatsoever ye do, do all to the glory of God." But it is common prudence which is to make the application of this in a thousand particular cases.

"But these," said another, "are all man's inventions." This is but the same objection in another form. And the same answer will suffice for any reasonable person. These are man's inventions. And what then? That is, they are methods which men have found, by reason and common sense, for the more effectually applying several Scripture rules, couched in general terms, to particular occasions. (*A Plain Account of the People Called Methodists* [1748], in Coll. C, 180-81)

SELF-DEFENSE

When abundance of persons have for several years laid to my charge things that I knew not, I have generally thought it my duty to pass it over in silence, to be *as one that heard not*. But the case is different when a person of your Lordship's character calls me forth to answer for myself. Silence now might be interpreted contempt. It might appear like a sullen disregard, a withholding honor from him to whom honor is due, were it only on account of his high office in the church. More especially, when I apprehend so eminent a person as this, to be under considerable mistakes concerning me. Were I now to be silent, were I not to do what was in my power for the removal of those mistakes, I could not have a conscience void of offense, either toward God or toward man. (Letter to the bishop of London [June 11, 1747], in *Works*, 12:406)

If you fall upon people that meddle not with you, without either fear or wit, you may possibly find they have a little more to say for themselves than you were aware of. I "follow peace with all men," but if a man set upon me without either rhyme or reason, I think it my duty to defend myself, so far as truth and justice permit. (Letter to the Rev. Mr. Downes [November 17, 1759], in Coll. C, 248)

SIN

(1) Not only *sin properly so called* (that is, a voluntary transgression of a known law) but sin improperly so called, that is, an involuntary transgression of a divine law, known or unknown, needs the atoning blood. (2) I believe there is no such perfection in this life as excludes these involuntary transgressions which I apprehend to be naturally consequent on the ignorance and mistakes inseparable from mortality. (3) Therefore *sinless perfection* is a phrase I never use, lest I should seem to contradict myself. (4) I believe a person filled with the love of God is still liable to these involuntary transgressions. (5) Such transgressions you may call sins, if you please; I do not, for the reasons above mentioned. (*A Plain Account of Christian Perfection* [1767; rev. 1777], in *Works* [WL], 11:396)

Nothing is sin, strictly speaking, but a voluntary transgression of a known law of God. Therefore, every voluntary breach of the law of love is sin; and nothing else, if we speak properly. . . . There may be ten thousand wandering thoughts and forgetful intervals without any breach of love, though not without transgressing the Adamic law. (Letter to Mrs. Elizabeth Bennis [June 16, 1772], in Coll. B, 540)

SINS, FORGIVENESS OF

I cannot find anything in the Bible of the remission of sins, past, present, and to come. (*The Principles of a Methodist Farther Explained* [1746], in *Works*, 12:343)

SLANDER

Hitherto you have succeeded extremely ill. You have brought five accusations against me and have not been able to make one good. However, you are resolved to throw dirt enough that some may stick. . . .

"Corporal severities or mortification by tormenting the flesh" . . . is the next thing you charge upon me. Almost two sentences you bring in proof of this. The one, "Our bed being wet" (it was in a storm at sea), "I laid me down on the floor and slept sound till morning, and I believe I shall not find it needful to go to bed, as it is called, any more." But whether I do or not, how will you prove that my motive is to "gain a reputation for sanctity"? I desire (if it be not too great a favor) a little evidence for this. . . .

. . . I cannot receive scurrilous invective, instead of Scripture: nor pay the same regard to low buffoonery, as to clear and cogent reasons. . . .

What could the god of this world do in such a case to prevent the spreading of this serious, sober religion? The same that he has done from the beginning of the world. To hinder the light of those whom God hath thus changed, from shining before men, he gave them all in general a nickname: he called them Methodists. And this name, as insignificant as it was in itself, effectually answered his intention. For by this means, that light was soon obscured by prejudice, which could not be withstood by Scripture or reason. By the odious and ridiculous ideas affixed to that name, they were condemned in the gross, without ever being heard. So that now any scribbler, with a middling share of low wit, not encumbered with good nature or modesty, may raise a laugh on those whom he cannot confute, and run them down whom he dares not look in the face. (*A Letter to the Author of* The Enthusiasm of Methodists and Papists Compared [1750], in *Works*, 13:5-6, 10, 15)

And are you afraid of hard names? Then you have not begun to be a disciple of Jesus Christ. (*Predestination Calmly Considered* [1752], in *Works* [T], 9:396)

Now, let all the world judge between Mr. Hill and me. I do not say all the religious world, but all that have the smallest portion of common sense and common humanity. Setting everything else aside, suppose him to be my superior in rank, fortune, learning, and understanding. Is this treatment for a young man to give to an old one who, at least, is no fool and who, before Mr. Hill was born, was in a more honorable employ than he is ever likely to be? What can inspire this young hero with such a spirit and fill his mouth with such language? Is it any credit to his person or to his cause? What can men think either of one or the other? If he does not reverence me or common decency, should he not reverence himself? . . . If he writes any more, let him resume the scholar, the gentleman, and the Christian. Let him remember him who "left us an example, that we might tread in his steps: in meekness instructing those that oppose themselves, peradventure God may bring them to the knowledge of the truth." (*An Answer to Mr. Rowland Hill's Tract, Entitled, "Imposture Detected"* [June 28, 1777], in *Works* [WL], 10:454)

But what does this smooth, candid writer endeavor to prove, with all the softness and good humor imaginable? Only this point (to express it in plain English), that I am a double-tongued knave, an old crafty hypocrite, who have used religion merely for a cloak and have worn a mask for these fifty years, saying one thing and meaning another.

A bold charge this, only it happens that matter of fact contradicts it from the beginning to the end. (Letter to the printer of the *Dublin Chronicle* [June 2, 1789], in *Works* [S], 7:322)

SLAVERY

After Christianity prevailed, it gradually declined in almost all parts of Europe. This great change began in Spain about the end of the eighth century and was become general, in most other kingdoms of Europe, before the middle of the fourteenth.

. . . From this time slavery was nearly extinct, till the commencement of the sixteenth century; when the discovery of America and of the western and eastern coasts of Africa gave occasion to the revival of it. (*Thoughts on Slavery* [1774], in *Works*, 16:443)

Such is the manner wherein our African slaves are procured; such the manner wherein they are removed from their native land and wherein they are treated in our plantations. I would now inquire whether these things can be defended on the principles of even heathen honesty? Whether they can be reconciled (setting the Bible out of the question) with any degree of either justice or mercy?

. . . The grand plea is, "They are authorized by law." But can law, human law, change the nature of things? Can it turn darkness into light or evil into good? By no means. Notwithstanding ten thousand laws, right is right and wrong is wrong still. There must still remain an essential difference between justice and injustice, cruelty and mercy. So that I still ask, Who can reconcile this treatment of the Negroes, first and last, with either mercy or justice?

Where is the justice of inflicting the severest evils on those that have done us no wrong? Of depriving those that never injured us in word or deed of every comfort of life? Of tearing them from their native country and depriving them of liberty itself? . . . Yea, where is the justice of taking away the lives of innocent, inoffensive men? Murdering thousands of them in their own land by the hands of their own countrymen? many thousands, year after year, on shipboard, and then casting them like dung into the sea! And tens of thousands in that cruel slavery to which they are so unjustly reduced?

. . . But waving, for the present, all other considerations, I strike at the root of this complicated villainy. I absolutely deny all slave-holding to be consistent with any degree of natural justice. (*Thoughts on Slavery* [1774], in *Works*, 16:454-55)

"However this be, it is necessary when we have slaves to use them with severity." What, to whip them for every petty offense till they are all in a gore of blood? To take that opportunity of rubbing pepper and salt into their raw flesh? To drop burning sealing wax upon their skin? To castrate them? To cut off half their foot with an axe? To hang them on gibbets that they may die by inches with heat and hunger and thirst? To pin them down to the ground and then burn them by degrees, from the feet to the head? To roast them alive? When did a Turk or a heathen find it necessary to use a fellow creature thus?

I pray to what end is this usage necessary? "Why, to prevent their running away and to keep them constantly to their labor, that they may not idle away their time. So miserably stupid is this race of men, yea, so stubborn and so wicked." Allowing them to be as stupid as you say, to whom is that stupidity owing? Without question it lies altogether at the door of their inhuman masters: who gave them no means, no opportunity of improving their understanding and indeed leave them no motive, either from hope or fear, to attempt any such thing. They were no way remarkable for stupidity while they remained in their own country; the inhabitants of Africa, where they have equal motives and equal means of improvement, are not inferior to the inhabitants of Europe, to some of them they are greatly superior. . . . Certainly the African is in no respect inferior to the European. Their stupidity, therefore, in our plantations is not natural, otherwise than it is the natural effect of their condition. Consequently it is not their fault, but *yours*. You must answer for it before God and man. (*Thoughts on Slavery* [1774], in *Works*, 16:459-60)

Is there a God? You know there is. Is he a just God? Then there must be a state of retribution, a state wherein the just God will reward every man according to his works. Then what reward will he render to *you*? [Oh,] think betimes! Before you drop into eternity! Think now, "He shall have judgment without mercy that hath showed no mercy." Are you a *man*? Then you should have a *human* heart. But have you indeed? What is your heart made of? Is there no such principle as compassion there? Do you never *feel* another's pain? Have you no sympathy? No sense of human woe? No pity for the miserable? When you saw the streaming eyes, the heaving breasts, or the bleeding sides and tortured limbs of your fellow creatures, were you a stone or a brute? Did you look upon them with the eyes of a tiger? When you squeezed the agonizing creatures down in the ship or when you threw their poor mangled remains into the sea, had you no relenting? Did not one tear drop from your eye, one sigh escape from your breast? Do you feel no relenting *now*? If you do not, you must go on till the measure of your iniquities is full. Then will the great God deal with *you* as you have dealt with *them* and require all their blood at your hands. And at that day it shall be more tolerable for Sodom and Gomorrah than for *you*! (*Thoughts on Slavery* [1774], in *Works*, 16:462-63)

My dear sir, unless the divine power has raised you up to be as Athanasius *contra mundum,* I see not how you can go through your glorious enterprise, in opposing that execrable villainy which is the scandal of religion, of England, and of human nature. Unless God has raised you up for this very thing, you will be worn out by the opposition of men and devils; but, *if God be for you, who can be against you?* Are all of them together stronger than God? [Oh]! *be not weary in well doing.* Go on in the name of God and in the power of his might till even American slavery (the vilest that ever saw the sun) shall vanish before it.

Reading, this morning, a tract written by a poor African, I was particularly struck by that circumstance—that a man who has a black skin, being wronged or outraged by a white man, can have no redress; it being a *law* in our colonies that the *oath* of a black, against a white, goes for nothing. What villainy is this?

That he who has guided you, from your youth up, may continue to strengthen you in this and all things, is the prayer of, dear sir, your affectionate servant, John Wesley. (Letter to William Wilberforce [February 24, 1791], in *Letters,* 489-90 [Wesley's last letter, written six days before his death])

S SOCIETY AND CHRISTIANITY

Christianity is essentially a social religion and to turn it into a solitary religion is indeed to destroy it. ("On Our Lord's Sermon on the Mount: Discourse 4" [1748], Sermon 26, in *Works* [T], 5:254)

SOUL

The soul seems to be the immediate clothing of the spirit, the vehicle with which it is connected from its first existence and which is never separated from it either in life or in death. Probably it consists of ethereal or electric fire, the purest of all matter. It does not seem to be affected by the death of the body but envelopes the separate, as it does the embodied, spirit; neither will it undergo any essential change when it is clothed upon with the immortal body at the resurrection. (*Some Thoughts on an Expression of St. Paul, in the First Epistle to the Thessalonians, Chapter 5, Verse 23* [March 31, 1786], in *Works* [WL], 11:447-48)

SPIRIT (OF MAN)

May not *the spirit* mean (so it has been understood by the Christians in all ages) the highest principle in man, the immortal spirit made in the image of God, endued (as all spirits are, so far as we can conceive) with self-motion, understanding, will, and liberty? (*Some Thoughts on an Expression of St. Paul, in the First Epistle to the Thessalonians, Chapter 5, Verse 23* [March 31, 1786], in *Works* [WL], 11:447)

SUFFERING

What a blessing it is to have these little crosses, that we may try what spirit we are of! We could not live in continual sunshine. It would dry up all the grace of God that is in us. (Letter to Ebenezer Blackwell [April 29, 1755], in *Works* [WL], 12:167)

It is a happy thing, if we can learn obedience by the things which we suffer. Weakness of body and heaviness of mind will, I trust, have this good effect upon you. (Letter to Miss Furly [December 22, 1756], in *Works* [WL], 12:181)

It is plain God sees it best for you frequently to walk in a thorny path. By this means he aims at destroying your pride of heart and breaking your stubborn will. (Letter to Miss Furly [September 25, 1757], in *Works* [WL], 12:185-86)

May we not in every trial, great and small, observe the hand of God? And does he send any sooner than we want it or longer than we want it? (Letter to Ebenezer Blackwell [April 26, 1760], in *Letters*, 342)

So the Lord has chastened and corrected you, but he hath not given you over unto death. It is your part to stand ready continually for whatever he shall call you to. Everything is a blessing, a means of holiness, as long as you can clearly say, "Lord, do with me and mine what thou wilt and when thou wilt and how thou wilt." (Letter to Miss Bosanquet [August 16, 1767], in *Works* [S], 7:60)

I am not sorry that you have trials. They are intended to show you your own helplessness and to give you a fuller confidence in him who has all power in heaven and earth. You have reason to cast all your care upon him, for he has dealt bountifully with you. When any trial comes, see that you do not look to the thing itself, but immediately look unto Jesus. Reason not upon it, but believe. (Letter to Miss Jane Hilton [August 20, 1768], in *Works* [WL], 12:355)

You shall have exactly as much pain and as much disappointment as will be most for your profit . . . Never make it matter of reasoning that you have not either a larger or a smaller share of suffering. You shall have exactly what is best both as to kind, degree, and time. [Oh,] what a blessing is it to be in his hand who "doeth all things well"! (Letter to a young disciple [June 20, 1772], in Coll. C, 371-72)

All the trials you suffered, while you were there, are now passed away like a dream. So are all the afflictions we endured yesterday; but they are noted in God's book, and the happy fruit of them may remain when heaven and earth are passed away. Trials you are likewise to expect where you are now, for you are still in the body and wrestle, if not with flesh and blood, yet with "principalities, and powers, with the rulers of the darkness of this world, with wicked spirits in high places"; and it is good for you that every grain of your faith should be tried; afterward you shall come forth as gold. See that you never be weary or faint in your mind; account all these things for your profit, that you may be a full partaker of his holiness. (Letter to Miss Pywell [December 29, 1774], in *Works* [WL], 12:348-49)

You have indeed had a series of trials, one upon the back of another. It is well you know in whom you have believed, otherwise you would have been weary and faint in your mind. For it is not an easy thing always to remember (then especially when we have most need of it) that "the Lord loveth whom he chasteneth, and scourgeth every son whom he receiveth." Who could believe it, if he had not told us so himself? It is well that he never fails to give us strength according to our day and that we know these "light afflictions, which are but for a moment, work for us a far more exceeding and eternal weight of glory." (Letter to Mrs. Jane Barton [June 11, 1788], in *Works* [S], 7:49)

I am acquainted with several persons whom I believe to be saved from sin. But there is great variety in the manner wherein God is pleased to lead them. Some of them are called to act much for God, some to rejoice much, some to suffer much. All of these shall receive their crown. But when the Son of Man shall come in his glory, the brightest crown will be given to the sufferers. (Letter to Miss Bolton [January 9, 1789], in Coll. C, 377-78)

TALKING

Speaking too loud . . . is disagreeable to the hearers, as well as inconvenient for the speaker. For they must impute it either to ignorance or affectation, which is never so inexcusable as in preaching.

Every man's voice should indeed fill the place where he speaks, but if it exceeds its natural key, it will be neither sweet nor soft nor agreeable—were it only on this account, that he cannot then give every word its proper and distinguishing sound. . . .

. . . Above all take care . . . to vary your voice according to the matter on which you speak. Nothing more grates the ear than a voice still in the same key. And yet nothing is more common; although this monotony is not only unpleasant to the ear but destroys the effect of what is spoken. (*Directions Concerning Pronunciation and Gesture* [1749], in *Works* [S], 7:488-89)

Be temperate in speaking—never too loud, never too long—else Satan will befool you and on pretense of being more useful, quite disable you from being useful at all. (*Advice to Dr. Coke* [November 18, 1765], in Coll. B, 527)

TEMPTATION

Satan hath indeed desired to have us, that he may sift us as wheat, but our Lord hath prayed for us, so that the faith of few has failed. Far the greater part of those who have been tempted has come as gold out of the fire.

It seems to me a plain proof that the power of God is greatly with this people, because they are tempted in a manner scarce common to men. No sooner do any of them begin to taste of true liberty, but they are buffeted both within and without. The messengers of Satan close them in on every side. Many are already turned out of doors by their parents or masters; many more expect it every day. But they count all these things dung and dross that they may win Christ. (Letter to Ebenezer Blackwell [August 23, 1739], in *Letters,* 294)

TONGUES: GIFT OF

Whether these gifts of the Holy Ghost were designed to remain in the church throughout all ages, and whether or no they will be restored at the nearer approach of the "restitution of all things," are questions which it is not needful to decide. But it is needful to observe this, that even in the infancy of the church God divided them with a sparing hand. Were all even then prophets? Were all workers of miracles? Had all the gifts of healing? Did all speak with tongues? No, in no wise. Perhaps not one in a thousand. Probably none but the teachers in the church, and only some of them [1 Cor. 12:28-30]. ("Scriptural Christianity" [August 24, 1744], sermon, in Coll. C, 138)

TOTAL DEPRAVITY

This, then, have I learned in the ends of the earth—that I am fallen short of the glory of God; that my whole heart is altogether corrupt and abominable; and, consequently, my whole life (seeing it cannot be that an evil tree should bring forth good fruit); that alienated as I am from the life of God, I am a child of wrath, an heir of hell; that my own works, my own sufferings, my own righteousness, are so far from reconciling me to an offended God, so far from making any atonement for the least of those sins which are more in number than the hairs of my head, that the most specious of them, need an atonement themselves, or they cannot abide his righteous judgment. (*Journal,* January 29, 1738)

Coeval with our being and as old as the fall, our evil nature; a strong and beautiful expression for that entire depravity and corruption which by nature spreads itself over the whole man, leaving no part uninfected. This in a believer is *crucified with Christ,* mortified, gradually killed, by virtue of our union with him. *That the body of sin*—All evil tempers, words, and actions which are the *members of the old man* [Col. 3:5] *might be destroyed.* (*NT Notes*, 372, comment on Rom. 6:6)

We learn one grand, fundamental difference between Christianity, considered as a system of doctrines, and the most refined heathenism. Many of the ancient heathens have largely described the vices of particular men. They have spoken much against their covetousness or cruelty, their luxury or prodigality. Some have dared to say that "no man is born without vices of one kind or another." But still, as none of them were apprised of the fall of man, so none of them knew his total corruption. They knew not that all men were empty of all good and filled with all manner of evil. They were wholly ignorant of the entire depravation of the whole human nature, of every man born into the world, in every faculty of his soul, not so much by those particular vices, which reign in particular persons, as by the general flood of atheism and idolatry, of pride, self-will, and love of the world. This, therefore, is the first, grand, distinguishing point between heathenism and Christianity. The one acknowledges that many men are infected with many vices and even born with a proneness to them but supposes withal that in some the natural good much overbalances the evil. The other declares that all men are *conceived in sin* and *shapened in wickedness*: that hence there is in every man a *carnal mind which is enmity against God, which is not, cannot be subject to* his *law*, and which so infects his whole soul that *there dwelleth in* him, *in his flesh*, in his natural state, *no good thing*; but *all the imagination of the thoughts of his heart*, is *evil*, only *evil*, and that *continually*.

. . . Hence we may, secondly, learn, that all who deny this, call it original sin or by any other title, are but heathens still, in the fundamental point which differences heathenism from Christianity. They may indeed allow that men have many vices, that some are born with us, and that consequently we are not born altogether so wise or so virtuous as we should be: there being few that will roundly affirm, "We are born with as much propensity to good as to evil, and that every man is, by nature, as virtuous and wise as Adam was at his creation." But here is the shibboleth: Is man by nature filled with all manner of evil? Is he void of all good? Is he wholly fallen? Is his soul totally corrupted? Or, to come back to the text, is "every imagination of the thoughts of his heart evil continually"? Allow this, and you are so far a Christian. Deny it, and you are but a heathen still. ("Original Sin" [1759], Sermon 20, in *Works* [T], 5:194-95)

TRADITION, APOSTOLIC

You cannot but know it has always been the judgment of learned men . . . that the far greater part of those spurious books have been forged by heretics; and that many more were compiled by weak, well-meaning men, from what had been orally delivered down from the apostles. But there have been in the church from the beginning men who had only the name of Christians. And these doubtless were capable of pious frauds, so called. But this ought not to be charged upon the whole body. (*A Letter to the Rev. Dr. Conyers Middleton Occasioned by His Late "Free Inquiry"* [January 4, 1749], *Works* [S], 5:713)

The fact being . . . cleared, that infant baptism has been the general practice of the Christian church in all places and in all ages, that it has continued without interruption in the church of God for above seventeen hundred years, we may safely conclude it was handed down from the apostles, who best knew the mind of Christ. (*A Treatise on Baptism* [November 11, 1756], in Coll. B, 233)

Let us, therefore, hold fast the sound doctrine "once delivered to the saints" and delivered down by them, with the written Word, to all succeeding generations. ("On Sin in Believers," March 28, 1763, Sermon 13, in *Works* [T], 5:127)

TRADITIONS OF MEN

Yet the Papists add tradition to Scripture and require it to be received with equal veneration. By traditions they mean, "Such points of faith and practice as have been delivered down in the church from hand to hand without writing." And for many of these they have no more Scripture to show than the Pharisees had for their traditions. (*Popery Calmly Considered* [1779], in *Works*, 15:178)

TRINITY, HOLY

I know not how anyone can be a Christian believer till he hath (as St. John speaks) the witness in himself, till "the Spirit of God witnesses with his spirit that he is a child of God"; that is, in effect, till God the Holy Ghost witnesses that God the Father has accepted him through the merits of God the Son, and having this witness, he honors the Son and the blessed Spirit, "even as he honours the Father." . . .

Therefore, I do not see how it is possible for any to have vital religion who denies that these three are one. ("On the Trinity," May 8, 1775, Sermon 59, in *Works* [T], 6:213)

Mr. Jones's book on the Trinity is both more clear and more strong than any I ever saw on that subject. If anything is wanting, it is the application, lest it should appear to be a merely speculative doctrine, which has no influence on our hearts or lives; but this is abundantly supplied by my brother's *hymns*.

After all the noise that has been made about *mysteries*, and the trouble we have given ourselves upon that head, nothing is more certain than that no child of man is required to believe any mystery at all. With regard to the

Trinity, for instance; what am I required to believe? Not the *manner* wherein the mystery lies. This is not the object of my faith. But the plain *matter of fact*, "These Three are One." This I believe, and this only. (Letter to Mary Bishop [April 17, 1776], *Letters* [JT], 6:213)

Bishop Bull has indisputably proved that this [Trinitarian] faith was delivered to the saints long before the Nicene council sat and before Athanasius was born. . . .

For the term *person* I contend not. I know no better; if any does, let him use it. (*Thoughts on the Writings of Baron Swedenborg* [May 9, 1782], in *Works* [S], 7:429)

TRUST IN GOD

It is a little thing to trust God as far as we can see him, so far as the way lies open before us. But to trust in him when we are hedged in on every side and can see no way to escape, this is good and acceptable with God. This is the faith of Abraham our father and, by the grace of God, this is your faith! (Letter to Miss Jane Hilton [December 18, 1772], in *Works* [S], 7:43)

As long as you trust, not in yourself, but in him that has all power in heaven and in earth, you will find his grace sufficient for you and his strength made perfect in your weakness. Look to him continually and trust in him that you may increase with all the increase of God. (Letter to Mrs. Elizabeth Bennis [February 12, 1773], in *Works*, 16:180)

TRUTH

I am sensible . . . how extremely difficult it is so to speak, as neither to say too little nor too much, neither more nor less than the cause of God requires. I know also that it is absolutely impossible, so to speak as not to give offense. But whosoever is offended I dare not be silent; neither may I refrain from plainness of speech: only I will endeavor to use all the tenderness I can consistently with that plainness. (*A Farther Appeal to Men of Reason and Religion* [1745], pt. 2, in *Works*, 12:192)

It is very possible that many good men now also may entertain peculiar opinions, and some of them may be as singular herein as even Jehonadab was. And it is certain, so long as *we know* but *in part*, that all men will not see all things alike. It is an unavoidable consequence of the present weakness and shortness of human understanding that several men will be of several minds in religion as well as in common life. So it has been from the beginning of the world, and so it will be "till the restitution of all things."

Nay, farther: although every man necessarily believes that every particular opinion which he holds is true (for to believe any opinion is not true is the same thing as not to hold it), yet can no man be assured that all his own opinions, taken together, are true. Nay, every thinking man is assured they are not, seeing *humanum est errare et nescire*: "To be ignorant of many things, and to mistake in some, is the necessary condition of humanity." This, therefore, he is sensible is his own case. He knows, in the general, that he himself is mistaken; although in what particulars he mistakes, he does not, perhaps he cannot, know. ("Catholic Spirit" [1750], Sermon 41, in *Works* [T], 5:412)

T

UNCONDITIONAL ELECTION (FALSITY OF CALVINIST VERSION)

"This is the key: Those that hold, 'Everyone is absolutely predestinated either to salvation or damnation,' see no medium between salvation by works and salvation by absolute decrees." It follows that whosoever denies salvation by absolute decrees, in so doing (according to their apprehension) asserts salvation by works. . . .

. . . Let us consider it more attentively. If the salvation of every man that ever was, is, or shall be finally saved depends wholly and solely upon an absolute, irresistible, unchangeable decree of God, without any regard either to faith or works foreseen, then it is not, in any sense, by works. But neither is it by faith, for unconditional decree excludes faith as well as works since, if it is either by faith or works foreseen, it is not by unconditional decree. Therefore, salvation by absolute decree excludes both one and the other; and, consequently, upon this supposition, salvation is neither by faith nor by works. (*Thoughts on Salvation by Faith* [1779], in *Works* [WL], 11:493-94)

WAR

But wherever war breaks out, God is forgotten, if he be not set at open defiance. (Letter to Thomas Rankin [May 19, 1775], in *Letters,* 251)

WHITEFIELD, GEORGE (CALVINIST DIFFERENCES)

Having heard much of Mr. Whitefield's unkind behavior since his return from Georgia, I went to him to hear him speak for himself that I might know how to judge. I much approved of his plainness of speech. He told me that he and I preached two different gospels and, therefore, he not only would not join with or give me the right hand of fellowship but was resolved publicly to preach against me and my brother wheresoever he preached at all. Mr. Hall (who went with me) put him in mind of the promise he had made but a few days before, that, whatever his private opinion was, he would never publicly preach against us. He said that promise was only an effect of human weakness, and he was now of another mind. (*Journal,* March 28, 1741)

Here was the first breach, which warm men persuaded Mr. Whitefield to make merely for a difference of opinion. Those, indeed, who believed universal redemption had no desire at all to separate; but those who held particular redemption would not hear of any accommodation, being determined to have no fellowship with men that "were in so dangerous errors." (*A Short History of Methodism* [1764], in Coll. C, 202)

In every place where Mr. Whitefield has been, he has labored in the same friendly, Christian manner. God has indeed effectually broken down the wall of partition which was between us. Thirty years ago we were one, then the sower of tares rent us asunder. But now a stronger than him has made us one again. (Letter to Mrs. Emma Moon [December 6, 1767], in *Works* [WL], 12:256)

But who made that division? It was not I. It was not my brother. It was Mr. Whitefield himself; and that notwithstanding all admonitions, arguments, and entreaties. Mr. Whitefield first wrote a treatise against me by name. He sent it to my brother, who endorsed it with these words: "Put up again thy sword into its place." It slept a while; but after a time he published it. I made no reply. Soon after Mr. Whitefield preached against my brother and me by name. This he did constantly both in Moorfields and in all other public places. We never returned railing for railing, but spoke honorably of him at all times and in all places. . . .

   . . . Did not Mr. Whitefield proclaim, upon the housetop, the difference between us and him? And yet it was not merely the difference of doctrine that caused the division. It was rather the *manner* wherein he maintained his doctrine and treated us in every place. Otherwise difference of doctrine would not have created any difference of affection; but he might lovingly have held particular redemption, and we general, to our lives' end. (*A Letter to the Rev. Mr. Thomas Maxfield; Occasioned by a Late Publication* [February 14, 1778], in *Works* [WL], 11:481-82)

W

WORKS AND GRACE; CO-LABORERS WITH GOD

"All our works, thou, O God! hast wrought in us." These, therefore, are so many more instances of free mercy . . .

   Wherewithal then shall a sinful man atone for any, the least of his sins? With his own works? No. Were they ever so many or holy, they are not his own, but God's. . . .

   . . . Neither is salvation of the works we do when we believe: for *it is then God that worketh in us* and, therefore, that he giveth us a reward for what he himself worketh, only commendeth the riches of his mercy, but leaveth us nothing whereof to glory. ("Salvation by Faith" [June 18, 1738], sermon, in Coll. C, 17, 25)

With regard to the former of these assertions, "If man has any free will, then God cannot have the whole glory of his salvation," is your meaning this: "If man has any power to *work out his own salvation*, then God cannot have the whole glory?" If it be, I must ask again, What do you mean by God's "having the whole glory"? Do you mean "his doing the whole work, without any concurrence on man's part"? If so, your assertion is, "If man do at all *work together with* God, in *working out his own salvation,* then God does not do the whole work, without man's *working together with him.*" Most true; most sure; but cannot you see how God nevertheless may have all the glory? Why the very power to "work together with him" was from God. Therefore, to him is all the glory. . . .

. . . If, then, you say, "We ascribe to God alone the whole glory of our salvation," I answer, so do we too. If you add, "Nay, but we affirm that God alone does the whole work, without man's working at all," in one sense, we allow this also. We allow it is the work of God alone to justify, to sanctify, and to glorify, which three comprehend the whole of salvation. Yet we cannot allow that man can only resist and not in any wise *work together with God* or that God is so the whole worker of our salvation as to exclude man's working at all. This I dare not say, for I cannot prove it by Scripture; nay, it is flatly contrary thereto, for the Scripture is express that (having received power from God) we are to "work out our own salvation" and that (after the work of God is begun in our souls) we are "workers together with him." (*Predestination Calmly Considered* [1752], in *Works* [T], 9:397-98)

Suffer me to warn you of another silly, unmeaning word. Do not say, *I can do nothing.* If so, then you know nothing of Christ; then you have no faith. For if you have, if you believe, then you "can do all things" through Christ who strengtheneth you. You can love him and keep his commandments, and to you his "commandments are not grievous." Grievous to them that believe! Far from it. They are the joy of your heart. Show then your love to Christ by keeping his commandments, by walking in all his ordinances blameless. Honor Christ by obeying him with all your might, by serving him with all your strength. Glorify Christ by imitating Christ in all things, by walking as he walked. Keep to Christ by keeping in his ways. Trust in Christ to live and reign in your heart. Have confidence in Christ, that he will fulfill in you all his great and precious promises, that he will work in you all the good pleasure of his goodness and all the work of faith with power. Cleave to Christ till his blood have cleansed you from all pride, all anger, all evil desire. Let Christ do all! Let him that has done all *for you* do all *in you.* Exalt Christ as a Prince to give repentance: a Savior both to give remission of sins and to create in you a new heart, to renew a right spirit within you. This is the gospel, the pure, genuine gospel; glad tidings of great salvation. Not the new, but the old, the everlasting gospel—the gospel not of Simon Magus but of Jesus Christ. (*A Blow at the Root* [1762], in *Works* [T], 9:457)

Again, you say, "I who believe am authorized to expect life, not through any condition or act, inward or outward, performed by me." *"I who believe."* But cannot you as well expect it without believing? If not, what is believing but a condition? For it is something *sine qua non*. And what else do you, or I, or anyone living, mean by a condition? And is not believing an inward act? What is it else? But you say, *"Not performed by me."* By whom then? God gives me the power to believe. But does he believe for me? He works faith in me. But still is it not I that believe? And if so, is not believing an inward act performed by me? (Letter to Mr. Hart [July 11, 1763], in *Works,* 16:102)

If we were not utterly impotent, our good works would be our own property, whereas now they belong wholly to God, because they proceed from him and his grace. While raising our works and making them all divine, he honors himself in us through them. (*A Plain Account of Christian Perfection* [1767; rev. 1777], in *Works* [WL], 11:440)

No good is done or spoken or thought by any man without the assistance of God, working together *in* and *with* those that believe in him . . . all good tempers and, remotely, all good words and actions are the fruit of the good Spirit. ("Of Evil Angels" [January 7, 1783], Sermon 77, in *Works* [T], 6:362)

"But (say some) . . . if it is God that worketh in us both to will and to do, what need is there of our working? Does not his working thus supersede the necessity of our working at all? Nay, does it not render our working impracticable, as well as unnecessary? For if we allow that God does all, what is there left for us to do?"

Such is the reasoning of flesh and blood. And at first hearing, it is exceedingly plausible. But it is not solid, as will evidently appear, if we consider the matter more deeply. We shall then see there is no opposition between these—"God works; therefore, do ye work"—but, on the contrary, the closest connection; and that in two respects. For, first, God works; therefore you *can* work; secondly, God works, therefore you *must* work.

First, God worketh in you; therefore you *can* work. Otherwise it would be impossible. If he did not work, it would be impossible for you to work out your own salvation. . . .

Yet this is no excuse for those who continue in sin and lay the blame upon their Maker, by saying, "It is God only that must quicken us, for we cannot quicken our own souls." For allowing that all the souls of men are dead in sin by *nature,* this excuses none, seeing there is no man that is in a state of mere nature. There is no man, unless he has quenched the Spirit, that is wholly void of the grace of God. No man living is entirely destitute of what is vulgarly called *natural conscience.* But this is not natural; it is more properly termed *preventing grace.* Every man has a greater or less measure of this, which waiteth not for the call of man. . . .

W

Secondly, God worketh in you; therefore you *must* work. You must be "workers together with him" (they are the very words of the apostle), otherwise he will cease working. The general rule on which his gracious dispensations invariably proceed is this: "Unto him that hath shall be given, but from him that hath not"—that does not improve the grace already given—"shall be taken away what he assuredly hath" (so the words ought to be rendered). Even St. Augustine, who is generally supposed to favor the contrary doctrine, makes that just remark. . . . "He that made us without ourselves, will not save us without ourselves." He will not save us unless we "save ourselves from this untoward generation"; unless we ourselves "fight the good fight of faith, and lay hold on eternal life"; . . . and labor by every possible means to make our own "calling and election sure." (Quoted in "Of Salvation," chap. 3 in Coll. D, 217-18, 220)

WORKS (IN GRACE) AND SALVATION

(1) That none shall finally be saved who have not, as they have had opportunity, done all good works; and (2) That if a justified person does not do good, as he has opportunity, he will lose the grace he has received, and if he "repent" not and "do the former works," will perish eternally. But with regard to the unjustified (if I understand him) we wholly disagreed. He believed it is not the will of God that they should wait for faith *in doing good.* I believe this is the will of God and that they will never find him, unless they seek him in this way. (Quoted in "Of Justification by Faith," chap. 11 in Coll. A, 76-77; the other person was Mr. Ingham, a Moravian Methodist)

And in fact, every believer, till he comes to glory, works *for* as well as *from* life. . . . We have received it as a maxim that "a man is to do nothing in order to justification." Nothing can be more false. (*Minutes of Several Conversations, 1744-1789,* quoted in Coll. C, 243n)

Good works (properly so called) cannot be the conditions of justification, because it is impossible to do any good work *before* we are justified. And yet, notwithstanding, good works may be (and are) conditions of final salvation. (*Answer to the Rev. Mr. Church's "Remarks on the Rev. Mr. Wesley's Last Journal"* [February 2, 1745], in *Works,* 12:298)

Instead of teaching men that they may be saved by a faith which is without good works, without "gospel obedience and holiness of life," we teach exactly the reverse, continually insisting on all outward as well as all inward holiness. For the notorious truth of this we appeal to the whole tenor of our sermons, printed and unprinted; in particular to those upon "Our Lord's Sermon on the Mount," wherein every branch of gospel obedience is both

W

asserted and proved to be indispensably necessary to eternal salvation. (Letter to the Rev. Mr. Downes [November 17, 1759], in Coll. C, 243-44)

It is undoubtedly true that nothing avails for our final salvation without . . . *a new creation*, and consequent thereon, a sincere, uniform keeping of the commandments of God. This St. Paul constantly declares. (Letter to the Rev. Dr. Horne [1762], in *Works,* 13:109)

We have received it as a maxim that "a man is to do nothing, *in order to* justification." Nothing can be more false. Whoever desires to find favor with God should "cease from evil and learn to do well." Whoever repents should do "works meet for repentance." And if this is not *in order* to find favor, what does he do them for? Is not this "salvation by works"? Not by the *merit* of works but by works as a *condition*. What have we then been disputing about for these thirty years? I am afraid, *about words.* As to *merit* itself, of which we have been so dreadfully afraid: we are rewarded "according to our works," yea, *because* of our works. How does this differ from "for the sake of our works"? And how differs this from *secundum merita operum?* — As our works *deserve?* Can you split this hair? I doubt, I cannot. (Quoted in "Of Justification by Faith," chap. 11 in Coll. A, 79-80)

W

And who can deny that both inward good works (loving God and our neighbor) and outward good works (keeping his commandments) are a condition of this? What is this more or less than *"Without holiness no man shall see the Lord"?* (Letter to several preachers and friends [July 10, 1771], *Letters* [JT], 5:264)

No one is a real Christian believer (and consequently cannot be saved) who doeth not good works, where there is time and opportunity. (Minutes of the Methodist Conference at Bristol, August 9, 1771, quoted in "The Life of the Rev. John Wesley, A.M.," in *Works* [WL], 1:xxxii)

I believe . . . that final salvation is "by works as a condition." And let anyone read over the twenty-fifth chapter of St. Matthew and deny it if he can. (*Some Remarks on Mr. Hill's Farrago Double-Distilled* [March 14, 1773], in *Works* [T], 9:520)

[My brother and I] set out upon two principles: (1) None go to heaven without holiness of heart and life; (2) Whosoever follows after this (whatever his opinions be) is my "brother, and sister, and mother," and we have not swerved a hair's breadth from either one or the other of these to this day. (Letter to Samuel Sparrow, Esq. [December 28, 1773], in *Works* [S], 7:113)

None of us talk of being accepted for our works; that is the Calvinist slander. But we all maintain we are not saved without works, that works are a condition (though not the meritorious cause) of final salvation. It is by faith in the righteousness and blood of Christ that we are enabled to do all good works, and it is for the sake of these that all who fear God and work righteousness are accepted of him. (Letter to Mrs. Elizabeth Bennis [March 1, 1774], in *Works* [S], 7:59)

When the Son of Man shall come in his glory and assign every man his own reward, that reward will undoubtedly be proportioned, (1) to our inward holiness, our likeness to God; (2) to our works; and (3) to our sufferings. Therefore, whatever you suffer in time, you will be an unspeakable gainer in eternity. (Letter to Ann Bolton [December 15, 1790], in *Works* [WL], 12:472)

WORSHIP

My dear friend, consider, I am not persuading you to leave or change your religion, but to follow after that fear and love of God without which all religion is vain. I say not a word to you about your opinions or outward manner of worship. But I say, all worship is an abomination to the Lord unless you worship him in spirit and in truth—with your heart, as well as your lips; with your spirit, and with your understanding also. Be your form of worship what it will, but in everything give him thanks; else it is all but lost labor. Use whatever outward observances you please, but put your whole trust in him; but honor his holy name and his word and serve him truly all the days of your life. (*A Letter to a Roman Catholic* [July 18, 1749], in Coll. C, 307)

A catholic spirit is not any kind of *practical* latitudinarianism. It is not indifference as to public worship or as to the outward manner of performing it. This, likewise, would not be a blessing but a curse. Far from being a help thereto, it would, so long as it remained, be an unspeakable hindrance to the worshipping of God in spirit and in truth. But the man of a truly catholic spirit, having weighed all things in the balance of the sanctuary, has no doubt, no scruple at all, concerning that particular mode of worship wherein he joins. He is clearly convinced that this manner of worshipping God is both scriptural and rational. He knows none in the world which is more scriptural, none which is more rational. Therefore, without rambling hither and thither, he cleaves close thereto and praises God for the opportunity of so doing. ("Catholic Spirit" [1750], Sermon 41, in *Works* [T], 5:418)

WORSHIP: METHODIST

The longer I am absent from London, and the more I attend the service of the [Anglican] Church in other places, the more I am convinced of the unspeakable advantage which the people called Methodists enjoy. I mean with regard to public worship, particularly on the Lord's Day. The church where they assemble is not gay or splendid, which might have been a hindrance on the one hand; nor sordid or dirty, which might give distaste on the other; but plain as well as clean. The persons who assemble there are not a giddy crowd who come chiefly to see and be seen; nor a company of goodly, formal, outside Christians whose religion lies in a dull round of duties; but a people most of whom do, and the rest earnestly seek to, worship God in spirit and in truth. Accordingly they do not spend their time there in bowing and curtsying or in staring about them, but in looking upward and looking inward, in hearkening to the voice of God, and pouring out their hearts before him.

It is also no small advantage that the person who reads prayers (though not always the same, yet) is always one who may be supposed to speak from his heart, one whose life is no reproach to his profession; and one who performs that solemn part of divine service, not in a careless, hurrying, slovenly manner, but seriously and slowly, as becomes him who is transacting so high an affair between God and man.

Nor are their solemn addresses to God interrupted either by the formal drawl of a parish clerk or the screaming of boys, who bawl out what they neither feel nor understand, or the unseasonable and unmeaning impertinence of a voluntary on the organ. When it is seasonable to sing praise to God, they do it with the spirit, and with the understanding also. (Letter to a friend [September 20, 1757], in *Letters*, 113-14)

WRITING

I am under some difficulty from Dr. Taylor's manner of writing. It is his custom to say the same thing (sometimes in different, sometimes in nearly the same words) six or eight, perhaps twelve or fifteen times, in different parts of his book. Now I have accustomed myself for many years to say one and the same thing once only. (Preface [November 30, 1756], *The Doctrine of Original Sin: According to Scripture, Reason, and Experience* [1757], in *Works* [T], 9:167)

I have had many thoughts, since we parted, on the subject of our late conversation. I send you them just as they occur. "What is it that constitutes a good style?" Perspicuity, purity, propriety, strength, and easiness joined together. When any one of these is wanting, it is not a good style. Dr. Middleton's style wants easiness; it is stiff to a high degree. And stiffness in writing is full as great a fault as stiffness in behavior. It is a blemish hardly to be excused, much less to be imitated. He is pedantic. "It is pedantry," says the great Lord Boyle, "to use a hard word, where an easier will serve." Now, this the Doctor continually does, and that of set purpose. His style is abundantly too arti-ficial: *Artu est celare artem* ["It is the highest art to conceal art"]; but his art glares in every sentence. He continually says, "Observe how fine I speak," whereas a good speaker seems to forget he speaks at all. . . .

As for me, I never think of my style at all, but just set down the words that come first. Only when I transcribe anything for the press, then I think it my duty to see every phrase be clear, pure, and proper. Conciseness (which is now, as it were, natural to me) brings *quantum sufficit* ["as much as suffices"] of strength. If, after all, I observe any stiff expression, I throw it out, neck and shoulders.

Clearness in particular is necessary for you and me because we are to instruct people of the lowest understanding. Therefore we, above all, if we think with the wise, yet must speak with the vulgar. We should constantly use the most common, little, easy words (so they are pure and proper) which our language affords. When I had been a member of the university about ten years, I wrote and talked much as you do now. But when I talked to plain people in the castle, or the town, I observed they gaped and stared. This quickly obliged me to alter my style and adopt the language of those I spoke to. And yet there is a dignity in this simplicity, which is not disagreeable to those of the highest rank.

I advise you sacredly to abstain from reading any stiff writer. A bystander sees more than those who play the game. (Letter to the Rev. Samuel Furley [July 15, 1764], in *Letters*, 436-38)

I have delayed writing thus long because I was not inclined to draw the sword of controversy, particularly on a subject not very important and with a person not very easy to be convinced. I simply told you my thoughts concerning style and concerning yourself. If you can profit by them, well; if not, there is no harm done. I wanted to have you write in the most excellent way: if you prefer any other, you may. I have no prejudice for or against any writer; but I may say, without much vanity, I know a good style from a bad one, and it would be a shame if I did not, after having spent five-and-forty years (with some natural understanding, much attention, and a free acquaintance with many eminent men) in reading the most celebrated writers in the English tongue.

Observing *you* to want one of the things essential to a good style, namely, *easiness*, I warned you of it, and to make the reason of my caution more clear, enlarged a little upon the head. You reply, "*Harmony* is essential to a good style." It may be so; I have nothing to say to the contrary. In the very lines I quoted there is admirable harmony: . . . the soul of music breathes in them; but there is no stiffness. The lines are as easy as harmonious. This is the perfection of writing. . . .

That "poor people understand long sentences better than short" is an entire mistake. I have carefully tried the experiment for thirty years, and I find the very reverse to be true. Long sentences utterly confound their intellects; they know not where they are. If you would be understood by them, you should seldom use a word of many syllables or a sentence of many words. Short sentences are likewise infinitely best, for the careless and indolent. They strike them through and through. I have seen instances of it a hundred times. Neither are the dull and stupid enlightened nor the careless affected by long and labored periods half so much as by such short ones as these, "The work is great; the day is short; and long is the night wherein no man can work." (Letter to the Rev. Samuel Furley [October 11, 1764], in *Letters*, 438-39)

W

ZEAL (CHRISTIAN)

I detest all zeal which is any other than the flame of love. Yet I find it is not easy to avoid it. It is not easy (at least to me) to be "always zealously affected in a good thing," without being sometimes so affected in things of an indifferent nature. Nor do I find it always easy to proportion my zeal to the importance of the occasion, and to temper it duly with prudence, according to the various and complicated circumstances that occur. . . . and yet I daily experience a far greater danger of the other extreme. To this day, I have abundantly more temptation to lukewarmness than to impetuosity; to be . . . a philosophical sluggard, than an itinerant preacher. And, in fact, what I now do is so exceeding little, compared with what I am convinced I ought to do, that I am often ashamed before God and know not how to lift up mine eyes to the height of heaven! (Letter to John Smith [probably one of the archbishops of Canterbury, Thomas Herring or Thomas Secker] [June 25, 1746], in *Works* [WL], 12:71)

I am, to this day, ashamed before God that I do so little to what I ought to do. . . . I do not spend all my time so profitably as I might, nor all my strength; at least, not all I might have, if it were not for my own lukewarmness and remissness; if I wrestled with God in constant and fervent prayer. (Letter to John Smith [probably one of the archbishops of Canterbury, Thomas Herring or Thomas Secker] [March 25, 1747], in *Works* [WL], 12:81-82)

Why [are] the generality of Christians . . . less zealous and less active for God when they are middle aged than they were when they were young[?] May we not draw an answer to this question from that declaration of our Lord . . . , "To him that hath," uses what he hath, "shall be given; but from him that hath not, shall be taken away that he hath?" A measure of zeal and activity is given to everyone when he finds peace with God. If he earnestly and diligently uses this talent, it will surely be increased. But if he ceases . . . to do good, he insensibly loses both the will and the power. So there is no possible way to retain those talents, but to use them to the uttermost. (Letter to Miss Elizabeth Ritchie [August 19, 1784], *Works* [S], 7:182)

Z

TOPICS INDEX